Understanding ADHD
in Girls and Women

by the same author

Supporting Kids and Teens with Exam Stress in School
A Workbook
Joanne Steer
Illustrated by Suzy Ross
ISBN 978 1 78592 467 5
eISBN 978 1 78450 851 7

Helping Kids and Teens with ADHD in School
A Workbook for Classroom Support and Managing Transitions
Joanne Steer and Kate Horstmann
Illustrated by Jason Edwards
ISBN 978 1 84310 663 0
eISBN 978 1 84642 923 1

of related interest

ADHD – Living without Brakes
Martin L. Kutscher
ISBN 978 1 84310 873 3
eISBN 978 1 84642 769 5

Understanding ADHD in Girls and Women

Edited by JOANNE STEER

Foreword by Andrea Bilbow OBE

Jessica Kingsley Publishers
London and Philadelphia

First published in Great Britain in 2021 by Jessica Kingsley Publishers
An Hachette Company

2

Copyright © Jessica Kingsley Publishers 2021

A CIP catalogue record for this title is available from the British Library and the Library of Congress

ISBN 978 1 78775 400 3
eISBN 978 1 78775 401 0

Jessica Kingsley Publishers' policy is to use papers that are natural, renewable and recyclable products and made from wood grown in sustainable forests. The logging and manufacturing processes are expected to conform to the environmental regulations of the country of origin.

Jessica Kingsley Publishers
Carmelite House
50 Victoria Embankment
London EC4Y 0DZ

www.jkp.com

This book is dedicated to girls and women with ADHD and the networks that support them. We all stand with you.

All author royalties from the sale of this book will be donated to ADHD Richmond and Kingston. This is a charity set up to provide support and information to parents, carers, families and young people impacted by ADHD.

Contents

Foreword

— ANDREA BILBOW OBE —

I have been waiting for this book for a very, very long time; and yes, it's personal. It is a book which tells the story of my life and of the lives of so many brilliant and talented women. And it is a book like no other in its ability to take you, the reader, on a journey of discovery. The pages not only reveal individual experiences but, taken as a whole, weave together a rich and colourful tapestry of knowledge illustrating what it is, as a woman, young lady or girl, to live with ADHD.

It has long been accepted that the prevalence rate in boys and girls is in a ratio of 4:1 But we now know this is not the case. The diagnostic tools for assessment in children have a very strong male bias. Experience tells us that many more women are being diagnosed mainly through self-awareness and self-referral. So many teenage girls have been suffering in silence as their ADHD goes unrecognized, often misdiagnosed as conduct disorder, hormonal changes, mood disorders or depression. These late and incomplete diagnoses lead to missed opportunities for education and employment, broken relationships and unwanted teen pregnancies. It is just so unfair. There is so much hidden, untapped talent amongst these women who consider themselves to be a failure, a failure as a wife and mother or simply just as a woman.

Because this is my story too. My ADHD has been a loyal friend and mortal enemy, and I am both humbled and honoured to have been invited to write this foreword. As someone who has travelled the same path, I relate so well to the many women and girls who are still struggling. I have stumbled often and been knocked back by the same challenges faced by other women speaking here. The feelings of inadequacy, of worthlessness, of having aspirations and dreams that could not be realized. Like so many others after me, I saw only through the diagnosis of my children that this is what had been at the root of all my childhood problems. I grew up in a warm and loving, secure family but felt different and apart from my peers. Receiving my diagnosis in my early 30s, I can honestly say it has been so empowering. When you know what is wrong, you know how to fix it. When you know your limitations, you know where to stop or redirect yourself. I had to put aside the education I craved, but that strong feeling of injustice and passion to impart knowledge that so many of us have took over. I found my mission. It was intense. And I too have finally become fearless and confident in my dedication to fighting for others.

This is an urgent book about learning and understanding, a book covering new ground, shedding a bright light on a condition which has been misunderstood in women for far too long. It offers a factual look at the route to assessment and diagnosis as well as offering a treasure trove of tips and ideas for anyone working with ADHD. It is original in its view of ADHD and women from several different perspectives. The chapters stand alone and offer a chance to dip in and take away a particular piece of knowledge. What does it mean to have ADHD in school? How do I get an assessment? Why do I struggle with friends? When read together, the chapters present a journey from experience and assessment through to diagnosis and treatment.

The reality of living with ADHD presents mighty organisational challenges and distractions, and this is voiced beautifully by the girls and women themselves throughout the book. Rather like living life on a board of 'Snakes and Ladders', daily life with ADHD can be an emotionally challenging matter. Severe premenstrual tension can lead to actions in the short term which can destroy relationships long term. Feelings of failure run deep. These voices are important, they are urgent. What they have to say really matters.

The chapters ahead offer readers, for the first time in the UK, a comprehensive map of the people, places and experiences girls and women will encounter on their own journey to diagnosis. There is no 'one size fits all' presentation of being a girl with ADHD; described as the condition where the only consistency is inconsistency, it makes accurate assessments critical.

Many will discover this only in their teens, and some, like myself, when they are women. The joy of this book is that it will speak to many other women who have always wondered if, perhaps, they too might have the condition and perhaps feel more reassured to seek a diagnosis. It provides you with the right information about where to go and what you can expect.

Written by professionals who have worked with girls, teens and women with ADHD over many years, the book offers the reader a sympathetic, honest and clear insight into what it really means to have ADHD.

Think on this shy little girl, who climbed under the table with embarrassment as her friends sang happy birthday to her, who hid behind her mother's skirts when meeting new people. A girl who struggled every day at school and underperformed despite her obvious intelligence. A teenager with awkward friendships and low self-esteem, how did she end up running a national charity for 25 years, sit at the head of a European ADHD organisation as President for six years and lecture internationally to large audiences without so much as a single butterfly in the stomach?

Getting my diagnosis changed everything and the key is education. The education I lost is not the education that would have allowed me to be the person I am today. I went on a different path. When I work with parents and adults with ADHD, I make it very clear: you are the one who will make the difference in your life and your child's life. Become the expert in ADHD. Take ownership of it. Read everything you can. Go to conferences, join support groups. Educate yourself. You can never know enough. After 25 years of learning I know there is still more to learn. This knowledge will be your superpower. It will give you confidence and it will give you courage to be the person you are meant to be.

This book is essential, it may save lives, and it is long overdue.

Andrea Bilbow OBE is the founder and Chief Executive of the National Attention Deficit Disorder Information and Support Service ADDISS, the national ADHD patient advocacy group in the UK, and is Vice President of the Board of ADHD Europe.

Chapter 1

Introduction

Girls and Women Have ADHD Too!

— DR JOANNE STEER —

My best friend at school was the first person to suggest that I might have ADHD. I had not heard of this condition before, but after she explained what it was, it greatly resonated with me. My diagnosis was confirmed shortly after my 15th birthday and medication was commenced immediately. The effects were astounding. I was able to engage properly with lessons for the first time in my life and was surprised by how interesting I found them. My relationships with my teachers (as well as my parents) flourished as I discovered I was able to make them proud as well as making them laugh.

With medication and support, I managed to gain almost all A* and A grades in my GCSEs and A levels, and am now just over halfway through medical school, contrary to many of my teachers' expectations. I have conducted a research project related to ADHD, for which I earned a Bachelor of Medical Science (BMedSci) degree, and am considering specialising as a psychiatrist in the future. I would not be who I am without ADHD, but I would not be where I am without adequate diagnosis and treatment.

Natalia

Attention deficit hyperactivity disorder (ADHD) is a neuro-developmental condition which creates significant difficulties with attention and concentration, restlessness and impulsivity. These difficulties are so significant that they interfere with everyday functioning and development. There are three categories of ADHD in the *Diagnostic and Statistical Manual of Mental Disorders*, known as DSM-5 (American Psychiatric Association 2013):

- Combined type: for those who display inattention, hyper-activity *and* impulsivity

- Predominantly hyperactive/impulsive: for those who are much more hyperactive and impulsive but not inattentive

- Predominantly inattentive: for those who are inattentive but are not hyperactive-impulsive, this was previously known as Attention Deficit Disorder (ADD).

Unfortunately, there are lots of stereotypes and assumptions made about ADHD, particularly when it comes to ADHD in girls or women. The biggest mistake most commonly made is that girls and women cannot and do not have ADHD. So, let us set the record straight now: girls and women can have ADHD, as Natalia so eloquently describes. Every individual with ADHD will of course have a different profile of needs within their difficulties with attention, restlessness and impulsivity.

Why is it that so much less attention is given to ADHD in girls and women? We know that females may hide or mask their difficulties from those around them. We also know that the presentation of ADHD in females can be different from that of their male counterparts and so people are less likely to consider ADHD as a hypothesis to explain the difficulties which are apparent. We also know that a huge amount of the literature is written about males – whether this is research, case studies or books – and so often clinicians, teachers and parents are looking out for male indicators of ADHD. This book explores the world of ADHD for girls and women from assessment and diagnosis to treatment, education and support. We hope this is a step towards balancing the literature on ADHD in girls and women.

GENDER

This book is all about girls with ADHD. There are of course young people with gender dysphoria who very much identify with a different gender to the one they were assigned at birth. They may have been born biologically male, but identify as female, or born biologically female and identify as male. Some young people identify on a spectrum somewhere between male and female. It is difficult to know how young people with both gender dysphoria and ADHD will present. The vast majority of the research to date has focused on young people who do not have gender dysphoria. Interpreting this research for young people with gender dysphoria is a challenge.

However, supporting any young person, whatever their gender, should really be based on how they present as an individual. Research is incredibly good at looking at large groups, and the overall differences within these groups. It is not so good at predicting how an individual will present. There are plenty of young men with ADHD who will present in very similar ways to those described in this book, just as there are plenty of young women who will present in ways more typically described in ADHD books about boys. This has nothing to do with their gender or their sexuality, but more to do with who they are as a person, and how their ADHD presents. In this book we will be using the terms 'young women' and 'girls' for ease, but this should not be taken as excluding boys or young people with gender dysphoria who may identify with a range of gender identities but still present with similar issues to those we will go on to discuss.

PREVALENCE

In the UK, ADHD is estimated to be prevalent in 1.9–5% of children (Murphy *et al.* 2014). Across the world the average rate of prevalence in children is reported to be 5%, ranging between 2% and 7% (Sayal *et al.* 2017). The rates reported in the literature vary significantly, and this is thought to be due to when and which country the study was carried out in and which diagnostic criteria were used. For example, data can be derived from parental reports, population studies or clinical databases. Polanczyk *et al.* (2014) looked at prevalence rates of ADHD across 30 years. They found that when only studies that used strict clinical criteria were analysed, the prevalence rates between 1985 and 2012 remained virtually unchanged. There is a perception that ADHD is on the rise; however, in the UK the condition is largely under-identified in children. This under-identification is a particular issue for girls and results in many girls coming forward for formal assessments only as teenagers and adults. Prevalence rates reported for adults are also variable. Research has looked at combining data from several sources. The prevalence rate across these studies (pooled prevalence) is estimated to be 2.7% in adults (Simon *et al.* 2009) and 2.8% in older adults (Michielson *et al.* 2012).

There are large variations in the reporting of gender ratios within ADHD, although all studies agree that the prevalence is higher in males than in females. A large European study of gender ratios (Nøvik *et al.* 2006) reported some ratios as low as 1:3 (Norway) and others as high as 1:16 (Austria) in females to males (see Figure 1.1 for further details).

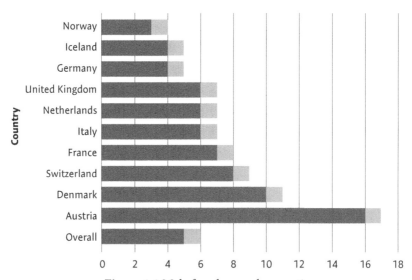

Figure 1.1 Male:female prevalence ratio

The gender ratios reported in the literature appear to be linked to the research sample. The ratio of males to females is much higher in those studies which used a clinic-based sample (those already in services) compared with those that used a population-based sample. This suggests that ADHD is affecting a greater proportion of females than those referred to services.

In adulthood, there is a shift and the ratio of males to females with ADHD is closer to 1:1 (Kessler *et al.* 2006). This suggests that ADHD is potentially underdiagnosed in girls. This hypothesis is supported by the women who are diagnosed in adulthood and report their girlhood experiences.

The NICE guidelines for ADHD (National Institute for Health and Care Excellence 2018) highlight in 2018 that ADHD is under-recognised in girls and that they are less likely to be referred for an assessment, more likely to have undiagnosed ADHD, and are more likely to receive an incorrect diagnosis of a mental health condition or other neurodevelopmental condition.

SCREENING TOOLS AND DIAGNOSTIC CRITERIA

Screening tools are subjective and based on the views of parents and teachers, who are often central to the process of assessment and diagnosis. It is always important to hold in mind that screening tools are just that; they are not diagnostic, they are not a complete assessment, but part of building a picture of what is happening and what other people are concerned about for a particular child. Mowlem *et al.* (2019a) found that parents may not be as good at judging impairment of symptoms of ADHD in girls in comparison with boys. This may lead to an under-estimation of impairment, which in turn may lead to parents not taking their daughters for assessments or perceiving there to be less of an impact of their symptoms compared with boys. Ohan and Johnston (2005) had previously shown that parents perceived the criteria for ADHD outlined in DSM-IV as descriptive of boys. This potentially leads to a gender stereotype of ADHD, further fuelling the challenge to recognise ADHD in girls.

Many of the factors which will be outlined throughout this book influence the perception of girls and their challenges, potentially leading to under-rating and under-reporting. It is essential to give girls themselves a voice, as they are indeed the only ones fully aware of their struggles. The opportunity for self-report rather than relying on teachers and parents is of utmost importance. Nadeau, Littman and Quinn (2016) helpfully have developed several rating scales and questions for girls and teenage girls that facilitate screening and assessment, which are well worth exploring. The role of screening tools in the assessment of ADHD is further explored in Chapter 2.

Could it be that clinicians more readily diagnose ADHD in boys than girls, which leads to the unequal gender ratios? A diagnosis should be based on the criteria outlined in DSM-5 or ICD-11; however, it is recognised that clinicians are influenced by biases and rules of thumb (Bruchmüller, Margraf and Schneider 2011). Boys with certain ADHD symptoms are likely to be seen as 'typical' and representative of ADHD. Bruchmüller *et al.*'s study looked at the hypothesis that clinicians are likely to make their diagnosis based on the most prominent symptoms of ADHD (which are exhibited more in boys). They presented case vignettes to clinicians which were identical other than the gender of the child. Indeed, boys were diagnosed more with ADHD than the girls, and gender was a significant predictor of diagnosis. This clinician bias is best overcome through the use of structured interviews and standardised tools for assessment. Claire Berry and Jess Brunet provide further details around this in Chapter 2.

It is important to be mindful that much of the research on ADHD is carried out with predominantly (and at times entirely) male participants. The diagnostic criteria laid out in DSM-IV for ADHD were largely based on observations of males (Lahey *et al.* 1994), and field studies for DSM-5 included a greater percentage of males (Clarke *et al.* 2013). Much of the research completed uses participants from clinics, yet we know that females are referred less often to these very clinics. Those girls with ADHD who are flying under the radar for all the reasons we are exploring here are not included in these research studies. Studies which do focus on ADHD in females are more likely to utilise a population-based approach. However, this often goes hand in hand with parent or teacher rating scales. As we have just explored, these rating scales are often completed with 'male ADHD' stereotypes at the forefront of the mind of the parent or teacher. This creates a real challenge for all our thinking and research around ADHD in girls and women.

The challenges of getting a formal diagnosis of ADHD can be difficult to overcome, so it is important to start implementing strategies to help as soon as possible and not wait for the formal assessment. If a girl ends up not meeting the criteria, you are still likely to have a girl who struggles with attention and possibly impulsivity and hyperactivity. The strategies outlined in Chapter 3 on treatment (with the exception of medication) and Chapter 6 on coaching will be helpful for this broad group of girls, with or without a diagnosis. It is sensible to be proactive both at home and at school by putting in support around these symptoms.

BEHAVIOURAL PRESENTATION

In the research literature, gender differences in the identification of ADHD are consistently attributed to the differences in the presentation or expression of the disorder among boys and girls (Gaub and Carlson 1997). Females with ADHD are reported to have fewer symptoms of hyperactivity and impulsivity and more symptoms of inattention when compared with males. When considering ADHD, people have a typical image in their minds of boys unable to sit down and bouncing off the walls. If a girl does not act like this, then they assume she does not have ADHD. A girl who is quietly daydreaming and not achieving does not come to the attention of teachers or parents in the same way, and ADHD is unlikely to be high on the list of possible explanations. Females more often present with the inattentive subtype of ADHD than males in clinic-based samples. This data means that we might consider a different presentation for girls and women. Chapter 2 explores the assessment of ADHD in girls including what to consider as a parent, clinician and member of school staff.

It is not the case that girls and women are not inattentive, hyperactive and impulsive but that these symptoms may be expressed in a different way. A girl with ADHD may not be as physically restless as a boy but her mind may be constantly on the go and restless. It is much harder to spot this in a child and difficult for a child to express this to those they are close to. A girl may be 'hyper-social', 'hyper-talkative' or 'hyper-emotional' rather than hyperactive. The 'hyper-talkative' girl can be verbally impulsive, interrupting others, talking excessively and frequently changing topics during conversations. These are different difficulties and challenges to identify and recognise as ADHD.

In girls, common symptoms of inattention include daydreaming, disorganisation, forgetfulness and low arousal. Impulsivity can appear as interrupting others, speaking without seeming to think first, and acting on impulse when making decisions (both big and small!). These symptoms in girls and women are often put down to emotional difficulties, learning problems or discipline issues rather than ADHD.

There is a good amount of literature that discusses the inattentive type presentation of ADHD in girls and attributes the low rates of identified girls to this cause. It is likely that even boys with this presentation are being missed, too. What is often less of a focus is the combined type presentation of ADHD in girls. These are girls with inattentive and hyperactive symptoms who are at increased risk of self-destructive behaviours and mental health difficulties in adolescence and adulthood. Hinshaw *et al.* (2012) reported that girls with ADHD combined type had significantly higher rates of self-harm and attempted suicide.

It is also of note that these challenges in girls can sometimes be put down to character or personality rather than ADHD, leading to their being labelled 'Little Miss Chatterbox' or 'Chatty Kathy', or being called ditzy or lazy. Ringer (2019) reported that in interviews with children about their experiences of ADHD, three of the older girls perceived aspects of their ADHD as personality traits: 'Being hyperactive, having difficulty paying attention, and being emotionally explosive were perceived like any other personality trait.' Inevitably, this can lead to low self-esteem, self-blame and emotional well-being difficulties in these girls and women, and this will be discussed in Chapter 4, in which Alex Doig clearly outlines the important role of self-esteem and how this is a real issue for this group of girls. Women and girls are far more likely to blame themselves when things go wrong. For example, if a boy does badly on a school test, he says to himself, 'stupid test'; however, if a girl does badly, she says, 'I'm so stupid.'

Many women and girls with ADHD meet the criteria for another mental health condition and this can often create a confusing picture for everyone involved. The literature highlights that girls with ADHD often present with more internalising symptoms such as anxiety and depression (Quinn 2008). This contrasts with boys, who are described as presenting as more hyperactive and impulsive and display externalising presentations in their behaviour (Quinn 2008). These mental health difficulties in girls should not be used to rule out ADHD diagnoses. It is important that they are explored and treated where appropriate, as Alex Doig will explain further.

The co-occurrence of ADHD and autism spectrum disorder (ASD) is also an important complex issue and diagnostic question. The changes made in DSM-5 have meant that clinicians can now diagnose both ADHD and ASD. Young *et al.* (2020) have published some helpful guidance and recommendations for clinical practice for the assessment and treatment of this particular group of children and adults. This includes the importance of always considering both ADHD and ASD when assessing for either disorder. It is also of note that girls are consistently under-identified for a diagnosis of ASD (Lai *et al.* 2015), with some similar issues as ADHD contributing to this picture.

Nadeau *et al.* (2016) highlight that symptoms of ADHD in girls appear to increase during puberty. It is thought that increasing demands on executive functions (e.g. the need to independently organise themselves and their equipment for school or plan increasingly complex assignments) highlight the challenges of ADHD at this age. It may be that as ADHD becomes unmanageable for girls at this age, they then are more likely to present to services for formal assessment or with other mental health difficulties. It is also worth considering how the structure and format of secondary or high school is not well suited to those with ADHD. There is a high level of demand for organisation and concentration alongside enforced study of subjects which hold little interest.

Society expects a lot from women (and men). There is an expectation that girls and women will demonstrate what might be considered traditional feminine traits such as being skilled in relationships and interactions, obedience, kindness, empathy, and being maternal and organisers of the home. In addition, society expects women to demonstrate characteristics that might be considered more masculine such as being focused on academics and their careers, being driven and determined, assertive and competitive. Features of ADHD such as hyperactivity, disruptive behaviour, impulsivity and disorganisation are judged harshly by society in girls and women. It is reported that in order to avoid judgement and social embarrassment, girls and women work hard to hide their problems (Quinn 2008), thus further increasing the challenge of recognition and diagnosis.

It is of note that there are few females in the public eye who talk about their ADHD. This contrasts with a wide selection of men ranging from celebrity chefs to Olympians, comedians, actors and entrepreneurs. Is it that the gender ratio is being represented in the data of famous faces or could it be that the harsh judgement from society of women extends into this arena? Perhaps females in the public eye with ADHD have not yet been identified and diagnosed or perhaps they have a fear of judgement in 'coming out' about their ADHD publicly. Young girls who have been newly diagnosed with ADHD report how helpful and comforting it is to know that the actress Emma Watson and gymnast Simone Biles have ADHD, too. Both women have talked openly about being diagnosed in childhood and taking medication as part of their treatment for the condition.

🖐 KEY POINTS

> » Prevalence data indicates that ADHD is more common in boys than in girls.

» There is evidence that ADHD in girls is underdiagnosed and many girls are 'missed'.

» Differing presentation, culture and additional mental health difficulties are potential factors in the under-recognition of ADHD in girls.

ASSESSMENT OF ADHD IN ADULTHOOD

Typically, ADHD is diagnosed later in females than in males (Grevet *et al.* 2006), which means that high-quality assessment in adulthood is crucial. A common scenario is that a woman comes to recognise her own ADHD as one of her children undergoes assessment and treatment. In reading and researching about the condition, she might recognise herself and her childhood experiences in what she is reading. Alternatively, a woman accesses mental health services for anxiety or depression and during the course of this support it becomes clear that she has experienced long-standing difficulties throughout her childhood and beyond. It is only then that ADHD is recognised and diagnosed, and treatment can commence. It is documented that a late or missed diagnosis for ADHD actually increases the risk for these girls and women to develop other mental health difficulties such as anxiety, low self-esteem, sleep difficulties, depression, substance misuse and eating disorders (Glaser Holthe and Langvik 2017). The impact is also felt in all aspects of life such as difficulties in parenting, conflict at work or home, an increased risk of divorce and single parenting, and difficulties holding down a job.

Chapter 7 focuses on the assessment of ADHD in women, and Sally Cubbin and Allyson Parry provide some comprehensive tips to consider when assessing women. One focus is the common experience of emotional dysregulation in women with ADHD. This challenge of overblown reactions to small setbacks can be a significant impairment for girls and women. Emotional regulation difficulties are not outlined in diagnostic criteria for ADHD but are an extremely common experience that should be explored at assessment. Often the emotional reactivity has been present throughout childhood, but in adolescence the 'hyperreactivity' can become more pronounced. It may be frustration over homework, a falling out with a friend, annoyance at a sibling or anger at parents; the emotions experienced around these typical adolescent experiences are often more extreme for a girl with ADHD. These emotional experiences can often dominate the clinical presentation in adolescence and onwards into adulthood. The consideration of these emotional symptoms associated with ADHD is critical to ensure accurate diagnosis and treatment of ADHD.

Women with ADHD are more likely to report a history of mental health difficulties such as anxiety, depression, eating disorders, post-traumatic stress and personality disorders. It is important to consider that unrecognised and untreated ADHD may lead to these mental health problems. However, even when ADHD is diagnosed and treated a significant number of women experience comorbid mental health presentations. There is also a small area of research (Adelizzi 1998) looking at post-traumatic stress in these women from childhood and their experiences of the classroom. This connection between the everyday challenges of the classroom and mental health later in life needs to be heard. A group of young women have recently produced a film for teachers talking about girls and ADHD in school. One of the most memorable lines from this film is 'my teacher was the bully'. These daily stressful experiences for some girls with ADHD must be a priority. To view the film in full, please visit www.adhdrichmond.org/our-videos.

Sally Cubbin and Allyson Parry also discuss the association of physical health conditions in women with ADHD. There are well-documented associations between a number of conditions, such as asthma, obesity, insomnia and other sleep conditions, and ADHD, which are explored in Chapter 7. Given the underdiagnosis of ADHD in girls and women, this association may offer an alternative route to the detection of ADHD through physical health physicians and clinics. There is a real opportunity to use this different pathway to services to screen and refer women for ADHD assessments.

✋ KEY POINTS

» Emotional dysregulation is a common in experience in women with ADHD.

» Women with ADHD are more likely to experience mental health difficulties.

» There are a number of physical health conditions associated with ADHD in women and therefore a thorough physical health review plays an important part in the assessment of ADHD in women.

TREATMENT OF ADHD

The gender differences reported in the diagnosis of ADHD can also be seen in the treatment of the condition. Males are more likely to receive medication for the treatment of their ADHD than females (Derks, Hudziak and Boomsma 2007). In 2017–18 it was reported that in the UK less than a fifth of prescriptions for medication for ADHD were for females (NHS Business Services Authority 2018). However, this may be due to the higher proportion of combined type presentations in males than females. It is certainly something to explore further, and Chapter 3 considers both medication and non-pharmacological treatment for girls.

Psychoeducation around ADHD is seen as the first step and foundation of treatment for ADHD. Psychoeducation means providing clear, good-quality information about a condition. A clear and comprehensive understanding of what ADHD is (and isn't) and how it impacts on the specific individual concerned by the whole system can go a long way. The whole system should include the individual themselves, their family (parents, siblings and extended), school (teachers, support staff and leaders), childcare providers and instructors at extra-curricular activities. Tailoring this psychoeducation to reflect the differences in ADHD for girls and using examples relevant to girls is critical. Many parts of the system may have come across ADHD before, but perhaps not in girls. The assumptions made about ADHD and what will be useful to implement to support the child may need to be challenged. It may be that movement breaks are not necessary but instead a doodle notebook is essential. The analogy of a 'Ferrari engine brain with bicycle brakes' made famous by Dr Edward (Ned) Hallowell may need to be adapted (it may also not, as many girls are also interested in cars). The humorous yet super-useful *All Dogs Have ADHD* by Kathy Hoopman (2008) brings to life the typical characteristics of ADHD and can be a great way to start conversations about the strengths and challenges that ADHD may bring.

Young people report that when a particular professional (usually a teacher) has really taken the time out to try to understand their needs, this has made a huge difference in terms of their learning and self-esteem. As individuals, our words and responses to these children with ADHD can have either a positive or a detrimental impact. I cannot over-emphasise the importance of taking the time to understand each child, young person or adult and *their* ADHD.

ADHD medication helps many girls manage their symptoms; however, there is also an appetite from parents and girls themselves to develop strategies and skills to help them overcome the difficulties. Cognitive behavioural therapy (CBT) can support the development of organisational skills and emotional regulation. There are some excellent CBT and psychoeducation resources available (Steer and Horstmann 2009; Taylor 2006; Young and Smith 2017) but many utilise boys in their examples. In order to engage girls with the materials, it is so important that the examples are relatable and reflective of their lives. Peter Hill in Chapter 3 explores how social media and YouTube can provide some relevant material.

In addition, coaching for girls and women can have many benefits and is seen as complementary to medication. Valerie Ivens in Chapter 6 describes and explains the coaching she has provided to girls and women over the years. Coaching is an excellent tool to help girls and women understand their personal challenges of ADHD in a focused and goal-orientated way, to develop skills to help them manage and progress. Valerie's reflections on her work with adolescents emphasises the importance of coming alongside these girls and seeing the world through their eyes. The challenges of societal expectations, social pressures, years of judgement and school life take their toll. Yet Valerie explains how to set up coaching and engage with these girls in a way that can significantly impact on their lives forever.

Coaching is often focused on making practical changes to improve daily life. A key area for coaching is on executive functioning (EF). The ADHD literature is clear that ADHD significantly impacts on EF in children, adolescents and adults. EF is a set of skills that we use every day to learn, work and manage daily life. These skills include planning and prioritising, task initiation, self-monitoring, impulse control, organisation, working memory and emotional control. Coaching can offer a supportive opportunity to develop a personalised approach to overcome some EF challenges.

Females with ADHD are also more likely to engage in risky sexual behaviour, which leads to an increased rate of unplanned pregnancies in this group. This is one aspect of the very real dark side of ADHD. Barkley and Fischer (2018) report that those with severe ADHD can see their life expectancy reduced by up to 12.7 years. Factors that contribute to this statistic are that people with ADHD are more likely to follow unhealthy diets and be overweight, be less careful and therefore involved in more accidents, and are more prone to suicide. This statistic highlights the importance of recognising and treating ADHD as soon as possible.

In Chapter 8, Sally Cubbin goes on to talk about the treatment of ADHD in adulthood. Effective treatment for women involves a multimodal approach, which may include medication, psychotherapy and coaching. There are complexities in the management of medication for women with ADHD, the most widely discussed being hormonal changes, whether during a woman's menstrual cycle, during pregnancy or later in life during the menopause. It is highlighted that the fall in oestrogen as women approach menstruation, following pregnancy and during the menopause can lead to worsening of ADHD symptoms. It is crucial that teenage girls and women (plus the health professionals looking after their care) are made aware of this issue, so that they can anticipate and make sense of what they are noticing. Sally clearly explains the issues and makes some helpful suggestions on how best to manage them.

A further complexity in the treatment of ADHD in women is the high number of mental health comorbidities. Women with ADHD are very likely to be misdiagnosed or experience an additional mental health problem. In Chapter 8, Sally Cubbin discusses the common examples and explains the importance of treating the comorbidities in order to improve overall health and mental health outcomes for these women.

✋ KEY POINTS

> » Psychoeducation and psychological therapy for girls with ADHD should be tailored.

> » Coaching provides an excellent opportunity for skills development, particularly in the area of executive functioning.

> » Changing oestrogen levels can affect women's ADHD symptoms.

> » Additional comorbidities are common in women and need effective identification and treatment alongside ADHD.

EDUCATION

Education and school are an important factor in every child's life, but for those girls with ADHD it can often make or break them. School may be the first place to identify any concerns, since placing a child among their peers of a similar age can reveal the differences in their behaviour, learning and interactions. Teachers who have a good knowledge of ADHD in girls may well identify and refer on to specialists for assessments. However, even teachers who have a good knowledge of ADHD in boys can overlook a girl with ADHD, particularly an inattentive type girl who is of average or above average ability. Indeed, the brighter a girl is, the more easily she can manage to progress through primary or elementary school without displaying any obvious symptoms of ADHD. Girls with ADHD are reported to have fewer learning problems or manifest symptoms in school than boys (Mowlem *et al.* 2019b). This only adds to the challenge of identification. Typically, schools are most concerned with those pupils who are falling behind academically. This leaves those 'average' girls who have potential for above average attainment lower down the list of priorities even if they are performing below their potential. It is not an easy job for a teacher to observe just one child in their large class and notice their attention wandering, their struggle to get started with their work and the fact that they are slower than their peers to complete their tasks. This is made only more challenging when the child utilises strategies such as copying her neighbour, quickly finishing up at the end of the session and fidgeting with her hair.

Girls often report that they don't want to stand out from the crowd, they want to be like their friends, and they feel stupid for asking additional questions. So, they work hard to hide the difficulties they have and find strategies and solutions to get them through. Living like this every day is hard work. So, it is inevitable that once home, these girls let out the frustration, the embarrassment and the anxieties and have a 'meltdown'. It is not uncommon to have disparate reports of ADHD from home and school for girls and this creates several issues. It creates a real challenge in assessment, where clinicians are looking for evidence from two settings (typically home and school) of the symptoms which will be explored in Chapter 2. It can also create a real tension between home and school. Schools report 'no problems here' and 'she is doing fine', while parents report quite the opposite. The risk is that schools can appear to blame parents and see issues as a 'home problem', and parents can feel blamed and unsupported. There is no easy answer to this difficult situation but remaining curious and open to different views about the situation is paramount. The bottom line is that everyone wants the child to be happy, healthy and achieve their potential.

Chapter 4 looks in detail at education for girls with ADHD, with a focus on accessing support in school. Eva Akins has personal experience of managing the challenges of school with ADHD as a child and as a parent. Eva offers a wealth of information and guidance which provides both parents and professionals with a good grounding in the legal frameworks surrounding school and accessing the most appropriate support for girls. Eva's 101 reasonable adjustments are comprehensive and a must-read for those working in schools, those working with schools and for parents. They also offer plenty of ideas which can equally be applied to the workplace for women with ADHD.

Girls with ADHD do struggle in school and therefore getting the support right in the classroom can make a significant impact. Research tells us that ADHD impacts on educational attainment. Loe and Feldman (2007) report that ADHD is associated with poor grades, poor reading and poor maths attainment. Despite the evidence, support is variable from school to school and even from classroom to classroom in one school. In the UK, limited (if any) time is spent supporting teachers in training to understand about ADHD. There are still teachers who question whether ADHD is a real diagnosis. This often total lack of understanding of the condition and its impact on children and their families can significantly affect the support offered those girls who have a confirmed diagnosis, and can mean no referral takes place for those girls presenting with difficulties who are yet to be assessed. Children with ADHD present with a range of difficulties in the classroom, from behaviour, peer relations, mood and organisation, to compliance with rules, and the subtleties of language. ADHD can impact across the board. Organisations such as ADDISS and the ADHD Foundation in the UK have worked tirelessly to educate and train school staff.

✋ KEY POINTS

» Girls often work hard to mask their difficulties in school, so as not to stand out from the crowd.

» Training for school staff on understanding and managing ADHD is critical.

The penultimate chapter of this book (Chapter 9) is dedicated to and written by girls and women with ADHD. Every aspect of this book is reflected in their accounts. If you are feeling low on concentration yourself, skip to Chapter 9 and read their words. These stories of late diagnosis, missed opportunities, a lifetime of adaptations and the power of recognition and treatment will motivate you to read on and explore the other chapters. As a clinician who has worked in the field of ADHD for over 15 years, I am never more motivated to strive to do better than when I hear from girls and women directly about their lives with ADHD.

REFERENCES

Adelizzi, J.U. (1998) *Shades of Trauma*. Plymouth, MA: Jones River Press.

American Psychiatric Association (2013) *Diagnostic and Statistical Manual of Mental Disorders: DSM-5*, 5th edn. Arlington, VA: American Psychiatric Association.

Barkley, R.A. and Fischer, M. (2018) 'Hyperactive child syndrome and estimated life expectancy at young adult follow up: The role of ADHD persistence and other potential predictors.' *Journal of Attention Disorders 23*, 9, 907–923.

Bruchmüller, K., Margraf, J. and Schneider, S. (2011) 'Is ADHD diagnosed in accord with diagnostic criteria? Overdiagnosis and influence of client gender on diagnosis.' *Journal of Consulting and Clinical Psychology 80*, 128–138.

Clarke, D.E., Narrow, W.E., Regier, D.A., Kuramoto, S.J. *et al.* (2013) 'DSM-5 field trials in the United States and Canada, Part I: Study design, sampling strategy, implementation, and analytic approaches.' *American Journal of Psychiatry 170*, 43–58.

Derks, E.M., Hudziak, J.J. and Boomsma, D.I. (2007) 'Why more boys than girls with ADHD receive treatment: A study of Dutch twins.' *Twin Research & Human Genetics 10*, 765–770.

Gaub, M. and Carlson, C.L. (1997) 'Gender differences in ADHD: A meta-analysis and critical review.' *Journal of the American Academy of Child & Adolescent Psychiatry 36*, 8, 1036–1045.

Glaser Holthe, M.E. and Langvik, E. (2017) 'The strives, struggles, and successes of women diagnosed with ADHD as adults.' *Sage Open 7*, 1, 1–12.

Grevet, E.H., Bau, C.H., Salgado, C.A., Fischer, A.G. *et al.* (2006) 'Lack of gender effects on subtype outcomes in adults with attention-deficit/ hyperactivity disorder: Support for the validity of subtypes.' *European Archives of Psychiatry Clinical Neuroscience 256*, 5, 311–319.

Hinshaw, S.P., Owens, E.B., Zalecki, C., Huggins, S.P. *et al.* (2012) 'Prospective follow-up of girls with attention-deficit/hyperactivity disorder into early adulthood: Continuing impairment includes elevated risk for suicide attempts and self-injury.' *Journal of Consulting and Clinical Psychology 80*, 6, 1041–1051.

Hoopman, K. (2008) *All Dogs Have ADHD*. London and Philadelphia: Jessica Kingsley Publishers.

Kessler, R.C., Adler, L., Barkley, R., Biederman, J. *et al.* (2006) 'The prevalence and correlates of adult ADHD in the United States: Results from the National Comorbidity Survey Replication.' *American Journal of Psychiatry 163*, 716–723.

Lahey, B., Applegate, K., Mcburnett, J., Biederman, L. *et al.* (1994) 'DSM-IV field trials for attention deficit hyperactivity disorder in children and adolescents.' *American Journal of Psychiatry 151*, 1673–1685.

Lai, M.C., Lombardo, M.V., Auyeung, B., Chakrabarti, B. and Baron-Cohen, S. (2015) 'Sex/gender differences and autism: Setting the scene for future research.' *Journal of the American Academy of Child & Adolescent Psychiatry 54*, 1, 11–24.

Loe, I.M. and Feldman, H.M. (2007) 'Academic and educational outcomes of children with ADHD.' *Journal of Pediatric Psychology 32*, 6, 643–654.

Michielson, M., Semeijn, E., Comijs, H.C., Van de Ven, P. *et al.* (2012) 'Prevalence of attention-deficit hyperactivity disorder in older adults in the Netherlands.' *British Journal of Psychiatry 201*, 4, 298–305.

Mowlem, F.D., Agnew-Blais, J., Taylor, E. and Asherson, P. (2019a) 'Do different factors influence whether girls versus boys meet ADHD diagnostic criteria? Sex differences among children with high ADHD symptoms.' *Psychiatry Research 272*, 767–773.

Mowlem, F.D., Rosenqvist, M.A., Martin, J., Lichtenstein, P., Asherson, P. and Larsson, H. (2019b) 'Sex differences in predicting ADHD clinical diagnosis and pharmacological treatment.' *European Child & Adolescent Psychiatry 28*, 481–489.

Murphy, M.J., McCarthy, A.E., Baer, L., Zima, B.T. and Jellinek, M.S. (2014) 'Alternative national guidelines for treating attention and depression problems in children: Comparison of treatment approaches and prescribing rates in the United Kingdom and United States.' *Harvard Review of Psychiatry 22*, 3, 179–192.

Nadeau, K.G., Littman, E.B. and Quinn, P.O. (2016) *Understanding Girls with ADHD*, 2nd edn. Washington DC: Advantage Books.

National Institute for Health and Care Excellence (2018) *Attention Deficit Hyperactivity Disorder: Diagnosis and Management (NICE Guideline NG87)*. Accessed on 27 July 2020 at https://www.nice.org.uk/guidance/ng87.

NHS Business Services Authority (2018) Freedom of Information Request from Guardian Newspaper.

Nøvik, T.S., Hervas, A., Ralston, S.J., Dalsgaard, S. *et al.* (2006) 'Influence of gender on attention-deficit/hyperactivity disorder in Europe–ADORE.' *European Child & Adolescent Psychiatry 15* (suppl. 1), I15–I24.

Ohan, J.L. and Johnston, C. (2005) 'Gender appropriateness of symptom criteria for attention-deficit/hyperactivity disorder, oppositional-defiant disorder, and conduct disorder.' *Child Psychiatry & Human Development 35*, 359–381.

Polanczyk, G.V., Willcutt, E.G., Salum, G.A., Kieling, C. and Rohde, L.A. (2014) 'ADHD prevalence estimates across three decades: An updated systematic review and meta-regression analysis.' *International Journal of Epidemiology 43*, 2, 434–442.

Quinn, P.O. (2008) 'Attention-deficit/hyperactivity disorder and its comorbidities in women and girls: An evolving picture.' *Current Psychiatry Reports 10*, 419–423.

Ringer, N. (2019) 'Young people's perceptions of and coping with their ADHD symptoms: A qualitative study.' *Cogent Psychology 6*, 1.

Sayal, K., Prasad, V., Daley, D., Ford, T. and Coghill, D. (2017) 'ADHD in children and young people: Prevalence, care pathways, and service provision.' *The Lancet Psychiatry 5*, 2, 175–186.

Simon, V., Czobor, P., Bálint, S., Mészáros, Á. and Bitter, I. (2009) 'Prevalence and correlates of adult attention-deficit hyperactivity disorder: Meta-analysis.' *British Journal of Psychiatry 194*, 3, 204–211.

Steer, J. and Horstmann, K. (2009) *Helping Kids & Teens with ADHD in School: A Workbook for Classroom Support and Managing Transitions.* London and Philadelphia: Jessica Kingsley Publishers.

Taylor, J.F. (2006) *The Survival Guide for Kids with ADD or ADHD.* Minneapolis, MN: Free Spirit Publishing.

Young, S. and Smith, J. (2017) *Helping Children with ADHD: A CBT Guide for Practitioners, Parents & Teachers.* Chichester: Wiley Blackwell.

Young, S., Hollingdale, J., Absound, M., Bolton, P. *et al.* (2020) 'Guidance for identification and treatment of individuals with attention deficit/hyperactivity disorder and autism spectrum disorder based upon expert consensus.' *BMC Medicine 18*, 1, 146.

Chapter 2

Assessment of ADHD in Girls

Unlocking Hidden Superpowers through Understanding ADHD

—— CLAIRE BERRY AND JESS BRUNET ——

Attention deficit hyperactivity disorder (ADHD) as a diagnosis is diverse in its presentation and therefore affects different people in different ways, depicting a different pattern of strengths (or superpowers!) as well as areas of need where more support is required. Symptoms of ADHD can vary from the preschool years through to adolescence, with girls typically thought of as presenting with more of an inattentive type presentation; although we will explore how symptoms of inattention, hyperactivity and impulsivity can present in girls.

In this chapter we will look at ADHD symptoms in relation to girls with the aim of providing an insight from a clinical perspective into everything from what is important to include in the initial referral information screening to the assessment process itself and how ADHD in girls may present at school, and how we gather this information. As we go through the chapter, we will provide tips you may wish to consider along your assessment journey, whether you're a parent or professional supporting a child or young person with an ADHD diagnosis or a suspected diagnosis.

REFERRING FOR ASSESSMENT AND SCREENING REFERRALS

The first stage of the assessment process is for a referral for assessment to be made to the relevant local service. The role of assessment is ordinarily held by a local Community Paediatric Service or a local Child and Adolescent Mental Health Service (CAMHS). Referrals are ordinarily made by GPs or schools (often the Special Educational Needs Co-ordinator or SENCO) but at times self-referrals from family are received. Whilst each team is likely to have its own referral criteria (which should be identified by the referrer prior to sending the referral), the following information will provide an insight into some of the core information most services will require and subsequently assess.

As part of the screening process for ADHD referrals, information is collected from parents/carers, the school and the young person. This is because symptoms of ADHD need to be seen across more than one setting and there needs to be some evidence of ADHD consistent with the diagnostic criteria, as per DSM-5 (American Psychiatric Association 2013) or ICD-11 (World Health Organization 2018).

In some circumstances the idea of an ADHD assessment will have been suggested by a professional such as a teacher or paediatrician; however, it may be the parents who are the first ones to consider this. In some cases, the young person themselves may want to pursue the assessment, particularly those in their teenage years who may have heard about ADHD. Sometimes young people have learnt about ADHD through unlikely superheroes such as those in the *Percy Jackson* books. These books depict a 12-year-old boy who has ADHD and dyslexia and is descended from a Greek god. He goes on epic quests and discovers how his difficulties may actually be his strengths.

☼ **TIP:**
You can find out more about Percy Jackson on the website of the author, Rick Riordan: www.rickriordan.com.

Different services use different screening tools for ADHD. A commonly used measure is the Conners 3 questionnaire (parent, teacher and self-report version) (Conners 2008), which looks at the core symptoms of ADHD including inattention, hyperactivity, impulsivity, defiance/aggression, executive functioning and peer relationships. The Conners 3 comes in both long and short versions; the long version also considers comorbidities (conditions which co-occur with ADHD) such as anxiety, depression, conduct disorder and oppositional defiant disorder. The parent and teacher versions are validated within the age range 6–18 years, and the self-report version is validated in the age range 8–18 years. In clinical settings, the Conners 3 questionnaire often scores highly across the domains of inattention, hyperactivity/impulsivity and defiance/aggression for boys. In comparison, girls will tend to reach clinically significant scores predominantly for inattention and, on the long Conners 3, within the domains of depression, anxiety and oppositional behaviours (usually linked to emotional lability). Peer relationships tend to score highly in both genders.

Conners 3 questionnaires completed by schools can often not reach clinically significant scores for girls. The reason for this is that whilst girls may be chatty, daydreamy or have difficulty with their social relationships, from their teachers' perspective these may not be identified as being linked to traits of ADHD. It is therefore important to use the self-report versions of outcome measures such as the Conners 3 so that information is collected from the young person themselves, which reflects more accurately the areas in which they are struggling. Girls completing the self-report Conners 3 will frequently score themselves significantly across the majority of domains, which can present as disparate from teacher and parent/carer questionnaires but highlights the internalised, cognitive aspects of the condition which the girls may be masking.

The Conners 3 questionnaire is not the only ADHD screening measure available, and families and teachers may also be asked to complete an alternative screening tool. Examples of some alternative measures are as follows:

- **SNAP-IV 18 or 26**: This is an abbreviated version of the SNAP questionnaire (Swanson *et al.* 2001). The 18-question measure looks only at hyperactivity/impulsivity and inattention whereas the 26-item measure also looks at oppositional symptoms. Both home and school complete the same measure of the SNAP-IV. There is also a longer, 90-question version of the measure available. The measure is validated for 6- to 18-year-olds.

- **ADHD-RS**: The ADHD Rating Scale (also known in different forms as the ADHD RV IV/mADHD-RS) (DuPaul *et al.* 1998; Barkley *et al.* 1999) comes in home and school versions. Norms (scores) are calculated differently for different ages, boys and girls, and home and school. The measure is validated for 6- to 18-year-olds; however, there is also a Preschool ADHD-RS for ages 3–5 years (McGoey *et al.* 2007).

- **Vanderbilt ADHD Diagnostic Rating Scale**: The Vanderbilt (Wolraich *et al.* 2003) again comes in parent and teacher versions and is predominantly used in the assessment of children aged 6–12 years.

☀️TIP:

The SNAP-IV, ADHD-RS and Vanderbilt are freely available to download online. If you are a parent/carer of a child you feel would benefit from an ADHD assessment, or a teacher of a pupil you feel would benefit from an assessment, submitting completed home and school rating scales with a referral can support your referral information.

It is often recognised in assessment teams that there are higher referral rates for ADHD in boys than for girls. The chapter authors looked at the prevalence of girls either referred for ADHD assessments or accessing treatment within their own services. Within one service (CAMHS) girls made up 33% of the referrals for ADHD over a period of a year compared with 67% for boys; in the other service

(Community Paediatrics), girls made up 25% of the children and young people being treated with medication for ADHD.

Within a Child and Adolescent Mental Health (CAMHS) setting, ADHD symptoms are often picked up by a clinician when they have started a talking therapy intervention for depression or anxiety. Clinicians may note the executive function deficits and mind wandering linked with ADHD or excessive chattiness and find themselves on tangents within the therapy session. The girls are then subsequently referred for further assessment.

In a Community Paediatric setting, if a girl is attending for assessment of autism spectrum disorder (ASD), symptoms of ADHD may also be identified during the assessment process.

In clinical practice, girls are often referred at a later stage and therefore tend to be assessed in their teenage years as compared with boys, who will present to services at a much younger age. It should be noted that it is not uncommon for a girl's brother to be assessed initially and the family subsequently to consider that their daughter may also have aspects of the condition not previously picked up on.

With increased awareness of the female presentation of ADHD available online, girls and young women are beginning to request exploration of their symptoms themselves, having watched a YouTube channel or read about symptoms online which, for them, explain why they might have been struggling at school and/or been having difficulties at home.

☼TIPS:

When seeking a referral for ADHD – whether it is for a child of preschool age, primary school age or at secondary school – you will strengthen your referral information by showing that the symptoms are present in more than one setting (e.g. home and school) and have an impact on your child's or pupil's functioning. Remember that being 'bright' doesn't mean ADHD is not present; if the child in question is not reaching their potential due to symptoms of inattention, hyperactivity and/or impulsivity, then an assessment may be beneficial. Consider getting reports from nursery or school. Observations are normally the most beneficial piece of information on a referral form – what does that GP, teacher, scout leader, etc. see when they are with the child being referred? For young people who are old enough, asking if they're able to write down what it feels like at school and at home from their perspective is even more valuable. Pair this with a home rating scale and school rating scale (as mentioned above) and you have got a comprehensive referral. Ensure that the person completing the referral forms is someone who knows the child well and sees them on a regular basis.

✋ KEY POINTS

» ADHD symptoms need to be evidenced in more than one setting.

» There are a range of screening tools available for completion by parents, teacher and girls.

ASSESSMENT PROCESS
What to expect

The main thing for families to expect when engaging their young person in an assessment for ADHD is an assessment that is both holistic and comprehensive. It is acknowledged that some NHS services have long waiting times for assessment, and families may choose to seek a private assessment for ADHD due to the level of concern they have for their child. If seeking a private assessment for ADHD, it is important to ensure that the clinician conducting the assessment is experienced in completing ADHD assessments with children and young people.

Whether families are seeking NHS or private treatment, it should be noted that whilst the ADHD assessment focuses on concluding if a child meets the diagnostic criteria for ADHD or not, the process of assessment should also focus on ruling in or out whether there are any other conditions which may occur alongside ADHD, or which are causing the symptoms the family or school have identified as areas of concern and believe may be ADHD.

It is good practice to look at a range of aspects at both school and home which may be leading to impairment or may be the cause of behaviours seen. A thorough assessment will consider the child in the context of their whole family alongside any learning or health needs. The assessment should not focus on the child only, and families should be aware that it is a normal part of the assessment process to consider family functioning and dynamics. Sometimes additional difficulties within the family and/or school context are identified. If present, these should be assessed further so the impact on the child can be ascertained. This enables the assessing clinician to understand if ADHD is contributing to the difficulties at home or school; or if difficulties at home or school are contributing to or leading to the child's symptoms.

Clinicians will often provide the option of the child or young person being seen alone so that the girl is able to openly discuss any social or emotional difficulties commonly associated with ADHD and to explore her mental health.

Families and other professionals can identify what is expected from the assessment process by looking at the NICE guidance for ADHD. The National Institute for Health and Care Excellence (NICE) collates current research and best practice, and provides guidance on what is advised for assessment and treatment of health conditions. The current NICE Guidance for ADHD is NG87 (2018) but it is regularly updated.

☀TIPS:

If your child is assessed privately for ADHD but requires ongoing treatment within the NHS for their condition, or if your original assessment was completed in the NHS but you have moved and require treatment by a new team in a new area, it is likely that the report will be checked to identify if it is 'NICE compliant'. This means that from reading the report, the new team will be able to identify how the original assessors concluded a diagnosis of ADHD. A NICE compliant report will often include the following:

- information from home and school about the child's functioning

- an early developmental history (or reference to a report which provides this)

- the breakdown of scores from the screening questionnaires used and what these show

- that the assessing team has considered other conditions as well as ADHD and ruled these in or out or made alternative referrals

- if available (and therefore not always included), the outcome of a QbTest completed. The QbTest or QbCheck is a computerised assessment tool that monitors for movement and can aid the assessment process by informing clinicians about a person's level of hyperactivity, impulsivity and inattention based on their responses to the continuous performance task completed on screen. The QbTest results should be integrated into the assessment alongside information gathered from home and school and not used to diagnose as an assessment on their own (Hall *et al.* 2017)

- that the rationale for the diagnosis or no diagnosis is stated clearly

- an observation from in clinic and possibly from school (or comments of observations reported by school or extracurricular clubs)

- a care plan and recommendations.

If this information is not provided, in order to safely take over the care of the young person, the new team may need to complete elements of their own assessment to confirm the diagnosis and produce a NICE compliant report.

Developmental history

Whilst it is important to gain information on key milestones when obtaining the child's developmental history, consideration of the child's temperament will often highlight that from an early age boys have experienced problems with aggression, hyperactivity and impulsivity, resulting in obvious and externalised problems. Girls, on the other hand, can tend not to have the same sort of behavioural problems as their male counterparts, and a common report from parents is that the child has always appeared to be in a world of her own. Other common reports from parents include their daughter having difficulties listening and following instructions, and being easily distracted as well as excessively chatty. Whilst these difficulties are often considered not to be as disruptive as the behaviour shown in boys, they can cause significant impairment in all areas of a child's life as they get older and become more independent. Another important aspect of the developmental history to ascertain is whether there are any other difficulties from early childhood which could mimic ADHD symptoms. These include the parents' early bonding with the child and whether there may be any attachment or mental health difficulties, including early childhood trauma, anxiety and depression. Such difficulties can be seen across both genders (Klein *et al.* 2014).

Part of obtaining a thorough developmental history includes gaining an understanding of factors which may increase the risk of ADHD, including substance misuse and/or smoking during pregnancy (Knopik *et al.* 2016). In addition to this, families should be aware they will likely be asked whether the child's mother was taking any medications during pregnancy, as well as about the home environment during pregnancy (and exposure to any violence), birth weight and whether the child was born premature or late.

Whilst not the classic developmental history, having the child give an insight into their own perspective on growing up, and ruling in or out any situations they found particularly 'scary' or challenges they have overcome at school and home, provides valuable information as part of the assessment process.

The first consideration of ADHD

The majority of girls who present to services will be thought to present with an inattentive type presentation, whereby they will struggle in the areas of attention, and many families who have requested an assessment will often refer to these symptoms as attention deficit disorder (ADD).

Whilst girls do not always have the overt hyperactivity and impulsivity that is commonly seen in boys, part of the assessment will be to discuss common features of hyperactivity in girls (such as being chatty, changing friendships a lot or finding themselves in dangerous situations).

Due to ADHD presenting differently across the genders, for some parents the beginning of the assessment process can be the first time they have thought about their daughter having ADHD. Parents will often report a stereotyped view of ADHD as a child who is very hyperactive and gets into trouble a lot, and so had not considered that their daughter's difficulties may be attributed to this. It is not uncommon to hear parents describe their daughter as a daydreamer or being in her own world. This is when it can be helpful to discuss the different ways ADHD can present between the genders.

This also highlights the importance of raising awareness in parents of what to look for in girls with ADHD. Some parents may be reluctant to pursue a diagnosis initially, if they are not aware of how ADHD presents in girls. As already mentioned earlier in the chapter, late diagnosis can have negative consequences for a young person. Other parents will report that whilst they have considered ADHD, this has been dismissed by others (such as other family members, teachers or health professionals), which has resulted in the referral not being made.

During the assessment process, it has been observed that particularly mothers of girls being assessed for ADHD can begin to consider their own difficulties, which are often similar to those of their daughters. They will therefore start to consider if they themselves could have ADHD. Mothers will often report that they have never considered their difficulties within the context of ADHD, but will speak of their own struggles throughout their life due to their difficulties with inattention and possibly impulsive behaviour. It is not uncommon for parents to subsequently think about their own assessment. Some parents who have their own challenges with ADHD symptoms, particularly organisational skills, have reported that they can find it hard to support their child as a result of this. Therefore, parents seeking out an ADHD assessment for themselves can have a real benefit in terms of treating their own symptoms, which can then have a positive impact on the child.

☀ TIP:

> If you are a parent of a child whom you think may have ADHD, but also feel you might have ADHD too, you could ask your child's clinician about the local processes for adults to get assessed for ADHD. Chapter 7 contains more information around assessment in women.

GETTING THE RIGHT CLINICAL APPROACH TO ASSESSMENT

From a clinical perspective, in order to complete a thorough assessment, it is important to get the young person's insight into the functional deficits and cognitive difficulties associated with ADHD, rather than focusing solely on their behaviour. Having the young person narrate a 'day in their life' and finding out how it feels inside their world and their brain gives rise to helpful understanding of how their ADHD affects them personally. Encouraging the use of anecdotes, drawings or even gestures can prove fruitful, with young people usually relating to characters such as the Duracell Bunny or Sonic the Hedgehog, or reverting to expressive arm movements to show how they can feel.

During the assessment, girls will often describe themselves as being very chatty, and share that in class they may be reprimanded by teachers for talking or whispering. Equally, where their mind frequently wanders in lessons, they might say they frequently lose track of what has been asked of them in lessons and so may end up chatting to find out what they are supposed to be doing. This often comes out in the assessment process, particularly if trying to engage them in a long task perceived as boring (e.g. a cognitive assessment); girls with ADHD will often deflect from the task, particularly when younger, by chatting and making excuses to leave their seat, such as wanting to show their parents how they are getting on or to use the bathroom. For older teens during prolonged assessments, you are more likely to notice low-level fidgeting such as a slight foot tap, picking at clothing, or fiddling with fingers or nails. Equally, you may notice they will ask questions to be repeated or might go off topic, chatting about friends, family members or events that have happened in a manner that assumes knowledge about them on your part.

In clinics, the combination of symptoms can often result in girls feeling low self-esteem, feeling not as good as their peers and not knowing why they can't do things in a way others can. From this perspective, considering the diagnosis can be a relief or at least a known 'thing' which they can begin to tackle with the support of their family, clinician and school.

It is imperative to have the young person's voice throughout your assessment; however, assessing risk associated with ADHD is also integral. Substance misuse and promiscuous behaviour are noted to be higher in young women with ADHD (Quinn 2005) and therefore sensitively exploring these topics alongside sexual health precautions being taken (and onward referral to sexual health clinics, if required) should be factored into the assessment process.

☀ TIPS:

Ensure that children and young people are given the opportunity to speak about their difficulties and experiences. Allowing a space to reflect on their difficulties away from their parents/carers can on occasion result in obtaining more information, particularly in relation to risk factors. Teenagers are likely to be able to articulate their difficulties and the impact these have on them. As parents and professionals, we can often assume we know how a child feels as a result of their difficulties, and what is causing them the most concern; however, the young person's views can often be different.

Focus on what is going well for the young person. Assessments can often be heavily focused on things the child is finding difficult and not doing so well at. All children and young people will have their own unique strengths and interests outside of academic performance, and it can be particularly helpful to focus on those. As a way of building young people's self-esteem and supporting them to see their hidden superpowers, this is a vital part of the assessment and diagnostic process. Some young people may find it hard to identify their own strengths, and so you may want to draw on others around the child who can share their views on the child's strengths, including teachers, parents and the assessing clinicians.

Focusing on positive aspects of ADHD early on during the assessment can make the idea of a diagnosis less daunting. Young people can be shown a list of famous people who have an ADHD diagnosis, which helps them to see how ADHD symptoms can serve as positive qualities for future success.

SCAFFOLDING

Parents will often take an active role in supporting children in their early years, which can mask symptoms of ADHD (particularly inattention), and this is something for clinicians to unpick during the assessment. Scaffolding can include parents supporting children to organise their school uniform and equipment, helping them with homework, and getting children to school and social events on time. When girls transition to secondary school there is more of an expectation for them to become independent in the areas of study and day-to-day organisation. Some young people will want to become more independent, even if this proves difficult, whereas others may not.

This scaffolding and areas of transition are also key points to discuss with the young person. Girls are quite often referred for assessment for ADHD once they have transitioned to secondary school, and will frequently tell you that in primary school, their teachers got to know them so would 'fill in the gaps' in the areas they struggled with, such as helping with reminders for equipment needed (or having extra available in the classroom) or ensuring that their role in the class was more physically active, for example being in charge or giving out and collecting books.

Young girls often highlight the transition to secondary school as a big step up due to the increasing demands on their executive function skills. Having multiple teachers, classrooms, subjects and deadlines as well as the social pressures of secondary school can lead to symptoms showing themselves more readily or feeling more overwhelming.

When considering ADHD, it is therefore important to consider if parents or teachers may be providing a lot of scaffolding for the child, which could be masking any ADHD symptoms. For example, parents will report that they will support the child to get their school equipment ready the night before by going through their planner with them, will make checklists with them, sit with them to complete homework and drive them to school to ensure they are on time. Or, they might enrol them in several extra-curricular activities to save the child from feeling bored and to give them an energy outlet in the evening. It may appear to others that the child is managing as they do not see the extra work that parents or other adults are putting in place to support them.

This highlights the importance of establishing what support is already being put in place for the child, as some strategies will be those that are recommended for use with young people with ADHD. This can therefore result in a reduction of ADHD symptoms, so it is important to consider the role of parents in supporting their child and to consider how the child would be managing without this support. Equally, it is important to identify what work-arounds and strategies the young person is already using to account for 'being forgetful' or taking too long in the shower in the morning. It is not uncommon for young people to be utilising apps on their phones, their phone calendar or reminder system as well as the alarm. For older teenage girls, asking them about how they prep for exams or big assignments will give a beneficial insight into their organisational skills and how they may use peers to scaffold them, for example studying with a friend to help them stay on track.

How young people's difficulties are understood is important. Some parents have reported that they have dismissed these difficulties as being due to laziness and a lack of motivation on the young person's part, which can then impact on how they respond to these impairments. Similarly, young people will pick up on this narrative and will relay to the assessor, 'I don't know why I can't do it; I'm just lazy' or 'I'm just stupid', which internalises the ADHD symptoms as being something that is wrong with them as a person, rather than as symptoms of a diagnosis that they are able to overcome. A negative narrative can be a source of tension within homes that not only causes added stress to parents, who are having to provide a lot more support for their daughter's day-to-day organisation, but also can lead to more emotional outbursts by the young person, who feels they are not achieving or are not good enough. This is also where tensions can heighten, as whilst some young people will accept help from their parents, others will strive for independence and reject any help, even if they know they are unable to manage without it.

When parents understand their child's difficulties within the context of an ADHD diagnosis, this can ensure that they are able to provide the right support. This can often result in parents responding differently to the child's symptoms as they understand them as being associated with ADHD rather than the child just not doing what they have been asked. Similarly, it can also be an opportunity for the young person to begin to understand their symptoms and start to externalise some of their difficulties as a way to begin to challenge them, for example seeing ADHD as something they can get to know and work with rather than their being 'stupid' or 'lazy'. This can have a positive impact on the child and in turn the parent–child relationship.

☀️TIPS:

Ask parents, teachers and young people what they think would happen if the support they are being given was not there. Would the young person still be able to complete the tasks they are currently able to or would this result in more noticeable difficulties?

Always ask for specific examples where a young person is reported to be able to carry out tasks and ask the parents what they will be doing at this time. It can often be the case that parents or young people will report that the child can do a task, but on further questioning it becomes evident that this is done only with the support or prompting of a parent.

✋ KEY POINTS

» Assessments should meet NICE guidelines and consider alternative explanations for the reported symptoms.

» Assessments should focus on the impact of the symptoms on a girl's functioning and cognition, not just her behaviour.

» Consider whether teachers and parents are scaffolding and therefore masking the extent of the concerns.

HYPERACTIVITY AND IMPULSIVITY

Whilst we have discussed how inattention can seem to be a predominant symptom of ADHD in girls, this is not to say that girls do not experience symptoms of hyperactivity and impulsivity. It is important to remember that whilst there are differences in relation to how hyperactivity and impulsivity can present in boys and girls, they can still cause significant impact, just in a different way. Being aware of hyperactivity and impulsivity in girls can also lead to earlier detection of ADHD as parents and young people will not always be aware that their hyperactive symptoms fall under this domain.

In preschool age children, hyperactivity and impulsivity may be the predominant behaviour that is initially noted by parents. As girls get older, inattention tends to become the main difficulty noticed or attributed to ADHD symptoms.

Parents of boys will report lots of overactivity in the classic sense of their child not being able to remain seated, constantly being on the go and running around. In girls, hyperactivity can tend to present in other ways; a main report from parents is in relation to emotional reactivity.

Pre-school and primary age children will find it harder to identify and express their emotions. Parents tend to report that as children get older, this is a skill they begin to develop; however, for some this can take longer. Extreme emotional responses are an aspect of hyperactivity that can present in girls with ADHD. Parents will often report that their daughters can have difficulties with regulating their emotions and their reactions can appear extreme and over-exaggerated, whilst it also takes them a long time to come down from them. These responses can present as extreme mood swings in teenage girls.

Young people will often report that they can find the school day exhausting as they are trying to navigate their way through a day which requires a lot of organisation, planning and focus. This can result in girls trying to suppress their emotions within the school environment so as not to appear different to their peers. As a result, they can display this pent-up emotion when they return home. Others will report feeling overwhelmed at school, and this can result in emotional outbursts occurring in the classroom environment.

Excessive talking can also be a symptom of hyperactivity in girls. When children are younger, this can present as the child being sociable; however, parents will report that as their daughter gets older, this can cause difficulties in their interactions with others as they can begin to be perceived as being dominant. Parents also report a common theme from parent evenings and school reports that their daughter talks too much in lessons.

Girls can present with restlessness, which is evidenced by fidgeting with their hands and legs. This form of hyperactivity is less disruptive in a class setting and therefore may go unnoticed. As girls get older, they start to develop ways to manage their hyperactivity and some will report that things such as doodling during lessons or the use of fidget toys can help with symptoms of hyperactivity and inattention. Parents and teachers will often notice this but as the child can remain seated, it is often not seen as disruptive or having a significant impact on the child.

When it comes to impulsive actions, girls can still find themselves in dangerous situations or acting without thinking. Examples can often crop up in social situations, with arguments being started quickly over something relatively minor or girls not being able to problem solve events that occur. Equally, trying to impress others, or becoming over-excited and shouting out comments that will get a laugh, or posting inappropriate or inconsiderate items on social media without realising the potential impact may all be factors in impulsivity. In younger girls, running off or climbing and jumping on things without being able to calm down again after can all be features of impulsivity.

☀ TIPS:

When a child or young person shows extreme emotional responses, try to think about what is going on for that young person and what they might be trying to communicate rather than just focusing on the negative aspects of the emotion or behaviour. Consider what was going on before the emotion was expressed and try to identify any common triggers. Younger children will find it harder to express their emotions so try using visual aids to support them in drawing and writing down how they feel.

WORKING STYLES

For adolescent girls with ADHD, parents will tend to report two differing types of working styles in relation to their schoolwork. The first is that the young person will spend excessive periods of time completing their work (often called having perfectionist traits), which can often result in late nights and working into the early hours of the morning as they are having to work much harder than their peers to keep up. In turn this can often further impact on the child's inattentive symptoms and their mental health. This can also suggest why difficulties may not be as apparent to the school as they are not seeing the amount of work that is being carried out behind the scenes.

During the assessment girls may describe feeling frustrated at school, and finding it really hard to start tasks, keep organised with homework or finding that they procrastinate long into the night by putting off their work in favour of researching obscure things on the internet or chatting on social media. It is also not uncommon for girls to discuss that when they can finally get into a task, they hyperfocus (which is being intensely focused on a task) alongside their perfectionist traits, which can lead to work being ripped up, thrown in the bin and/or impulsive emotional outbursts due to their studying not going as planned.

The second type of working style reported by parents is that the child has become avoidant of completing work altogether. This can often cause frustration and tension within the home, particularly when the child rejects the parent's support. A common report from parents is that homework can feel like a battle with their child. This can also lead to anxiety for the young person, and it is important to explore both with her and her parents/carers whether this struggle is impacting on her mental health. Young girls will often somatise, and experience stomach aches and/or become particularly clingy to a parent or carer, whereas older teens may miss lessons or school, become excessively tearful over schoolwork or experience panic attacks. Exploring with the young person any triggers linked to work and school during the assessment, and unpicking with them when and how these feelings started and what might help can be very therapeutic. There are often simple interventions, such as discussing with teachers or supporting the young person to organise their workload, which can help alleviate some of this stress and anxiety.

Younger children will find it harder to consider the impact that their difficulties have on them but they become more aware of this as they get older. Although this awareness can be helpful for children in terms of understanding their difficulties and finding ways to manage them, it can also bring about difficulties as adolescents will tend to start reporting that they feel different to their peers.

☀ TIP:

For parents and teachers of girls who are having emotional outbursts linked to work, it would be helpful to start keeping a diary or chart to record what was happening before the outburst (e.g. she was asked to complete a piece of work in a set period of time). Also note what the behaviour was (e.g. ripping up work, shouting) and finally the consequences of the behaviour (e.g. work avoided, got a behaviour point or detention, reprimanded at home). This can help to build up a picture of what might be the trigger to behaviours, but also what your young person is trying to convey. Is the work too hard? Does she not respond well to time pressures? Is she trying to get sent to her room to avoid homework?

ADHD AND COMORBIDITIES

Approximately 70% of people diagnosed with ADHD will have a comorbid condition (National Institute for Health and Care Excellence 2018) including ASD and anxiety. Within some clinical settings, such as that of the authors, it is mandatory that any referrals for neurodevelopmental assessments are screened for both ADHD and ASD due to how often these conditions co-occur, despite the original referral only requesting screening for one condition. For example, if a young person is referred for an autism assessment but the screening tools for ADHD show clinical significance across settings and there is evidence of tics, then all disorders would be assessed for. The rationale for this is that in order to optimally support the young person to identify their superpowers, we need to know and name the areas of need, so we get the strategies and support right. On a more functional level, this can also help the professionals around the young person make the right decision about their needs, for example what support should be put in place at school or whether an Education, Health and Care Plan (EHCP) should be applied for and updated. It will also aid DLA (Disability Living Allowance) and PIP (Personal Independent Payments) assessments if the young person's diagnosis and impact on function are clearly stated. Both DLA and PIP are benefits to support with health-related costs of a long-term health condition; DLA can be applied for on behalf of children and young people under 16 and PIP is the equivalent for over 16s.

Another factor to consider during an assessment is whether onward referral to any other agencies is needed to consider other conditions which may exist alongside the ADHD and could account for some of the difficulties the child is presenting with. Examples of comorbid conditions include mental health disorders, sensory processing disorder, learning difficulties and dyspraxia. Clinicians should be aware of the associated disorders that can occur alongside ADHD and be able to identify when a referral is needed for assessment by other agencies such as occupational therapy, paediatrics, educational psychology and Child and Adolescent Mental Health Services (CAMHS).

If other difficulties or disorders are not picked up during the assessment, then this can often result in the child not getting the right support and therefore not progressing as they should. For example, in some cases ADHD medication will be prescribed following an assessment but if other disorders have been missed, the medication alone will not be an effective intervention.

Assessments should not be rushed and may need to be carried out over several sessions. Due to girls not always displaying the overt behaviours of ADHD, this can mean a longer period of assessment is needed. Therefore, information around emotional symptomology and social adjustment, which is gained via interview with the young person, may take longer to gather than with boys where it is the overt behaviour that is identifiable.

It is important for clinicians and parents to be aware that the assessment process does not finish once a diagnosis has or has not been given. Assessment is ongoing, and some difficulties may not present until later in the child's life or not at all. It is important for everyone who is involved with the child to be aware of this and not to attribute all difficulties to the ADHD diagnosis. There is a danger that assuming all difficulties are linked to the ADHD diagnosis may result in other disorders being missed.

☀-TIPS for parents/carers:

If you feel that your child may have difficulties which are associated with another disorder, it can be helpful to raise this with the assessing clinician. It is also helpful to know about any family history of specific difficulties or disorders and to ensure that the assessing clinician is made aware of this.

☀-TIPS for clinicians:

When conducting an ADHD assessment, ensure you complete a holistic assessment of the young person and family, considering other things outside of ADHD that may either account for the ADHD symptoms or could be exacerbating them. It can be easy to focus solely on the ADHD aspect of the assessment; however, thorough assessments across all areas will result in a more accurate diagnosis and the most appropriate evidence-based interventions being used. Assessments do not need to be completed in one session so consider bringing the family back for further assessment if you still feel there is further information to be obtained following the first appointment.

ADHD, MENTAL HEALTH DIFFICULTIES AND ASD

Girls with ADHD tend to internalise their difficulties more than boys (Quinn and Madhoo 2014). It is for this reason that in the first instance many girls will often present to services with a mental health difficulty such as anxiety and/or depression. During a mental health assessment, clinicians may start to consider these difficulties within the context of a possible underlying neurodevelopmental condition such as ADHD. They will then refer these girls on for an ADHD assessment. As previously mentioned, these girls typically present to services in their teenage years.

Parents may not be fully aware of the extent of a young person's mental health difficulties, and therefore it is important to gain information from both parents and the young person in relation to this. Sometimes parents can score children low on screening measures for anxiety and depression and the child can score themselves more highly, or vice versa, and therefore having a dialogue around what each person has marked on the measure and why will help to unpick this.

There may also be some notable differences in terms of their eating and sleeping along with reports of self-harm and suicidal thoughts. Some parents may not be aware of the latter until the child discloses this at the assessment. It is therefore an important part of the assessment to consider the child's safety and to support parents in understanding these behaviours and how to support their child. This again highlights the need to identify if there is underlying ADHD as without treating this, the mental health difficulties are likely to remain. Chapter 4 looks in more detail at mental health difficulties and ADHD.

Parents who have a child with an ASD diagnosis will often report that ADHD might have been considered in the past, but that it was felt that the difficulties with inattention could be accounted for by the ASD and so assessment of ADHD was put on hold. As the child gets older, parents tend to notice more pronounced difficulties associated with ADHD, particularly inattention. A meta-analysis of community and clinic samples of children with ADHD found 21% also had ASD (Hollingdale *et al.* 2019).

Girls presenting with both ADHD and ASD can feel complex to assess. It is important to understand their specialist interests as these are the areas on which they are likely to become hyperfocused. Equally, understanding associated sensory needs and how the girl responds will be beneficial; for example, rocking and/or flapping in a crowded or stressful space may be assumed to be hyperactivity, whereas actually these are sensory-seeking behaviours linked to ASD. Autism may have gone undetected in girls with both conditions due to social masking, but also because their ADHD symptoms may aid them in social situations by helping them to feel more able to chat to others.

☀TIP:

If your child or pupil is presenting with suicidal thoughts or self-harm, it is important that she is seen as soon as possible by a health professional. This may be someone she is already working with, such as a CAMHS worker, otherwise contact her GP or local walk-in service so her mental health can be assessed. In an emergency, always go to Accident and Emergency or call 999.

TICS

Tics are involuntary movements, commonly vocal or motor, and can have a sudden onset (Oluwabusi, Parke and Ambrosini 2016). Examples include coughing, clearing of the throat, blinking and head jerking. Tourette's syndrome is diagnosed when there are multiple tics of both vocal and motor types which have been present for a period of over a year and are deemed chronic. Of those diagnosed with Tourette's syndrome, it has been estimated that 60% will also have a diagnosis of ADHD (Ogundele and Ayyash 2018).

In clinic, it has been observed that tics are more prevalent in the male population, but girls can still present with tics. Parents often report that tics come and go and the forms in which they present can change. Parents and young people will often note that tics tend to present at times of stress, which can include major transitions and exams.

When you are assessing children, parents will often report that there have been periods of time when the tics have not been present. It is helpful to keep this in mind as this may be the case at the time of the assessment. However, it is still important to consider what tics have been present previously, the age of onset and how they have impacted on the child when they have been present.

Parents may express concern as to whether they should highlight the tics to their child in order to try to stop them from engaging in them. Younger children will not always be aware of their tics but as they get older, peers can start to comment on these, especially if they become distracting in the classroom environment. Children can often report feeling self-conscious about their tics but struggle to prevent themselves engaging in them. This can have a negative impact on their mental health; children can report feeling anxious and depressed about it. It is helpful to identify tics at the earliest opportunity as it may be that a psychological intervention could be offered to treat these, especially as tics alone can have a significant impact on the young person. Identifying tics and Tourette's syndrome is also important in relation to prescribing the most appropriate ADHD medication.

☀ TIP:

Good conversations about tics between home and school are important. Tics will come and go and change over time but can also be exacerbated by anxiety such as school changes, exams, social pressures or stressors at home. Checking in with the young person if you notice an increase in tics and asking about any current worries may be helpful to them.

RISK AND ADHD

When assessing a young person for ADHD, whilst it can be a difficult subject, discussing risk will be one of the most important parts of the assessment process. Young women with ADHD are at a higher risk of teenage pregnancy, and both boys and girls with ADHD are noted on average to have sexual experiences at a younger age, have more sexual partners and be less likely to use contraception (Wehmeier, Schacht and Barley 2010). Sexual exploitation is another area of vulnerability which needs to be considered, especially if the young woman is known for 'acting in the moment'. Whilst these are challenging topics for parents to consider, they must be considered in order to help keep young people safe.

For young women, risk-taking behaviour may not seem obviously linked with ADHD; however, difficulty maintaining friendships or not feeling like they belong can lead to vulnerability to gang involvement (a risk which is greater in city areas), or for fallouts with friends to lead to violence. This is something which, in clinical practice, can feel more routinely considered in boys.

Drugs and alcohol needed to also be considered and approached delicately. Sometimes young people will inadvertently use illicit substances to manage their symptoms, such as using cannabis to help them sleep. If a young person is using drugs, the assessing clinician should attempt to identify where possible the rationale for this, what the pros and cons are for the young person of taking this medication and how willing are they to reduce their intake.

Asking open questions around mental health, self-harm and suicidal thoughts, especially in young people aged 12 years and upwards, is vital; remember that self-harm can take many forms from hitting themselves, burning and cutting, to putting themselves in risky situations because they no longer care about their well-being. Parents/carers may be asked to step outside during challenging conversations to enable the young person to speak freely. As difficult as this may be for parents/carers, not all young people are comfortable talking about these topics around their parents/carers. Clinicians always assess risk, and will disclose to you any need-to-know information whilst maintaining as much as the young person's confidentiality as possible as the main objective in these situations is to allow the adults and professionals around the young person to respond to and manage the risk.

Again, in order to best support the young person with any aspect of the above, further support may be required from mental health services or young people's drug and alcohol services, or from social workers around gang affiliation, and therefore onward referrals are likely to be discussed in this context.

☀ TIP for clinicians:

Using a motivational interviewing approach may be beneficial when looking at the young person's readiness to reduce and stop their drug intake.

☀ TIP for parents/carers:

If you have concerns about any of the risks mentioned above and want to discuss anything in confidence with your child or young person's assessing clinician, call in advance and make this known or request it at the time of your assessment.

ADHD AND PHYSICAL HEALTH

During the assessment process, considering other factors which could be impacting on or exacerbating the young person's symptoms is an important part of information gathering. Physical health conditions play a role in this, and whilst the following list of comorbidities is by no means exhaustive, they are commonly seen within a clinical setting.

Iron deficiency/ferritin

Ferritin is a protein in the blood which helps with the storage of iron in the body; serum ferritin levels can be used to indicate reduced iron levels with or without anaemia. Wang *et al.* (2017) identified a statistically significant result of serum ferritin being lower in people with an ADHD diagnosis (in the absence of low serum iron or anaemia) in comparison with controls (people without ADHD), which may suggest an association between serum ferritin levels and ADHD type symptoms. Whilst there is some variation in the research on the association between low serum ferritin levels and ADHD, young women who experience heavy menstrual bleeding may also experience low serum ferritin levels (Johnson *et al.* 2016), which may in turn impact on cognitive function and their behavioural presentation (Cortese *et al.* 2012). A blood test, usually completed via the GP, can indicate a young person's serum ferritin levels.

Epilepsy

The prevalence of ADHD in children with epilepsy is a minimum of 2.5 higher than in children who do not experience seizures (Aaberg *et al.* 2016). ADHD symptoms present as more severely and more commonly as inattentive type ADHD when a child also has epilepsy (Davis *et al.* 2010). Valproate, a common treatment for epilepsy, is also associated with difficulties with attention and so will need to be considered as part of the assessment if it is prescribed to the child being assessed.

Genetic conditions

Certain genetic conditions – such as Williams syndrome, Fragile X syndrome, neurofibromatosis type 1 and tuberous sclerosis complex, to name a few – are associated with ADHD symptoms (Lo-Castro, D'Agati and Curatolo 2011). It would be highly beneficial for families to disclose any genetic conditions they are aware of at the time of assessment to aid the clinical team with their assessment.

Sleep difficulties

Sleep difficulties are routinely reported during the ADHD assessment process; however, sleep difficulties do not always arise as a result of ADHD, but can be linked to a sleep disorder. Restless leg syndrome (an irresistible urge to move or jerk the legs eased with voluntary muscle movements), periodic limb movement in sleep (involuntary muscle movements or twitches often in the legs) as well as sleep onset insomnia (delay in falling asleep) are examples of this (Konofal, Lecendreux and Cortese 2010). Poor sleep, or poor quality of sleep, is likely to impact on the child's functioning, especially when at school.

☀️**TIP:**

> If your child has a known physical health condition, it would be beneficial to have this information ready at your assessment. If you are unsure of the names of conditions or medications your child is prescribed, your GP may be able to print out their summary information for you.

PEER RELATIONSHIPS AND SOCIAL SKILLS

It is not only family relationships that can be impacted by a child's ADHD. Peer relationships can also suffer, and this is something which can concern parents. When the child is younger, parents and teachers can support with building and maintaining relationships between children; however, as children get older, they manage these relationships independently. Peer conflict is commonly identified by parents of girls with ADHD. Parents will also take an active role when the child is younger in organising meet-ups with friends and getting them to these.

Parents of girls will report that they have concerns about their daughter being able to get herself to social events, due to the organisation and planning needed for this. They will report that their daughter can often turn up late to things and lose things needed for the day, such as bank or travel cards. This can then have an impact on their friendships. Boys will typically have more obvious peer relationship difficulties in their early years due to their hyperactivity and impulsivity. This can often be displayed as difficulties with turn taking and sharing, and aggression towards other children. Girls with more of an inattentive type ADHD presentation will not necessarily display disruptive behaviours in a social setting; however, due to their inattention, they may not appear fully engaged with their peers. This tends not to have a significant impact on their relationships when they are younger; however, parents will report that as their daughter gets older, they have become more concerned about their peer relationships. Parents have reported that their daughter's friends can feel that she does not listen due to her inattention, which is perceived as being rude and causes friction between the friends. Parents may also report that mental health difficulties impact on peer relationships as if the child is depressed or anxious as a result of their ADHD, this may make socialising more difficult and the child may want to isolate themselves more.

When speaking with young people about their peer groups during the assessment, younger children might say the whole class is their friend and reel off as many names as they can recall. From a young age, girls with ADHD often experience conflict or peer relationship difficulties, which they will discuss or be upset about in clinic. It can be challenging for girls with ADHD to maintain friendships for a number of reasons, whether it is due to impulsive actions leading to conflict, or not wanting to be bored so moving between groups of friends so they can play a number of games during play time.

Moving into teenage years, the relationships with peers can be mixed. Whilst some girls find their friendship niche, others can find themselves being 'easily led' or ending up in groups who display challenging behaviours as this is exciting and exhilarating. For others, managing large groups and maintaining multiple friendships becomes overwhelming and having a few friends they feel they can talk to suits them best. Girls frequently report in a clinical setting that they can find it hard to make or maintain friendships as they often feel other people do not understand what it is like inside their world and cannot relate to them. Some young people will find themselves more comfortable around others who are neurodiverse for this reason.

☀ TIPS:

Consider the quality of the child's relationships, including the ability to establish and maintain friendships. How do other children react to the child? If there is a noticeable theme of friendship difficulties, try to think about where the difficulties arise as it will be important to support children and young people in managing peer and family relationships. Social skills groups can be helpful for children with ADHD.

✋ KEY POINTS

» Hyperactivity and impulsivity can present differently in girls than in boys.

» Comorbidities are extremely common, particularly ASD and mental health difficulties.

» A comprehensive risk assessment is an important component of the overall assessment.

SCHOOL OBSERVATIONS

As part of the ADHD assessment, clinicians will gain consent to observe a young person within the school setting, which can include observing them during lessons, break times and assemblies. These observations are not only helpful in terms of looking for evidence of ADHD symptoms, they can also uncover difficulties that account for the ADHD symptoms or contribute to the ADHD picture, such as difficulties with learning, social communication and emotional health.

During a school observation it can be helpful to note the child's behaviour in relation to ADHD, including whether they are engaged for the duration of the lesson, are able to get started on tasks and are looking up when the teacher calls for attention or changes the task. When looking at symptoms of ADHD in the school setting, comparing the child's difficulties with those of the rest of their peers in the classroom can provide helpful information about whether there are more noticeable difficulties for that child or if certain difficulties are common to the majority of students. Alongside this, consideration of what other support is in the classroom, including whether there is a teaching assistant and what support they are providing for that particular child, will add to the assessment information.

Some children may already be in a more specialist provision where there are fewer children in a classroom, making it a quieter environment with fewer distractions, and they will receive more one-to-one support. Again, it is important to know this as this type of setting will be more likely to reduce symptoms of ADHD in children compared with a mainstream school setting, where there can be up to 30 children in the class and no one-to-one support.

When school observations are completed as part of the ADHD assessment, it is important that the clinician completing this observation is aware of how ADHD can present differently in girls than in boys. It will not always be evident from a distance that students are struggling. An example of this includes observing a child when the class is asked to complete a written task. From a distance, it may appear that the child is completing the work because they are writing on the paper; however, on closer observation, it becomes apparent that the child is drawing on the paper or doing something else unrelated to the task set by the teacher.

Children may also rely heavily on their peers to complete the work. If they have missed the instructions given by the teacher or have not been able to focus on the session, then they may copy the work of their peers. The teacher who sees the end result, which is that the child has completed the task, will not necessarily realise that the work has just been copied. This can often be picked up during the school observation as the clinician is able to focus their attention on that one child, whereas for a teacher this is much more difficult. Similarly with homework, support may be given by friends or family members which enables the child to complete the work.

As already mentioned, girls can present as being in a daydream, and this is another sign that can be picked up by clinicians who complete the school observation. It is often noted that the child will be asked a question by the teacher and will not be able to answer because they have been distracted. Teachers can describe girls as 'zoning out'.

During a school observation, clinicians will often report that whilst the boys show obvious signs of hyperactivity during lessons and break times, this is less evident with girls. They will observe more low-level fidgeting in girls, for example tapping their legs or fiddling with objects on the desk. Girls also tend to be more controlling of their peers, for example telling them what to do or leading them to do another activity.

As part of the observation, the clinician will speak with school staff. This can be helpful in eliciting more information about the child's strengths and difficulties. In primary school, where a child usually has one teacher for the week, or in some cases two teachers who split the week, teachers will usually know the child well as they spend a lot of time with them. In secondary school, this can be more difficult since young people often have numerous teachers whom they may see for only short periods of time each week. It may also be that a young person's behaviour is different depending on the lesson, which could be due to the teaching style or the child's interest in that particular subject.

☀️TIPS:

Is the child presenting with difficulties in the areas of hyperactivity, inattention and/or impulsivity, which difficulties are greater than those of the rest of the class?

- Are the child's difficulties more prominent with certain tasks or subjects? For example, a child with dyslexia is more likely to find written tasks challenging and therefore may be avoidant of completing these, but may not have this problem with other tasks.

- Note what strategies and support you observe the child getting in the classroom setting.

- Ask to see the work the child has completed at the end of the lesson to see the quality of this and whether the task was completed. Also, an example of handwriting can be beneficial to ascertain if their motor skills are holding them back.

- Speak to more than one teacher when you are observing the child in school to build up more information about the child's strengths and difficulties.

ADHD ASSESSMENT AND SUPPORT WITHIN THE SCHOOL SETTING

Some girls who present for an ADHD assessment will have already had their learning needs identified. For example, some will have already been diagnosed with dyslexia or highlighted as underachieving. It is not uncommon to see girls who are performing well academically even though this may not be to their full potential. It is important that an assessment for ADHD is not decided based solely on the child's learning ability. The emphasis is on the impact of symptoms and whether these affect the child's abilities, rather than on the overall academic achievement. In primary school, children are supported more with learning, whereas in secondary school, more independent study is expected and organisation and planning skills are tested. Parents may be alerted to their daughter's difficulties at this time by the school.

Other parents will report having queried ADHD for some time, but being told by the school that their daughter is performing well. Whilst a lot of girls we see might be achieving well academically, they are not reaching their full potential. Nationally, work is being done with schools to help them understand how ADHD can present differently in girls than in boys. Helping schools to become more aware of ADHD in girls throughout the different stages is likely to result in girls being referred for assessments much earlier.

It is important to consider what support is already being implemented within the school setting. As has been discussed earlier, parents can provide scaffolding for children and therefore mask their difficulties, and this can also occur in school. An observation of the child in school will often pick up where ADHD strategies are already being used with a child, and this is particularly important to know for the overall assessment. For example, if a child has an EHCP, they may have an allocated teaching assistant to support them in the classroom. This is likely to have a positive impact on the child's focus; however, if the assessing clinician does not know about the EHCP, they could be misled into thinking the child is able to focus for a longer period of time than they actually can or complete more work than they would do without that support.

For any strategies being implemented within school, it is important to consider whether they are being used consistently and how effective they are for that particular child. Another thing to consider is whether the child has been seen by an educational psychologist as any information on the child's learning can be useful to the assessment process. As mentioned earlier, children with learning disabilities can present with ADHD symptoms; we know that when children struggle to learn, they will be less focused on, and distracted from, the work.

☼TIPS:

Make a note of strategies that have been used in the past and those being used currently that are working well. Consider if the strategies have been trialled consistently, for example for a period of at least a few weeks.

- Ask children and young people what they find helpful and unhelpful.

- Remember to consider whether the child is reaching their full potential, rather than just whether they are doing well overall.

- Avoid labelling children and seeing their behaviours as lazy or naughty. Part of the assessment is to understand a child's behaviours and the reason behind these. Try to put yourself in the shoes of the young person.

POST-ASSESSMENT SUPPORT

Whilst the aim of the assessment is to conclude whether a child meets the diagnostic criteria for ADHD, it is also important that parents and young people understand the diagnosis and are directed to services which can support them in learning further about it and about how to support their child. Liaising with the school is also important post diagnosis as it is imperative that they can begin to understand the young person's difficulties within the context of ADHD. This in turn can lead to modifications to the environment and the academic work, which can have a positive impact on the young person. Further details on treatment and post-diagnostic support are detailed in the next chapter by Peter Hill.

☼TIP:

Organising a meeting with your child's school or their SENCO can be a helpful way to think about the outcomes of the assessment, any recommendations and support moving forward.

✋ KEY POINTS

» School observations can add a wealth of information to the assessment.

» Assessment is often the start of the ADHD journey for girls and their families.

CONCLUSION

It is important to remember that whilst symptoms of ADHD can present differently in girls than in boys, this does not mean that they are any less impairing; that being said, it also does not mean symptoms cannot be managed.

As has been discussed throughout this chapter, part of the assessment process is to understand a young person's difficulties, but it also provides the opportunity to uncover their strengths and hidden superpowers. The assessment process itself can be a powerful therapeutic tool for young people and their families and should not be underestimated.

Supporting systems around children to be able to notice ADHD in girls will result in girls being assessed and diagnosed earlier, which could have a significant positive and validating impact on their overall well-being. It is important for adults and role models supporting girls with a diagnosis or with suspected ADHD to encourage self-reflection and begin to teach girls to harness their superpowers and their strengths. Whilst ADHD does come with a series of differences which may feel challenging to overcome, it can also come with strengths and power when girls are encouraged to embrace their differences and learn how to harness their energy and project it into what they love.

REFERENCES

Aaberg, K.M., Bakken, I.J., Lossius, M.I., Søraas, C.L. *et al.* (2016) 'Comorbidity and childhood epilepsy: A nationwide registry study.' *Pediatrics 138*, 3, 1–12.

American Psychiatric Association (2013) *Diagnostic and Statistical Manual of Mental Disorders: DSM-5*, 5th edn. Arlington, VA: American Psychiatric Association.

Barkley, R., Gwenyth, E.H. and Arthur, L.R. (1999) *Defiant Teens: A Clinician's Manual for Assessment and Family Intervention.* New York, NY: Guilford Press.

Conners, C.K. (2008) *Conners 3rd Edition: Manual.* Toronto, ON: Multi-Health Systems.

Cortese, S., Azoulay, R., Castellanos, F.X., Chalard, F. *et al.* (2012) 'Brain iron levels in attention-deficit/hyperactivity disorder: A pilot MRI study.' *The World Journal of Biological Psychiatry 13*, 3, 223–231.

Davis, S.M., Katusic, S.K., Barbaresi, W.J., Killian, J. *et al.* (2010) 'Epilepsy in children with attention-deficit/hyperactivity disorder.' *Paediatric Neurology 42*, 5, 325–330.

DuPaul, G.J., Power, T.J., Anastopoulos, A. and Reid, R. (1998) *ADHD Rating Scale–IV.* New York, NY: Guilford Press.

Hall, C., Valentine, A.Z., Walker, G.M., Ball, H.M. *et al.* (2017) 'Study of user experience of an objective test (QbTest) to aid ADHD assessment and medication management: A multi-methods approach.' *BMC Psychiatry 17*, 66, 1–12.

Hollingdale, J., Woodhouse, E., Young, S., Fridman, A. and Mandy, W. (2019) 'Autistic spectrum disorder symptoms in children and adolescents with attention-deficit/hyperactivity disorder: A meta-analytical review.' *Psychological Medicine*, 1–14. DOI: 10.1017/S0033291719002368.

Johnson, S., Lang, A., Sturm, M. and O'Brien, S.H. (2016) 'Iron deficiency without anemia: A common yet under-recognized diagnosis in young women with heavy menstrual bleeding.' *Journal of Pediatric and Adolescent Gynecology 29*, 6, 628–631.

Klein, B., Damiani-Taraba, G., Koster, A., Campbell, J. and Scholz, C. (2014) 'Diagnosing attention-deficit hyperactivity disorder (ADHD) in children involved with child protection services: Are current diagnostic guidelines acceptable for vulnerable populations?' *Child Care, Health and Development 42*, 2, 178–185.

Knopik, V.S., Maceau, K., Bidwell, L.C., Palmer, R.H.C. *et al.* (2016) 'Smoking during pregnancy and ADHD risk: A genetically informed, multiple-rater approach.' *American Journal of American Genetics 171*, 7, 971–981.

Konofal, E., Lecendreux, M. and Cortese, S. (2010) 'Sleep and ADHD.' *Sleep Medicine 11*, 652–658.

Lo-Castro, A., D'Agati, E. and Curatolo, P. (2011) 'ADHD and genetic syndromes.' *Brain and Development 33*, 456–461.

McGoey, K.E., DuPaul, G.J., Haley, E. and Shelton, T.L. (2007) 'Parent and teacher ratings of attention-deficit/hyperactivity disorder in preschool: The

ADHD Rating Scale-IV Preschool Version.' *Journal of Psychopathology and Behavioral Assessment 29*, 269–276.

National Institute for Health and Care Excellence (2018) *Attention Deficit Hyperactivity Disorder: Diagnosis and Management (NICE Guideline NG87)*. Accessed on 27 July 2020 at https://www.nice.org.uk/guidance/ng87.

Ogundele, M.O. and Ayyash, H.F. (2018) 'Review of the evidence for the management of co-morbid tic disorders in children and adolescents with attention deficit hyperactivity disorder.' *World Journal of Clinical Pediatrics 7*, 1, 36–42.

Oluwabusi, O.O., Parke, S. and Ambrosini, P.J. (2016) 'Tourette syndrome associated with attention deficit hyperactivity disorder: The impact of tics and psychopharmacological treatment options.' *World Journal of Clinical Pediatrics 5*, 1, 128–135.

Quinn, P.O. (2005) 'Treating adolescent girls and women with ADHD: Gender specific issues.' *Journal of Clinical Psychology 61*, 5, 579–587.

Quinn, P.O. and Madhoo, M. (2014) 'A review of attention-deficit/hyperactivity disorder in women and girls: Uncovering this hidden diagnosis.' *Primary Care Companion for CNS Disorders 16*, 3. DOI: 10.4088/PCC.13r01596.

Swanson, J.M., Kraemer, H.C., Hinshaw, S.P., Arnold, L.E., Conners, C.K. and Abikoff, H.B. (2001) 'Clinical relevance of the primary findings of the MTA: Success rates based on severity of ADHD and ODD symptoms at the end of treatment.' *Journal of American Academy of Child Adolescent Psychiatry 40*, 168–179.

Wang, Y., Huang, L., Zhang, L., Qu, Y. and Mu, D. (2017) 'Iron status in attention-deficit/hyperactivity disorder: A systematic review and meta-analysis.' *PLoS ONE 12*, 1, e0169145.

Wehmeier, P.M., Schacht, A. and Barley, R.A. (2010) 'Social and emotional impairment in children and adolescents with ADHD and the impact on quality of life.' *Journal of Adolescent Health 46*, 3, 209–217.

Wolraich, M.L., Lambert, W., Doffing, M.A., Bickman, L., Simmons, T. and Worley, K. (2003) 'Psychometric properties of the Vanderbilt ADHD diagnostic parent rating scale in a referred population.' *Journal of Pediatric Psychology 28*, 559–567.

World Health Organization (2018) *ICD-11 for Mortality and Morbidity Statistics (ICD-11 MMS)*, 2018 version. Accessed on 27 July 2020 at https://icd.who.int/browse11/l-m/en.

Chapter 3

Treatment of ADHD in Girls

—— PROFESSOR PETER HILL ——

This chapter assumes some knowledge of the treatment of attention deficit hyperactivity disorder (ADHD) in general and some familiarity with the use (or not) of medication as part of this. The outline of what is authoritatively considered to be good treatment of ADHD in childhood and adolescence relies heavily on international scientific findings so, not surprisingly, national guidelines on treatment, whether from the English NICE, the American Academies of Paediatrics or Child and Adolescent Psychiatry, or CADDRA in Canada, are generally in agreement. Therefore, what is written here takes modern treatment of ADHD as described in publications like these for granted and focuses on how particular aspects of treating ADHD in girls under 18 years merit special attention.

At first sight there is little difference between girls and boys when it comes to how their ADHD is treated in a health service. Much the same treatment approaches are used across the board, though in the UK girls seem to be treated with medication less frequently than boys (Renoux *et al.* 2016). This is not now the case in the USA (Visser *et al.* 2014). Having said this, there are some subtle points to be considered even before treatment of ADHD in an individual girl is considered.

In any clinic or service for ADHD there will be fewer girls than boys, partly because ADHD is less common among them and partly because they are less likely to be referred. That means that treating clinicians will be a little less experienced with ADHD in a girl.

'When they assessed her, he was asking me about rudeness and disobedience but those were not the main issues and I was thinking about Anna's emotional state of mind and her crying in the evenings after school.'

It also means that a parent of a girl with ADHD is likely to be outnumbered by the parents of boys in any group meeting about the management of their children. In what used to be called a 'parenting group', the problems that parents of boys with ADHD experience can be slightly different.

'It was a bit pointless. They were all talking about stuff that I'd either been through with Jemma years ago or just didn't apply; screen combat games and so on when I wanted to know about managing being bullied and homework.'

As we have heard, girls tend to be diagnosed later than boys so an adolescent girl may find herself in a waiting room full of restless, noisy younger boys and wonder to herself why she is there and whether her diagnosis is correct.

There is also the issue of differences between the sexes in the likelihood of which subtypes of ADHD and which problems, conditions and disorders co-exist with ADHD and need active treatment, so the focus of clinical management is likely to differ. Nevertheless, the classic model for treatment of ADHD in the young is to apply a step-by-step approach so that any differences between the treatment of boys and girls come to light within each step.

STEP 1: PSYCHOEDUCATION
For girls themselves
Girls are more likely to be first seen by services when they are in secondary school or their early teens. That means that they are more able to both understand and participate in explanations and discussions of treatments than young boys. Actively including them in these discussions is therefore likely to be more possible than is the case with boys, and there are benefits from this as it means they

are more likely to co-operate with treatment (Ferrin *et al.* 2018). Not always, of course, but something not to be overlooked by a clinician who is more used to talking mainly to a parent about their difficult son. Quite often this means asking a girl directly what she thinks about, for instance, proposed medication, at which point, more than a hint of future difficulties with compliance may emerge. And an opportunity for psychoeducation.

> 'Yeah but what's the point of it? The drug. Why do I have to be turned into a zombie because his lessons are sooo boring?'

The point that so much of the history of ADHD has focused on boys and the problems they cause their families, teachers and friends has already been made earlier in this book. What seems to be particularly helpful is to find material that deals with the specific problems of girls from their point of view. In my experience, they are likely to use digital media to find out what other girls think about ADHD and its treatment and what is being said on internet forums (clinicians need to keep an eye on these). Fake news abounds. The misunderstandings that then arise are sometimes surprising and will only emerge if asked about – 'What have you found out from your friends or online?'

> 'And I read that there was this woman and all her hair fell out when she had medication. There's no way I'm having that happen.'

> 'Why can't I have Adderall? My cousin in Atlanta says it is so good and you don't get fat.'

> 'I've seen all about it and there are masses of side effects I'm going to get.'

> 'I don't need therapy. I'm not going to rehab. I say No, No, No.'

The American CHADD website (www.chadd.org) is a useful asset for parents and older girls, with several contributions on ADHD in girls and women. The classic and trailblazing book *Understanding Girls with ADHD* (Nadeau, Littman and Quinn 2016) may be too lengthy for the overwhelming majority of girls (or boys) with ADHD to read all the way through, but the questionnaires at the end include items that illustrate some of the issues that ADHD gives rise to where girls are concerned. I have found this a useful focus for discussions with teenage girls and their parents. These questionnaires seem to provide a more extended and personal view of ADHD from their perspective than simply the usual list of diagnostic items of DSM-5 or ICD-11.

Not all information about ADHD and its treatment needs to be given at the outset. Indeed, what emerged from an informal survey of teenagers attending ADHD clinics was that they would like to be told one new thing about ADHD or its treatment at each follow-up appointment. In my experience, suggesting to girls that they might read a book about their ADHD does not often result in them reading it; however, they just might glance at the information in Figure 3.1.

When talking with some teenage girls, who often have more advanced language than boys, a clinician may find they can use language that is a bit more subtle and metaphorical than the direct factual talk that goes down well with so many boys (e.g. to a boy: 'You have ADHD and that's why you can't concentrate'). A more appropriate approach might be for a clinician to use 'externalising' language in order to separate out the ADHD from the person and seem less critical. This might include 'The ADHD is stopping your brain organise things as well as you would like it to' or 'Your ADHD is what gets in the way when you're trying to listen in class' or 'It sounds as though you were getting on really well with your friends and then your ADHD popped up and wrecked everything by making you jump in too quickly and too loudly.'

Finding out about ADHD: for the girls themselves

First check out ADHD generally. Much will be about boys because it is commoner among them. You have to allow for that. The American websites are best, though often either too short or too wordy: www.chadd.org has *Information for Teens*. The UK sites for UKAP (www.ukadhd.com) or the ADHD Foundation (www.adhdfoundation.org.uk) have lots of information on their pages but this is not easy for girls with ADHD to read through on screen. It can feel like homework. Print out the good bits and read them bit by bit.

If you look at some of this information, you should become clear that:

- ADHD is when problems with paying attention, concentration, getting organised, reacting quickly to situations without thinking, and being hyperactive are extreme and stopping you doing what you or other people want you to do

- it is a brain problem but nothing to do with low intelligence or brain damage; some parts of your brain are developing more slowly

- it is not caused by parents, too much screen time, or fast food

- it's not your fault

- you can learn how to cope with it

- medicines help and will not change your personality.

Girls with ADHD very often also have difficulties with:

- getting organised and generally getting things done

- holding in mind what they have just been told while they think about it

- containing their emotions

- feeling good about themselves.

These may need separate treatment.

There has been a great deal of false ideas about ADHD but all countries are now in general agreement about what it is and how to treat it.

When it comes to girls with ADHD, I think the best source of information and advice is the YouTube collection by Jessica McCabe *How to ADHD*. There are a lot of videos, but start with *How to Recognize the Symptoms*. You might like her TED talk on YouTube too, but don't think that you will necessarily have ADHD when you are her age.

If you would like a book written for girls and young teenagers, then Dr Patricia Quinn's *Attention Girls!* (2009) is by an absolute expert and is full of helpful tips. It is, of course, written in American English for American girls.

Figure 3.1 Handout for girls with ADHD

Groups for parents

The idea that parents should be offered advice about ADHD and its management, preferably in a group (National Institute for Health and Care Excellence 2018), stems essentially from the fact that boys with ADHD are characteristically disruptive in their family setting and parents can be helped by guidance on the best management of this. Plenty of girls can also be impulsive and disruptive but that may not be the case with a girl if her ADHD is the predominantly (or entirely) inattentive subtype. The difficulties that her ADHD causes her family might be to do with personal disorganisation, taking too long to get tasks done, or repeatedly losing things.

Although the principles of successful management of ADHD and the value of peer support between parents apply across the age range and equally to boys and girls, it will require skilful management of a parents' group to ensure it is not taken over by the problems caused by hyperactive or hostile behaviour so common among the families of boys with ADHD. Parents' groups specifically for girls are likely to be possible only in a large service with many patients. Occasionally, there will be a sufficiently large and resourceful voluntary support group locally for a short-lived group for parents of girls with ADHD to be organised. Less structured than group sessions, the informal support offered by local and national family support groups for ADHD generally is invaluable. In the UK, ADDISS is long established and based on the American organisation CHADD.

Reading and watching for parents

There are websites that have sections on ADHD in girls. In particular, the contributions by Rae Jacobson on the Child Mind Institute site (www.childmind.org) are brief and to the point. The classic book *Understanding Girls with ADHD* (Nadeau *et al.* 2016) has a wealth of information for parents. Two of the authors, Ellen Littman and Patricia Quinn, have videos on YouTube for those who find reading books more challenging.

The diagnostic label attention deficit disorder (ADD), which implies that inattention exists without hyperactivity also being present, is no longer a formal diagnostic term. This is mainly because the majority of children and teenagers who come to the attention of services with predominantly attentional problems have previously had full ('combined') ADHD but have grown out of their previous hyperactivity. That means, from a scientific point of view which looks at the origins, neurology or associations of ADHD, they do not differ from ordinary combined ADHD.

Nevertheless, because so many girls have the predominantly inattentive form of ADHD, books that talk about 'ADD' or 'attention deficit disorder' (rather than 'ADHD') may seem more relevant to their parents, particularly Brown's (2005) classic *Attention Deficit Disorder* and the best-seller *Driven to Distraction* by Hallowell and Ratey (2011). Similarly, using the term 'ADD' may avoid the common assumption that ADHD is necessarily associated with hostile disobedience or aggression, especially in an educational setting where the 'ADD' term is still used.

'We can manage her if she's got ADD but ADHD would be a problem.' (Head teacher)

Because so many girls with ADHD have *problems with cognitive executive skills* (self-organisation, time management, planning, setting priorities, etc.; see Chapter 6), some reading in that area is helpful for their parents. Once again, the American books are best and the comprehensive *Smart but Scattered* series for parents and teachers by Dawson and Guare (or vice versa) building on their original (2009) book go down well, though UK readers are sometimes puzzled by the language and advice about dealing with specific situations that apply to American children. The same is true for the books by Joyce Cooper-Kahn, whose original book *Late, Lost and Unprepared* (Cooper-Kahn and Dietzel 2008) had an equally evocative title. In that book, 'Part 2: What You Can Do About It' provides 125 pages of excellent advice which goes way beyond helping a girl and her family manage her executive function difficulties and offers guidance on wider aspects of parenting. The Dawson and Guare books are based on a tried and tested teaching model for parents of children with weak executive skills. The two sets of authors cover slightly different problems and naturally have somewhat different styles. Some people prefer one, others the other. Horses for courses; best to buy both. No book on executive skills difficulties concentrates specifically on girls though it is inevitable that many of the examples each provides are indeed girls.

UK parents can access the Connections in Mind organisation (www.connectionsinmind.co.uk or www.cimfoundation.org.uk), which has a brief introduction to the concept on its website and offers coaching based on the Dawson and Guare model. Once again this is not specifically aimed at girls, but I do not think that this matters.

Psychoeducation for schools

This is tackled in Chapter 5 but I should add here that a 'slow drip' approach to providing information about ADHD is worth attempting. A letter from a clinic to a school asking for a rating scale to be completed, for instance, might contain sections such as:

- This rating scale was essentially designed around boys because they are more likely to have ADHD. Girls with ADHD may appear dreamy or lacking in motivation as part of their condition, yet the rating scale does not address this so observations and comments about whether Miley seems like this in class are very welcome.

- Teenage girls with ADHD are often disorganised in their work because of differences in how their brains work and it would be very helpful if a teacher could say whether this is true as far as Lila is concerned.

- Girls who have ADHD quite often have emotional symptoms as well as restlessness or concentration difficulties. Have members of staff noticed whether Mia has signs of anxiety, low mood or poor self-esteem?

Psychoeducation for siblings

What is said to brothers and sisters will depend on how old they are. Teenagers will do their own research and it pays to check what they have found out. One helpful move in talking to siblings is to use language like:

'Her ADHD makes it very hard for her not to yell back at you.'

It will help if there are routines to minimise unstructured time in which a girl with ADHD will be provoked by or provoke her siblings. Within such a structure there should be time for individual interaction between parent and a non-ADHD sibling to compensate for the amount of parental time their sister's ADHD consumes. Within this it may be possible to explain how their sister is different from them.

✋ KEY POINTS

> » It is important to take a step-by-step approach to treatment.
>
> » Psychoeducation should cover every aspect of the girl's network to be most effective: themselves, parents, wider family, school and activity club leaders.

THE NEXT STEP: PSYCHOLOGICAL OR PSYCHOSOCIAL TREATMENTS, DIETS AND EXERCISE

The term 'psychosocial interventions' is widely used to cover the fact that treatments for ADHD other than medication involve work with parents and schools as well as with the girls themselves. The problems caused by ADHD are essentially the result of how a girl with ADHD reacts to the demands her environment places upon her. Because the young cannot choose their own environments as freely as adults, it becomes important to consider the different settings of family, school and peer group as well as helping the girl herself directly with her ADHD and its associated problems and impairments.

Helping parents organise a more settled household

There is good advice to parents which is general (and therefore often forgotten), which underpins more specific strategies for living and rearing a girl with ADHD:

- calmness (not easy!)

- setting an example, modelling coping strategies

- adequate sleep at a predictable time

- routines and structure

- family rules, stated clearly

- positive and clear communication

- finding something that is fun which a parent and girl with ADHD can do together

- recognition and appreciation of small gains in skills, or improvement in behaviour

- use of praise focused on what has earned the praise

- maintaining self-esteem for both daughter and parents

- time for parents to look after their own friendships and activities.

'Once we'd all calmed down and got our days organised so she became more settled we could concentrate on the things I'd read about. Before that I'd got frustrated that the tips and things in the books weren't doing anything.'

'We got a babysitter who was experienced and so Jack and I got to go out for a curry on our own. It was the first time for ages, and we cleared up a whole load of stuff so we can now work together as a team.'

Going beyond these principles can then become more specific.

Helping parents manage their daughter and help her build skills

A local service may offer (should offer) a course for parents of young children with ADHD, which may follow a structured programme such as Triple-P, The Incredible Years, The New Forest Parenting Programme, Parent–Child Interaction Therapy or Parenting Special Children, to name but a few. Or they may have developed their own. CHADD's Parent-to Parent family training and support can be accessed online (www.chadd.org).

Apart from these programmes, there are several pieces of advice that parents welcome when it comes to helping them deal with the key features of ADHD. The key issue is to combine behavioural techniques that manage ADHD behaviours and impairments with measures that help the girl learn self-management skills. This should be done within an overall framework of structure and routine for each day with regular meals, bedtime and planned activities which are important underpinning for successful management.

Hyperactivity

The risk here is that restlessness escalates into uncontained, over-excitable or angry, under-controlled behaviour. The key interventions for the parents to learn are how to anticipate this and, importantly, to contain their daughter's behaviour as calmly as possible, not to flare up or over-react. This is not easy, to say the least. Certain situations such as boring journeys or meals out are risk situations and require some forward planning for how to manage mounting hyperactive behaviour by providing short breaks outside or settled occupational activities such as puzzles or even phone or screen games and videos. Spoken encouragement and praise for quiet behaviour is important.

If the girl is clearly unable to contain herself, then use this simple breathing technique: count 'one hippopotamus, two hippopotamuses, three hippopotamuses' over three seconds as she breathes in, count three hippopotamuses while she holds her breath, then a further three while she exhales slowly. With luck she will learn to do this for herself. (It does not have to be hippopotamuses; it could be crocodiles.)

Some families believe that allowing a large amount of physical activity will 'wear her out'. This is not likely to work in those terms (she can go on for ever) but regular opportunities for a short run, trampoline session outside or dancing can relieve the impatience that hyperactive girls feel when having to contain their restlessness.

Impulsiveness

This is, of course, potentially dangerous – running into a busy road, for instance – especially as girls with ADHD often enjoy risky excitement. Just as with hyperactivity, anticipation is half the answer, so that a parent who knows where temptation lies can set a limit ('hold my hand') or remind their daughter of a rule ('Do not take stuff off the shop shelves yourself', 'Do not hit back'). Alongside this, distracting an impatient girl in a queue or airport lounge reduces the chance of them doing something sudden and rash.

The language of 'choices' is helpful: 'Wait a minute, make a choice', 'That was a good choice, well done.' The crucial aspect of this is to teach a girl that there are usually *several* options they can choose from, not simply the first one that occurs to them (see 'Systematic problem solving' below). A parent talking out loud about how they are making a choice makes adult thinking about evaluating options something understandable to a young person.

Using non-verbal communication to indicate that self-restraint is needed is more acceptable than a spoken warning for older girls in public. A simple hand gesture to imply stop and think, agreed beforehand between girl and parent, can be a semi-private communication.

Inattention

In the home situation, this tends to revolve round a few particular issues. One is communication between parent and daughter. Using the daughter's name at the beginning of any instruction, using short instructions and breaking down more complex instructions into separate chunks are important.

> 'Lucy. Listen. Go upstairs now. Go into my bedroom cupboard. Find my grey jacket. Not the blue one. And bring it down to me.'

This may also need a summary and a check that the message has been fully received by asking for the instruction to be repeated (not just 'Did you get that?').

In parallel with this, using a similar chunking approach to tasks such as homework as well as actively organising the girl's environment to minimise distraction will help her achieve. Each chunk can be timed with a timer, written on a sticky note and separated from the next by a short break.

'Inattention' is a complex construct and much of what is dealt with below under the heading of 'Cognitive executive skills' applies to problems with focus, resisting distraction, motivation and persistence, which are included within the idea of clinical inattention.

Oppositional and disobedient behaviour

Although not a diagnostic component of ADHD, this is a common issue. Everything said so far about routine, structure, clear communication, and adequate nutrition and sleep applies.

It is important for parents to maintain a positive tone in dealings with their daughter both to promote self-esteem (use of encouragement and focused praise for achievement) and to provide something against which the use of time out can provide a contrast. The '1-2-3 Magic' principles (YouTube has videos) are widely used, learned either from the video or book or from a course or taught by a clinician.

SOCIAL SKILLS TRAINING

The peer group is especially important to girls, particularly in terms of providing support for coping with emotional distress. This cannot be taken for granted as ADHD itself makes socialising more difficult. Some girls with ADHD will antagonise their peers by impatience or boisterousness but others will drift to the periphery because of their slow processing of thoughts or language, or inattention to group talk.

Social skills training in groups has historically been offered but evidence for its benefit in ADHD is lacking (Storebø *et al.* 2019) and it is no longer a core treatment recommendation in NICE guidelines

(National Institute for Health and Care Excellence 2018). Group meetings for teenagers with ADHD are nevertheless popular with girls because of the ability to share and identify, though these are not always easy for a service to provide because a large number of patients is required to be able to gather a group of girls who are the same age. NICE (National Institute for Health and Care Excellence 2018) now recommends a CBT approach to young people who have benefited from medication but still have social relationship difficulties. Presumably, this would usually be delivered to individual girls.

COGNITIVE EXECUTIVE SKILLS

It is very likely that girls will have not only ADHD but weak executive skills, too; the two go hand in hand so often as far as girls are concerned but one does not completely explain the other. I have referred to this above but, to expand, girls, especially adolescents, with ADHD are likely to have difficulties with such tasks as:

- Self-organisation: not packing what is needed for school, having a markedly untidy room or schoolbag, forgetting appointments or arrangements, not handing in completed homework.

  'She (my 17-year-old daughter) is all over the place – I have to act as her alarm clock, her diary, her appointments secretary, her schoolbag monitor, clear her bedroom floor, cover her babysitting job she forgot about, make her apologies for her...'

- Time management: taking ages to get dressed or pack, leaving things to the last moment, not allowing enough time to complete a task. Procrastinating, especially by fiddling around with preliminaries (decorating the cover of a revision folder) rather than getting on with it.

  'I just sit there sometimes just staring into space when I have to write something. Or I do doodles – they're great doodles!'

- Planning: considering what needs to be done to solve a problem or make an arrangement. Getting things in the right order. Resisting distraction. Working out what is needed for a school project.

'I just can't think forwards.'

- Getting started: making choices between possibilities.

  'I find her sitting on her bed for ages with all her clothes out trying to decide what she's going to wear. I know we all do a bit of that but for her it takes up so much time she's going to be too late to get where she's going.'

- Setting and maintaining goals and priorities: allowing distractions to get in the way of getting something done (checking phone while getting dressed), not being able to identify an appropriate goal or hold it in mind.

  'I know I just forget why I'm doing something; I know. I get distracted and lose the point of what I'm doing.'

- Systematic problem solving: knowing what kit or information she needs at each point in a task. Completing one step or activity before moving on to the next.

  'She has this big piece of homework and although she's up for doing it, bless her, she starts in the middle and then finds she hasn't got the worksheets they've given her. So she rings (her friend) to borrow them and – then that's it – can't get her off the phone. Then she's lost interest. So I say, 'How far have you got, have you done the introduction?' And she says, 'I don't have to do that, I've already started doing what I have to do.' (But not at the beginning, apparently.)'

- Thinking about how well they are getting on with a task or assignment: checking realistically how far she has got with an assignment, considering the range of her own choices and the implications of each.

  'It's that I feel it's all too much. It's, like, a muddle in my mind, you know. I know I've got so far but I can't bear looking at it so I don't know how far I've got and what's got to be done. And I think what I've done's all rubbish anyway. For the next bit I can't work out what to say in any case: I could do this, I could do that…it's just too much, like I said.'

These are the core topics of cognitive executive function. It is clear they overlap with each other and in many ways are simply dimensions of a general problem of maintaining organisation and intent in thinking. Some academic authorities will add other dimensions such as that of weak working memory (a limited capacity to think about and digest what has just been heard or seen without losing track or forgetting it). Others include in the list of executive functions the ability to control impulsive responses, the use of visual imagery and mental self-talk, and the ability to regulate one's own emotional responses. Some authorities see ADHD as effectively the result of poor cognitive executive skill (Barkley 2018; Brown 2005), though when one tries to measure things experimentally there is not a complete overlap.

The existence of poor planning and self-organising skills on top of the inattention and impulsiveness of ADHD can make the parents of a scatty or dreamy girl with ADHD feel overwhelmed as to what they will have to do to help.

'Whoever thought a YouTube video 54 minutes long was a good idea for someone with ADHD?'

For their sake, I am going to stick to the core topics of executive functioning listed above and suggest that they can be considered as problems that commonly, though not always, exist alongside classic ADHD. For instance, although treating ADHD with medication will probably help with attention and reduce impulsive and hyperactive behaviour, it will not on its own do that much to help a girl manage her life. Valerie Ivens provides further thoughts on this topic in Chapter 6 on coaching.

Parents, by their nature, teach children how to live independently. They instruct, inspire, demonstrate and congratulate in order to build skills – from how to get dressed and wash oneself to how to manage homework. This is part of bringing up a child and it is enormously frustrating when it seems not to work. Parents can feel exasperated, irritated and can easily start to believe their daughter is simply lazy.

'I've heard enough of this ADHD stuff – she just needs to get off her arse.'

In turn this can rub off on her and lower her self-esteem.

'I don't know why it's so hard for me to get organised. They all shout at me because I'm the last one to get ready. Something's missing.'

'Have I got brain damage or am I just really thick and no one's told me? I know I keep forgetting to bring stuff home for school. Am I getting dementia?'

What can parents do?

Above all, *set an example* (not easy for a parent with ADHD, of course). List, plan, talk out loud about things such as making a shopping list, identify important and urgent matters and separate them.

'We've run out of milk and I've go to buy some (that's urgent), I need to get my hair done (possibly important but not that urgent), I should call Jenny and find out how she got on (probably neither), I must do my tax return (important but not urgent, but am I just putting a tedious task off?).'

Going through the list of executive functions above, there are tried and tested tips for girls to be taught.

Self-organisation

Checklists of what has to be done or what's needed. To be kept somewhere easily visible – a phone may not be as good as a written list on a post-it in this respect because not immediately catching the eye and phones can do other distracting things. Timed and sequenced routines and habits: back from school by 5pm, have snack, then 30 minutes' down time in bedroom, then get homework out on table downstairs at 6pm, complete and then file for handing in tomorrow, have supper together with mother and sister at 7.30 pm, etc.

Time management

Clocks on the wall, wearing a watch (probably not using a phone for this for obvious reasons though the timer function is theoretically helpful if the phone is then placed in sight but out of easy reach). Using a kitchen timer or, better, a Time Timer (www.timetimer.com) Teach her to ask herself: 'What do I need? What do I do first? How long have I got?'

Setting priorities and planning

Mutual discussion between girl and parent or teacher. Separate what is urgent from what's important. What is the point ultimately?

'My friends are so important. I really must see Georgie now because I haven't seen her all week.'

'Yes and they need to trust you so if you now break tonight's arrangement with Ella (impulsively!) to see Georgie, then Ella won't get why it's happened and she won't believe you next time. It's a good idea to build trust so your friends are there when you need them.'

Getting started

Got all the kit you need? But be wary of procrastination.

'I'll just call Ria and ask what she's got.'

Mind mapping to create a range of possible actions. 'Swiss cheesing' a school project by doing small parts of an activity (i.e. making holes in it) to prevent it seeming overwhelming without having always to start at the beginning. But not forgetting to put them in place in a progress plan ('road map'). And definitely not forgetting the beginning.

'OK it's a big project.

What bits can you do that will only take half an hour? Give me three.

And how do you now put these in order?

All right, would you do that first one now or in half an hour?'

Systematic problem solving

Teach your daughter to say to herself *SOCS*: 'What is the **S**ituation I am in? What are my **O**ptions (at least two)? What would the **C**onsequences of each be? **S**o what's the plan?'

Situation
I really want to go and see Leon. But you've just told me I can't until I've done the weekend homework.

Options

1. I could do the homework.

2. I could just go, and stuff the homework (and you).

3. I could call Leon and explain the problem.

4. I could get really, really angry so you'd give in.

Consequences (or 'what's Coming?' for each)

1. I gain points for being a good girl. And Leon's a **** in any case.

2. I get to see Leon. But I get grounded and I must get out on Sunday evening.

3. Yeah but he won't get it. Or he might.

4. I'd get grounded.

So what's the plan?

I'm going to sulk. Loudly. And then ring Leon in tears and explain. Then do the homework. *OK?*

Evaluating progress

Make a list of what has been done, in order. Then teach self-questioning with prompting. 'How far have I got? What does anyone else think about it? What next? Am I going the best way about it? Is it too late to change?'

'I'll never finish. There's just so much to do...'

'Yeah but you're nearly there. Look...'

In real life, it is indeed often about schoolwork and social activities but teaching a young adolescent daughter how to manage her periods also exemplifies what may be included.

INDIVIDUAL PSYCHOLOGICAL APPROACHES TO A GIRL

Individual and group work using psychological understanding and methods with adult women who have ADHD is rewarding and effective. Essentially, it is helping the girl to learn how to recognise and predict the impairments or maladaptive behaviours caused by ADHD (such as impulsive responses or being too easily distracted from a task), to alter her assumptions if these are unhelpful, and then to work out alternative ways of reacting, subsequently to test them (e.g. by behavioural experiments), and practise those that work until they become habitual. In its purest form, this is a cognitive behavioural therapy (CBT) approach.

It is not a direct treatment for inattention, yet it can help with impulsivity or hyperactivity by helping a girl learn self-management. But for a clinician working with a girl with ADHD in a clinic, getting CBT to work is difficult for several reasons:

- Healthcare services for the under-18s are typically accessed by parents on behalf of their child. A girl with possible ADHD is *brought* to a service; it is unlikely that she will present herself to it. Her motivation to work with a psychologist on a problem such as impulsivity will be limited by her motivation to spend time and effort on what she may well see as really a problem for others. If she comes to a service because she wants to resolve problems she experiences herself, then she will be more motivated. If she has been brought by parents, perhaps following a prompt by her school, she will not have the same will to work.

'It's not fair. They've just got to see me as I am.'

- Psychological treatments such as CBT require her to think hard, keep records and practise techniques. All too often in my experience she will see this as an extension of school homework. And these tasks to be carried out between sessions are, of course, called 'homework' within the language of CBT.

    'Where's all this going? Who said it's a good idea? It's not going to change anything. I've got enough that I've got to do already.'

- A girl needs a certain level of brain development and neuropsychological maturity to be able to think analytically about her own functioning and social relationships.

    'How do I know what I'm going to do? I just do it.'

- She has ADHD. Looking for quick fixes is part of what ADHD is about. Individual psychological work is not a quick fix.

If a psychological approach is possible, then there is a tension between working on targets that the girl wants to achieve (such as not forgetting arrangements with friends) and what the therapist considers might be important issues for early adult life (e.g. emotional self-regulation, self-esteem, thinking ahead). Realistically, one has to accept the girl's preference and negotiate.

For pre-teen girls who need to learn to use coping strategies, explanation, teaching and training are better done by parents or schools, as explained above (see 'What can parents do?') but progressively through the middle teenage years a direct treatment approach on CBT or interpersonal therapy (IPT) principles becomes more possible. The capacity to observe and reflect on one's thoughts and relationships improves with maturation, even though it will be hard for someone with ADHD. With increasing age through the later teenage years, the techniques correspond to those used with adult women (see Chapter 8), though the fact that most teenage girls live within families and go to school means that parents and teachers can support a psychologist or coach who is working therapeutically with an individual adolescent.

It is possible for parents to support individual CBT so long as the therapist informs them of what is being done. Even if individual work with their daughter is not getting off the ground, they can be instructed by a therapist to go beyond the coaching and modelling methods described above and promote some of the specific CBT techniques such as internal self-talk to help contain impulsiveness, reframing to defuse mounting anger, or keeping a thought chart and identifying positive thoughts which can be imposed upon negative ones.

DIET

Rather more girls than boys seem to be keen on modifying their diet for various reasons, and the question as to whether diet can help ADHD is often raised. If one takes a hard-headed approach and reviews the scientific evidence for benefit in ADHD, then one can confidently say that a good balanced diet is important. On the other hand, cutting out anything (E-numbers, gluten, 'red foods', sugar, dairy products, etc.) is not a recommended approach for most girls, and supplements such as zinc or magnesium have hardly any high-quality evidence to support them.

Having said that, there are some points to consider. Fish oils which contain the polyunsaturated fats EPA and DHA are probably safe (not for the fish) even though there is very little hard evidence about dosing, side effects and indeed benefit. The evidence that they work is conflicting and, by and large, the better-designed studies do not show much worthwhile benefit. In the light of this NICE (National Institute for Health and Care Excellence 2018) says they should not be recommended as a treatment for ADHD.

To illustrate the complexity of the field, a recent study (Chang *et al.* 2019) makes the point that it depends upon whether there are low or high blood levels of the polyunsaturated fatty acid EPA. If there are low levels, giving extra EPA improves cognitive functioning on some laboratory tasks but giving EPA to children with high blood levels results in worse functioning.

The exception to this negative take on supplements is iron. Menstruating teenagers are at risk of iron depletion and, according to some studies, this is associated with a variety of neurodevelopmental disorders. This needs documentation by a blood test. The key measure is ferritin, not serum iron or anaemia (Wang *et al.* 2017). One research group has shown improvement in ADHD when low body iron stores (as measured by ferritin level) are treated with oral iron (Konofal *et al.* 2004) and that low ferritin impairs the effect of stimulant medication (see Cortese *et al.* 2012). Going beyond iron-rich vitamin over-the-counter preparations is often not necessary and prescribing iron needs caution because of uncomfortable gastro-intestinal side effects.

There will often be a positive placebo effect from complicated diets because of the investment of effort involved but there are also drawbacks such as weight loss, vitamin deficiencies, unwarranted blaming of the child for breaking a diet should ADHD worsen, and expense.

On very general principles, it seems common sense to avoid encouraging young women to restrict their diet by cutting out certain foods because of the risk of initiating anorexia nervosa or sustaining an avoidant/restrictive food intake disorder. Yet these conditions have complex causes and it is not clear that this happens with diets that have been recommended for ADHD.

Given that slowing of weight gain or even weight loss can be a side effect of many ADHD medications, a restriction diet with specific foods or additives removed is risky when applied in addition to medication.

EXERCISE

There is ample proof that regular aerobic, whole-body exercise (i.e. not just hyperactivity!) improves ADHD. Just how much exercise is needed is not clear but perhaps 20–30 minutes several times a week at a minimum. The difficulty is arranging it in competition with other demands on time. Some families can organise joint activities such as cycling. For some girls, running or swimming with a parent, siblings or friends is possible but the most acceptable form for many teenage girls in my experience is dancing.

✋ KEY POINTS

» Supporting parents to facilitate a home environment which builds skills development in their daughter will be beneficial.

» Difficulties with executive function skills are common and strategies to support the development of these skills will provide essential groundwork for life.

» Individual psychological work can be hugely valuable but presents many challenges.

» Caution should be applied in considering changes to diet for ADHD as there is little consistent evidence around positive effects.

NEXT STEP: MEDICATION

Medication for ADHD is remarkably effective but should be offered alongside educational and psychological measures at the very least. It is not a 'cure' for ADHD but promotes brain functioning in the areas in which the ADHD brain is not functioning well. It should not be the only treatment intervention for any one girl and carefully considered for mild ADHD. The way in which ADHD medicines work and the general principles of how the medicines are used are part of mainstream orthodox medicine and well set out in a number of sources and books (see e.g. Coghill, Chen and Silva 2019) so I will not deal further with that here beyond a few brief statements.

The medicines used to treat ADHD fall into two broad groups. The *stimulants* methylphenidate and dexamfetamine (and amfetamine in the USA, where it is usually spelled amphetamine) are by far the most widely used. Methylphenidate was first manufactured as Ritalin but this is not so often used now as various other preparations exist, especially those which are extended release preparations which may need to be taken only once daily. Dexamfetamine and its extended release form lisdexamfetamine are used rather less frequently outside the USA and Canada as general guidance in many countries is for a prescriber to start medication treatment with methylphenidate. This is because for many children it offers a better balance of effectiveness against side effects. The effect of stimulants starts promptly within half an hour of being taken but lasts for a few hours only, and they are broken down by the body and leave it on the same day that they are taken. That means that they do not necessarily have to be taken every day if their benefit is not required on any particular day. They are remarkably effective in treating the core symptoms of ADHD but are likely to suppress appetite and usually keep children awake if given too late in the day. Both stimulant medicines are controlled drugs that usually require a prescription to be written every month.

The names of some methylphenidate preparations include the tag XL (e.g. Concerta XL, Matoride XL). It is wise to point out to an image-aware teenager that this is not because they are extra-large themselves.

Then there are the *non-stimulants*, used less frequently. They are rather less powerful in their effect on ADHD than the stimulants but have the advantage that their beneficial effect can extend across 24 hours without disturbing sleep much. Indeed, sleepiness is a not uncommon side effect. The most widely used are atomoxetine (Strattera) and extended release guanfacine (Intuniv). Both are effective treatments for ADHD though less powerful. Each works in a different way at a nerve cell level. Their side effects are different from the stimulants and from each other though it is important here to note that atomoxetine can reduce appetite. Non-stimulants are not controlled drugs but do need to be taken every day.

A much wider range of preparations of methylphenidate and amfetamine are available in the USA than in other countries, including patches and liquids for methylphenidate and an extended release form of clonidine (Kapvay) which is more effective than clonidine itself but which is little used for ADHD nowadays, apart from helping with sleep problems. Obtaining American ADHD medicines in the UK is very difficult as their manufacturers have often not applied for a British or European licence (an expensive business with less chance of financial return for the company since the UK–European ADHD market is a fraction of the size of the American one). Special arrangements can be made but these are expensive and exceptional and not usually available on the NHS.

There is nothing to suggest that girls respond to the conventional ADHD medicines in a manner any different from boys. Each conventional medication, stimulant or non-stimulant, is equally effective for boys and girls in controlling core ADHD symptoms. Although there is quite a bit of difference between individuals as to what dose suits them best, there is no significant difference between boys and girls of the same age. Nor is there any clear difference in the rate or type of side effects.

Puberty and medication

There is a repeated suggestion that the increased oestrogen and progesterone secretion at puberty can make stimulant medication less effective for adolescent girls though there are no scientific studies that confirm this. If 16- to 19-year-old boys and girls with ADHD are compared directly, methylphenidate is equally effective in both sexes (Mikami *et al.* 2009). Group studies can, of course, obscure individual differences, but if the effect of a medication seems to be wearing off in a pubertal girl, it pays to first consider the adverse situational factors that might affect young adolescents rather than automatically assuming a hormonal interaction with medication and increasing her dose (Smith *et al.* 1998).

> Lila, an immigrant child, started a new school at the age of 11 years. Previously her ADHD had responded well to methylphenidate. Her periods started after about 12 months and at about the same time she became more inattentive and less engaged in classwork. The paediatrician attached to the school wondered if her pubertal hormones were to blame but her year tutor was concerned that she had recently become the victim of bullying. When this was addressed, her ADHD came back under control and no change of medication was required.

An apparently contrasting, often-repeated statement is that oestrogen facilitates the effect of amfetamine. But this has only been shown for positive effects of amfetamine on mood in adult women, not when ADHD in pubertal girls is being treated. Interestingly, in the original study on this topic, progesterone secreted in the second half of the menstrual cycle appeared to cancel the positive effect of oestrogen (Justice and de Wit 1999) which is consistent with the overall lack of pubertal hormonal influence on ADHD medication.

Medication and eating

Teenage girls are, of course, so often preoccupied with body shape and size. The fact that stimulant medication and to a somewhat lesser extent atomoxetine suppress appetite can seem a distinct bonus. Occasionally, it becomes a fixation.

> 'I really, really need to take my (lisdexamfetamine) every day, even when I'm not at school.'
> (Why? It's there to help with your concentration in class.)
>
> 'No but I really must have it because, because...'
> (Mother asks, 'It helps you not eat so much?')

'Yeah well that's it, I'm so overweight.'

And indeed she was. I referred her to a dietician immediately and her fixation on her medication disappeared once she had a framework for sensible eating.

Conversely, the information on the pack insert leaflet for guanfacine states that a possible side effect is weight gain. I have seen so many girls flatly refuse to have anything to do with it once they have seen that, though in my experience it is not very common in common-sense terms (in spite of being described as 'common' in the leaflet, 'common' being a technical term in pharmacological studies meaning it can occur in up to 10% of children taking a medicine) and is easily reversed when the medication is stopped.

Normal medical practice for anyone on ADHD medication is to monitor weight and height growth regularly. On occasion a girl can become quite thin because of appetite suppression, especially with extended release stimulants. The question of anorexia nervosa will then arise. Sometimes it is straightforward to rule this out by asking the girl what she thinks about her weight; see Chapter 4 for further discussion on eating disorders.

'I hate being skinny, really hate it. Everyone keeps asking if I've got an eating disorder.'

Or:

'I don't mind losing weight but what I want to know is will it go on and on like this and get worse?'

There may not be a clearly voiced opinion, in which case the clinician needs to consider whether there is in fact a horror of normal body bulk and shape or a sense of shame about eating. If so, and there seems to be secrecy about eating and dressing, a resistance to regaining normal weight and selective carbohydrate restriction, then anorexia nervosa is likely, and withdrawal of stimulant medication would normally be indicated. In my experience, when this picture emerges there is usually co-existing, and perhaps previously unsuspected, high-functioning autism spectrum disorder (Anckarsater *et al.* 2012). While anorexia nervosa in girls with ADHD is not common, bulimia and binge eating disorder are more likely, due to the impulsive nature of the behaviours. Yet I have treated a few older teenagers and young adults with established anorexia nervosa and a late diagnosis of ADHD with highly controlled and supervised medication coupled with CBT and a whole family approach – it can be done, though the course is not likely to be smooth.

Measuring the effect of medication

Ordinarily, a prescribing clinician will assess whether a medication is effective by using a rating scale. This is often one of the questionnaires for parents and teachers that include the list of standard diagnostic items such as the Conners 3, the SNAP-IV or the ADHD-RS. Although this is good practice in the management of ADHD generally, there are problems with relying too much on this when girls are concerned.

The diagnostic items are skewed towards the picture of ADHD in boys, particularly those between the ages of 6 and 11 years. Girls are more likely to be affected by predominantly inattentive items so their initial score on the whole questionnaire will be low. This means that improvement is measured against a low baseline even though impairment is significant. Partitioning the questionnaire responses into the inattention and hyperactivity/impulsivity sub-scores is more helpful.

In addition, girls are more likely to be diagnosed at an older age. This poses well-known problems when asking teachers to complete a standard rating scale as there is the familiar problem of seeing so much variation between teacher ratings in a secondary school setting. It may be better to rate improvement on a simple, perhaps five-point, scale for the severity or frequency of a problem/solution such as:

- preparedness for school in the morning
- amount of homework completed

- number of times homework has been handed in appropriately
- observed daydreaming in class for a particular lesson by the same teacher.

If properly set up with agreed and described anchor points for each point on the scale, this is easier for a girl to interpret compared with the graphs or numbers from the scales above.

The subjective report of a teenage girl is also important:

'My mind is clearer.'

'I can concentrate now.'

'Though not always.'

'I don't think it's made a difference.'

(Contradicted strongly by mother: 'You can't say that, you sat down and did your homework for three-quarters of an hour like you've never done before.')

The girl's subjective report is also crucial for some side effects:

'I guess I'm getting in less trouble at school, but I feel weirdly out of it with my friends.'

'I just can't face eating. It's more than not feeling hungry; eating is really, really boring.'

'I feel really sick.'

Medication for associated conditions

Girls with ADHD are more likely than boys to also have emotional conditions: anxiety and depressive mood in particular. These can usually be treated by psychological methods in the first place but if they are severe or when psychological treatments are not available, then medicines come into play.

For emotional conditions, selective serotonin reuptake inhibitors (SSRIs) are the usual choice. Many prescribers consider sertraline (Lustral in the UK, Zoloft in the USA) the first choice when anxiety or panic is the major issue. This is partly because its dose can be managed more precisely than fluoxetine. Fluoxetine (Prozac), is preferred for depression because the evidence for its effect in the young as an antidepressant is the strongest of all the SSRIs.

For prescribers, it is important to note that most girls with ADHD who are also taking ADHD medication will tolerate an SSRI well but fluoxetine and lisdexamfetamine (Elvanse/Vyvanse) can interact unpleasantly. This is because fluoxetine blocks the metabolic breakdown of dexamfetamine in the liver (by CYP2D6 in the P450 enzyme system) and vice versa. If fluoxetine is the first medication to be given, then lisdexamfetamine can be cautiously introduced, but to give a girl who is already on lisdexamfetamine a standard dose of fluoxetine can result in a toxic reaction with agitation or even a serotonin syndrome. Fluoxetine and methylphenidate can be used together because methylphenidate is metabolised through a different system.

PARENTS SHOULD CONSIDER WHETHER THEY MAY HAVE SIMILAR DIFFICULTIES

There is a strong genetic contribution to the causes of ADHD (although there is no single gene responsible). This means that there is a chance that a girl with ADHD may have a parent with ADHD too. This complicates matters as:

- the advice that parents should create rules and routines will be a struggle for a parent with ADHD

- organising supplies of medicines may be hard to achieve

- comparing their daughter with themselves can lead to skewed judgement.

'Nothing wrong with her, I was like her at that age and I didn't need drugs.'

'OMG she's going to grow up feeling useless like me.'

The implication is that any parent of a daughter with ADHD should consider, especially by asking their partner, whether it is likely they have ADHD and ask for a referral for assessment. Treated parental ADHD, if it is present, makes parenting a great deal easier and helps their daughter manage her difficulties.

✋ KEY POINTS

» There is no difference in the response of girls to ADHD medication than that of boys.

» There are no scientific studies which evidence that stimulant medication is less effective for adolescent girls than it is for boys.

» Monitoring the impact of medication should be done both by using screening tools and by asking girls directly for their views.

REFERENCES

Anckarsater, H., Hofvander, B., Billstedt, E., Gillberg, I.C. *et al.* (2012) 'The sociocommunicative subgroup in anorexia nervosa: Autism spectrum disorders and neurocognition in a community-based, longitudinal study.' *Psychological Medicine 42*, 9, 1957–1967.

Barkley, R.A. (2018) *Attention Deficit Hyperactivity Disorder: A Handbook for Diagnosis and Treatment*, 4th edn. New York, NY: Guilford Press.

Brown, T.E. (2005) *Attention Deficit Disorder*. New Haven, CT and London: Yale University Press.

Chang, J.P.-C., Su, K.-P., Mondelli, V., Satyanarayanan, S.K. *et al.* (2019) 'High-dose eicosapentaenoic acid 1 (EPA) improves attention and vigilance in children and adolescents with attention deficit hyperactivity disorder (ADHD) and low endogenous EPA levels.' *Translational Psychiatry 9*, 1, 303.

Coghill, D., Chen, W. and Silva, D. (2019) 'Organizing and Delivering Treatment of ADHD.' In L.A. Rohde, J.K. Buitelaar, M. Gerlach and S.V. Faraone (eds) *The World Federation of ADHD Guide*. World Federation of ADHD. Accessed on 27 August 2020 at https://www.adhd-federation.org/publications/adhd-guide.

Cooper-Kahn, J. and Dietzel, L. (2008) *Late, Lost and Unprepared*. Bethesda, MA: Woodbine House.

Cortese, S., Angriman, M., Lecendreux, M. and Konofal, E. (2012) 'Iron and attention deficit/hyperactivity disorder: What is the empirical evidence so far?' *Expert Review of Neurotherapeutics 12*, 10, 1227–1240.

Dawson, P. and Guare, R. (2009) *Smart but Scattered*. New York, NY: Guilford Press.

Feldman, M., Charach, A. and Belanger, S. (2018) 'ADHD in children and youth: Part 2 – treatment.' *Paediatrics and Child Health 23*, 7, 462–472.

Ferrin, M., Moreno-Granados, J., Salcedo-Marin, M., Ruiz-Veguilla, M., Perez-Ayala, V. and Taylor, E. (2014) 'Evaluation of a psychoeducation programme for parents of children and adolescents with ADHD: Immediate and long-term effects using a blind randomized controlled trial.' *European Child & Adolescent Psychiatry 23*, 8, 637–647.

Hallowell, E.M. and Ratey, J.J. (2011) *Driven to Distraction: Recognizing and Coping with Attention Deficit Disorder from Childhood through Adulthood*. London: Penguin Random House.

Justice, A.J. and de Wit, H. (1999) 'Acute effects of d-amphetamine during the follicular and luteal phases of the menstrual cycle in women.' *Psychopharmacology 145*, 1, 67–75.

Konofal, E., Lecendreux, M., Deron, J., Marchand, M. *et al.* (2008) 'Effects of iron supplementation on attention deficit hyperactivity disorder in children.' *Pediatric Neurology 38*, 1, 20–26.

Mikami, A.Y., Cox, D., Davis, M., Wilson, H.K., Merkel, R.L. and Burket, R. (2009) 'Sex differences in effectiveness of extended-release stimulant medication among adolescents with attention deficit/hyperactivity disorder.' *Journal of Clinical Psychology in Medical Settings 16*, 3, 233–242.

Nadeau, K.G., Littman, E.B. and Quinn, P.O. (2016) *Understanding Girls with ADHD*, 2nd edn. Washington DC: Advantage Books.

National Institute for Health and Care Excellence (2018) *Attention Deficit Hyperactivity Disorder: Diagnosis and Management (NICE Guideline NG87)*. Accessed on 27 July 2020 at https://www.nice.org.uk/guidance/ng87.

Quinn, P. (2009) *Attention Girls!* Washington DC: Magination Press.

Renoux, C., Shin, J.-Y., Dell'Aniello, S., Fergusson, E. and Suissa, S. (2016) 'Prescribing trends of attention-deficit hyperactivity disorder (ADHD) medications in UK primary care, 1995–2015.' *British Journal of Clinical Pharmacology 82*, 3, 858–868.

Smith, B., Pelham, W., Gnagy, E. and Yudell, R. (1998) 'Equivalent effects of stimulant treatment for attention-deficit/hyperactivity disorder during childhood and adolescence.' *Journal of the American Academy of Child & Adolescent Psychiatry 37*, 3, 314–321.

Storebø, O.J., Andersen, M.E., Skoog, M., Hansen, S.J. *et al.* (2019) 'Social skills training for attention deficit hyperactivity disorder (ADHD) in children aged 5 to 18 years.' *Cochrane Systematic Review – Intervention.* Accessed on 27 July 2020 at https://doi.org/10.1002/14651858.CD008223.pub3.

Visser, S.N., Danielsson, M.L., Bitsko, R.H., Holbrook, J.R. *et al.* (2014) 'Trends in the parent-report of health care provider diagnosed and medicated ADHD: United States, 2003–2011.' *Journal of the American Academy of Child and Adolescent Psychiatry 53*, 1, 34–46.

Wang, Y., Huang, L., Zhang, L., Qu, Y. and Mu, D. (2017) 'Iron status in attention-deficit/hyperactivity disorder: A systematic review and meta-analysis.' *PLoS One 12*, 1, e0169145.

Chapter 4

Mental Health Comorbidities in Girls with ADHD

— DR ALEX DOIG —

MENTAL HEALTH AND WELL BEING

It isn't easy having attention deficit hyperactivity disorder (ADHD). There is the positive side, where young people with ADHD can be seen as funny, energetic and creative. They can gain popularity from their friends by being the creative driver in playground games, the sporty footballer or even the class clown. However, for a lot of young people with ADHD it is common for them, and those around them, to struggle with their difficulties in concentration, fidgetiness, poor impulse control and rapid mood changes. The effects of these core symptoms on their everyday activities and their relationships can have a negative impact on their mental well-being.

Good mental health, or well-being, is made up of a variety of factors. It includes good self-esteem, confidence, the ability to develop positive and secure relationships, being able to be resilient at times of stress and, above all, feeling good about yourself. Unfortunately, the experiences of a lot of young people with ADHD before their diagnosis can negatively impact on all these areas, knocking their confidence, and this can lead to low self-esteem.

Before the diagnosis of ADHD is known, it can be assumed by adults at school that the child with ADHD is naughty, careless or simply not very bright. The child doesn't pay attention to what is said, they forget what they have been asked or seem to learn something one day and act as if they have never heard about it the next. At home before their parents hear about ADHD, the child can be perceived as badly behaved, an annoyance or even as a disappointment. They are constantly in time out, or losing their toys, pocket money or phone as a consequence of impulsive behaviours. In frustration, parents may even end up saying to their child that they don't like them or want them to go away.

There can be difficulties with social skills, as outlined in Chapter 2. Within their friendship groups they can be over-controlling or too overwhelming. They may know that games often end badly, and so they may want to control the rules and their friends as an attempt to minimise this. Their peers soon learn that games end badly and can start backing away. The ADHD child's hyperactivity can be engaging and fun for the first five minutes but get too much very quickly. They can be quick to anger and find blame, but equally quick to get upset when there is a falling out. On the sports field they can be energetic and enthusiastic, but their impulsivity can lead to confrontation on the field and even fights and being sent off.

Unfortunately, it seems that girls with ADHD are more likely to be undiagnosed (Ramtekkar *et al.* 2010). This means that they are more likely to have more years of untreated ADHD and more exposure to negative comments and adverse life events. This can then have a greater knock-on effect on their self-esteem and overall mental health. Over time young people can pick up on the negative feedback and start seeing this as their identity. They can become convinced that they must be stupid, or there must be something wrong with them, leaving them feeling above all that they are not likeable and not good enough. I have had young women tell me that they always 'knew' that they were 'different' and that they assumed that they were 'broken' or that their brains were 'damaged'. These were their words, and this had started to become part of how they saw themselves.

As has already been explored in earlier chapters, the process of getting a diagnosis can be challenging in many ways. As girls don't always present as buzzy hyperactive children and can be more inattentive, it can be a long journey to get enough evidence to even access an assessment. Often the underlying difficulties with ADHD are not noticed at all until there is an effect on their mental health. When eventually an assessment of ADHD is suggested, some young women are relieved that there could be an explanation for their difficulties, that it isn't their 'fault'. However, some are frustrated at the possibility of 'yet another label' telling them how different they are. It is always important, particularly for adolescents, that the pros and cons of an assessment are discussed. The benefits of being better understood at school and home, having reasonable adjustments so that education is easier, and learning more about your own strengths and weaknesses are all helpful, but this is balanced against the potential downsides of being an adolescent and having a diagnosis and their possible worries at being seen as having special educational needs. It is important that adolescents have a say in their treatment, and this includes any assessments.

Once young people have a diagnosis of ADHD, they often have a sense of relief, despite any worries they may have had beforehand. The diagnosis can offer an explanation for their difficulties. They are not stupid, lazy or bad, they just have ADHD, which can then be dealt with.

☀ TIPS: What can you do to improve self-esteem and general mental health?

- Make sure that your child is getting enough sleep. A better night's sleep builds emotional resilience. Have a set bedtime routine and avoid screens (phones/laptops) for two hours before bedtime. Encourage them to take a warm bath as the cooling down after a bath makes it easier to fall asleep. Avoid pets in the bedroom, and make sure the room is cool and dark.

- Build on the skills your child is good at. When young people feel good at something this builds their confidence and self-esteem. If they are sporty, arty, enjoy performing or are good with animals, look for opportunities for them to practise and improve these areas.

    – Help your child work on their social skills. Have a few friends over to play rather than a large group and structure their time to give the best chance of a successful time together. Look for structured social groups, such as Brownies, Guides, Scouts, sports clubs and drama clubs, as structured play is more likely to be successful with fewer opportunities for conflict.

✋ KEY POINTS

» The core symptoms of ADHD can have a negative impact on emotional well-being.

» Girls are more likely than boys to have more years of untreated ADHD and more exposure to negative comments and adverse life events, further increasing the likelihood of additional mental health difficulties.

BEHAVIOURAL DISORDERS

When children are struggling, we often think about girls struggling inside with difficult emotions and boys showing how they feel by getting angry or acting out. These stereotypes do have some truth in them as in teenage years, young women are more likely to have anxiety and depression compared with boys, and boys are indeed more likely to have behavioural issues. However, each child is an individual and of course boys get depressed and girls can develop behavioural problems.

As a younger child, Lily was hyperactive and would often get in trouble at school for messing around in the classroom, talking to her friends and back-chatting to teachers. Frequently told off, she disengaged from school. At home she would often refuse to do as her mother asked and would get extremely angry very quickly, often about seemingly minor things. When she became a teenager, things went downhill. She was argumentative at school and would storm out of class or simply be sent home. She got in with a peer group that would hang around the town centre after school and harass passers-by for laughs. She started taking cannabis and moved on quite quickly to using ketamine with her friends. She got involved in shoplifting 'for laughs' and had received several cautions from police about antisocial behaviour.

A behavioural problem like this will be diagnosed only when the behaviour is repeated, persistent and much worse than would normally be expected for the child's developmental age. For example, it is common for 2-year-olds to misbehave, have temper tantrums and be defiant as they are figuring out independence but without having the language to be able to communicate this. A 2-year-old with temper tantrums and refusing to do what a parent asks would be considered normal. An 11-year-old doing the same, day in, day out, would be considered to have a behavioural problem. Typically for younger children, the behavioural problems tend to be 'oppositional' in that they will refuse to do what their parents ask, disobeying instructions and repeatedly having tantrums. This is often called 'oppositional defiant disorder'. For older teenagers, the challenging behaviour is often more extreme, with frequent angry outbursts, aggression towards others, destruction of property and frequent breaking of rules and laws. This is often termed 'conduct disorder'.

There can be a wide range of reasons why a young person is showing challenging behaviour. Anything from difficulties at home to arguments between parents, an angry or harsh parenting style, difficulties at school or generally struggling to succeed. It can be the result of a physical problem, like a lack of sleep, using drugs or alcohol, or low blood sugars. It can be because of other mental health reasons, such as anxiety or depression. It can also be because the young person has a neurodevelopmental issue such as an autistic spectrum disorder or ADHD.

We know that young people with ADHD commonly have behavioural issues. In fact, girls with ADHD are 11 times more likely to have oppositional defiant disorder, and 9 times more likely to have conduct disorder (Tung *et al.* 2016) compared with girls without ADHD. Sometimes this is the result of the emotional 'roller coaster', sometimes called 'emotional lability', where the feelings of someone with ADHD will be very changeable, with fast mood swings and frequent angry outbursts during the day. Sometimes it is because of the difficulties a young person will have with their impulse control, as they are likely to reply to a request with the first thing they think of, often a resounding 'No!', and only after responding will they have time to think it through. However, sleep, parenting style and emotional well-being are often factors as they are for any child with behavioural problems.

Managing this frequently requires a range of interventions from a range of services (National Institute for Health and Care Excellence 2017). School can often be a great help with younger children as a lot of schools run social and emotional groups for young children, particularly those identified as being at risk for developing behavioural difficulties. Parenting groups are often run in each area and will usually be age specific, as outlined in Chapter 3 on treatment. These groups are often the first intervention in trying to address the problem, as they support parents to try different ways of improving their child's behaviour. It can sometimes feel like a criticism if a parenting group is offered. It isn't. There are a range of behavioural strategies that have been shown to work well with behavioural disorders, and these groups are simply the best way of teaching parents such techniques. Sometimes the behaviour is so challenging that a child needs to get help from a range of services such as schools, social care, substance misuse teams and mental health teams.

If a young person has a behavioural disorder and ADHD, one helpful thing is to review their medication. If they have not been on medication, it may be worth thinking of starting; and if they are already on medication, it may be worth reviewing to see if there are other options in terms of dose or type. This would not be instead of all the interventions discussed above, but as well as them. Medication can improve emotional lability and poor impulse control, which in turn can make a big difference in a child's behaviour. If a young person is using recreational drugs, then medication might not be possible to prescribe until the drug taking has been addressed due to the risks of interactions.

☀ TIPS: What can you do to improve behaviour?

- Make sure that any difficulties with sleep, confidence and self-esteem are addressed as described above.

- 'Ignore the small stuff.' Minor infractions can easily become a constant complaint, and a young person can easily feel that they are never doing well enough. Focus on the important behaviours you want to change, be clear and precise on what good behaviour would look like, and catch every little positive, no matter how small.

- Catch the difficulties early if you can. Work alongside school and access the parent groups available in your area.

✋ KEY POINTS

» Girls with ADHD can present with behavioural difficulties.

» If behavioural difficulties are significant, then a co-ordinated approach and input from a range of services is important.

ANXIETY DISORDERS

Anxiety affects a lot of young people with ADHD, and girls in particular. Before their ADHD diagnosis a lot of young women describe always knowing that they were 'different' and struggling to fit in or finding it hard to keep up with their friends in the classroom. Often, they would think that there was something 'wrong' with them. They would try their best in lessons, but somehow would often get in trouble. Sometimes this shaped their thinking so that they would predict bad things would happen before anything had, making them anxious about even trying. Sometimes it would feel as if everyone was disapproving of them, even strangers in the street, making them anxious to go outside. Sometimes they would get so anxious about making mistakes at school that they developed a fear of school itself. Often the anxiety is noticed well before the ADHD itself is recognised, and it can take some time to recognise a young person has both conditions as the anxiety itself can mask the ADHD.

Anxiety affects one in three young women with ADHD (Masi and Gignac 2015). So, if they are commonly seen together, why does it sometimes take a while to recognise this? The reason is that the two conditions can look very similar. Both can present with fidgeting, distractibility and a lack of attention, irritability and a lack of sleep. With ADHD these symptoms have often been around for a long time. Sometimes with anxiety there is a very distinct start point for these symptoms, linked with a clear increase in anxiety thoughts and feelings. However, if you already have a child who is fidgety and doesn't sleep, it is easy to miss this change and assume it is all part of ADHD. Similarly, if you see a therapist or doctor to help with your child's anxiety, it would be reasonable for them to assume that the fidgetiness and insomnia are due to anxiety alone as the ADHD is masked. It is usually only after treating the anxiety, and when the anxious thoughts and feelings have improved but the fidgetiness is still present, that a question may be asked about a possible underlying ADHD diagnosis.

Inattentive and always described as being in a world of her own, Olivia always struggled at school. She would forget her books and PE kit, mislay her homework and really find it difficult to remember what had been spoken about in previous lessons, much to the frustrations of teachers. Her peers would get annoyed with her, and some of the girls would call her names or create games to deliberately exclude her. This subtle bullying went on for years, and Olivia kept it secret. She began finding it hard to sleep as she was worrying so much about school, and during the day she would hide in the bathroom. Her focus in class got worse, and she was doing poorly in her class tests and could see the disappointment in both her teacher and her parents. Every time she thought of school she would panic, and she started missing more and more school with tummy pains and headaches. She was then referred to Child and Adolescent Mental Health Services (CAMHS). After a few months in therapy, the therapist raised her fidgeting and poor attention with her parents and recommended that this was also looked into. She was found to have ADHD (inattentive subtype) and began treatment for this, too.

Treatment of anxiety would usually be with therapy, and if it is very severe, possibly anxiety medication alongside therapy. For young people with ADHD, therapy can sometimes be challenging. They sometimes struggle to articulate their feelings or get bored and distracted by a session that is too long. Often therapies such as cognitive behavioural therapy (CBT) can be adapted for ADHD with the introduction of activity breaks, the active involvement of the therapist supporting the young person to stay on task, the use of fiddle toys and shorter sessions. Visual aids and homework sheets are often helpful, as is involving parents in any practice activities between sessions. For some young people with severe ADHD, a problem solving style of therapy or family therapy may be easier to access than CBT.

Medication for ADHD can sometimes worsen anxiety, or even be a cause of the anxiety. This is rare, but it is always worth considering it if there appears to be a link with the starting of a new medication or a change in dose and the worsening or starting of anxiety symptoms. If there are issues with ADHD medication and anxiety, it may be worth considering a change to a non-stimulant medication if that has not been tried already.

☀ TIPS: What can you do to improve anxiety?

- Make sure that any difficulties with sleep, confidence and self-esteem are addressed as described above. Sleep is particularly important in anxiety disorders. If you are anxious, it is harder to sleep and more support to manage this is needed, and if you have not slept, you will feel less resilient during the day.

- Diet is often important in anxiety. Avoid drinking caffeinated drinks (energy drinks, coffee, fizzy drinks) as these will increase the anxiety.

- Help the child or young person understand that the physical symptoms of anxiety are just your body's reaction to your mind pressing the 'alarm button' and that the symptoms will pass. Often young people get frightened by the way their body responds in anxiety and this can make the anxiety bigger.

- Talk to the child or young person about their fears (or use a worry book, or a box to post worries) and help them find solutions.

- Distractions are a good way to help the anxiety pass. 'Square breathing', where you breathe in, hold your breath, breathe out and hold your breath again (the four steps are the same length like a square) before repeating the cycle, can be very helpful.

✋ KEY POINTS

- » Anxiety is common in girls with ADHD.

- » Therapy, usually CBT, is considered the most effective treatment for anxiety.

DEPRESSION

Depression, similar to anxiety, is very common in girls with ADHD. As described before, having ADHD is not easy. Before a diagnosis girls with ADHD can be thought of as 'lazy' or 'not trying' or even be told that they are 'stupid' all because they are distracted and unable to concentrate and struggle to keep up as a result. This can unfortunately be internalised as 'I am not good enough' by the young person, lowering their self-esteem. Socially, it can be harder to fit in and girls with ADHD can struggle to be accepted, which further compounds the difficulties. These challenges often make young women with ADHD more vulnerable to depression, and it takes only a bad family argument, a falling out with a friend or a break-up of a relationship to trigger more difficult feelings, and possibly lead to depression. Parents may notice that their daughter has become more irritable or that they are more withdrawn or tired. A common report from parents is that their daughter is extremely low in mood or angry on returning home from school. This is often linked to the amount of extra work and effort these girls are trying to put in to keep up with the demands of the day as well as fallouts with friends, which can be exhausting.

Depression can affect up to a third of young women with ADHD (Masi and Gignac 2015). Depression is more than low self-esteem, although low self-esteem is often part of it. Young people with depression will feel incredibly sad and possibly tearful or more irritable. Their moods can be more changeable, and in adolescence it is not uncommon for a teenager to appear bright and happy with friends while they are distracted, only to crash in mood moments after. Low energy, poor motivation, difficulties concentrating and losing interest or no longer enjoying things they used to are also common symptoms. Sleep is often affected, with young people finding it harder to sleep, or waking too early and still feeling tired. Some of these symptoms can seem very similar to ADHD, as motivation issues, poor concentration, irritability and mood swings, and difficulty sleeping are frequently seen in ADHD anyway. The difference is a change in mood: feeling sad along with a worsening of these areas; and the time frame, with ADHD having been around since early childhood and being long term, and depression being more of an episode with a later onset.

Self-harm and suicidal thoughts can be part of severe depression. Young people self-harm for many different reasons. Sometimes it is a way of dealing with difficult feelings, and young people will describe 'the physical pain being easier than the emotional pain' to deal with. Sometimes it is a distraction, sometimes a form of self-punishment. Occasionally, you will hear people question whether self-harm is 'attention seeking'. Sometimes this is from well-meaning people trying to understand what is happening, but sadly it is also used by people putting down someone who self-harms or minimising their distress. Rather than use the term 'attention seeking', it is better to speak to the young person and ask them why they self-harm, trying to understand from their perspective what is happening. Self-harm is almost always a communication of distress and difficulty.

Suicidal thoughts should always be taken seriously, particularly in girls with ADHD. Often, they are associated with a more severe depression, but they can arise in the midst of severe anxiety, or in response to an overwhelming incident or event. Girls with ADHD do seem to be more vulnerable to acting on these thoughts when they have them (Fitzgerald *et al.* 2019). Fitzgerald and her team found that young people with ADHD, and particularly those with additional mental health conditions, were more at risk of acting on these thoughts. This is important for young women with ADHD, who we already know are more likely to experience anxiety and depression. Young people with ADHD are more impulsive, and more likely to act on risky thoughts, which increases the risk of acting on the spur of the moment without thinking through the consequences. For any young girl with ADHD who is struggling with low mood, it is important to ask if they are finding it hard to manage thoughts of self-harm or suicidal ideas as outlined in Chapter 2. If they are asked, it will not 'put the idea in their head' or make them more likely to do it; in fact, it is often a relief for the young person that someone knows. If any young person is struggling with self-harm or suicidal ideas, it is a good idea to make an urgent appointment with your family doctor and get a referral to a specialist to get support.

Emily was 17 by the time she presented. She had broken up with her girlfriend and blamed herself. In her eyes it was yet another example of why she 'isn't good enough' and she had felt extremely upset. She saw a packet of medication on the window ledge and, without thinking it through, took all the tablets that were left. At the time she just wanted the horrible feelings to end, but as soon as she had taken the tablets she panicked and called a friend. Her friend immediately informed Emily's parents, and she was taken to the local hospital. Emily had been struggling with feeling sad for the last few years. Her energy was low, and everything felt difficult and it was hard some days to even get out of bed. She struggled to get off to sleep and would have constant negative thoughts swirling in her mind. At times she would cut herself as this seemed at first to numb the pain, but it didn't work for long and the dark thoughts still came back. Emily had not done as well as she had hoped in her exams, and had gone on to college to do a course she was not that interested in. She was snappy at home, and constantly arguing, and her negative thoughts often led her to think that everyone would be better off without her.

Emily was seen by CAMHS and started both therapy and medication. Her mood improved over time and she was able to challenge her negative thoughts. Feeling more positive, she decided to change her course and repeat some of her exams to enable her to do a course she wanted. Family life improved. However, even though Emily was feeling better, she continued to struggle with her memory and concentration, and it became clear that this was no longer related to any depression. She was assessed for ADHD and it was found that this was a big component of her difficulties with her attention and explained why she had struggled so much at school. Emily understood that her struggles were not because she 'was not good enough' but that there were other reasons, which could now be managed, which was a turning point for how she thought of herself. Emily started treatment of her ADHD, and several years later went on to university having overcome her depression.

Treatment for depression is again usually therapy, and if it is very severe, possibly antidepressant medication alongside therapy, as outlined in Chapter 3. The same issues in therapy apply to depression as to anxiety, and some modification to therapy is sometimes needed for young people with ADHD.

Stimulant medication for ADHD can be the cause of low mood, often termed 'dysphoria'. If the depression started only after ADHD medication was tried, or after an increase in dose, it is worth considering changing the dose or changing the type of medication. There is also a non-stimulant medication that has a very rare side effect of causing suicidal ideas. This would be discussed before starting this medication and should be monitored very carefully. However, any increase in suicidal ideas or self-harm after changing or starting medication should be explored further.

☀ TIPS: What can you do to improve depression?

- Make sure that any difficulties with sleep, confidence and self-esteem are addressed as described above. Sleep is particularly important in depression, as with anxiety. If you are depressed, it is harder to sleep and more support to manage this is needed, and if you have not slept, you will feel less resilient during the day.

- Try to encourage activities that the young person used to enjoy. Exercise can be extremely helpful, although it can be a struggle with motivation. Doing something together with a parent can help and also provide some one-to-one time. Distractions are often helpful to provide brief windows of respite from their low mood.

- It is often worth checking in with social media use. Bullying texts at 2am can be a trigger for depression and thoughts of self-harm. Some young people use unhelpful sites that encourage self-harm. Some restrictions around social media, particularly at night when a young person is more vulnerable, can be helpful if this is an issue.

- Ensure all medication, even ADHD medication, is locked away and kept safe from the young person. If a young person with ADHD does develop a suicidal thought, impulsivity can make them act rashly, and so making sure any medication is locked away can allow the extra five minutes that they may need to think things through and ask for help.

✋ KEY POINTS

» Depression is very common in girls with ADHD.

» Treatment for depression is usually talking therapy; if the depression is severe, antidepressant medication can be considered.

EATING DISORDERS

This is different from the loss of appetite that can happen with some ADHD medications. Often 'anorexia' is stated as a side effect, with 'anorexia' simply meaning loss of appetite in this context, and is different from anorexia nervosa, an eating disorder.

Eating disorders are rare in young people with ADHD, but far more common are concerns around body shape, particularly for young women but increasingly for young men as well. Today's society does promote thinness as an ideal body type, with social media glamorising and rewarding those who fit that mould. For a young lady with ADHD, there is the added burden of having her weight scrutinised at every ADHD clinic as weight needs to be monitored to see the impact of the medication. The management of this is the same as for any young woman in today's society: building resilience and self-esteem, modelling body confidence at home, avoiding any teasing related to weight and monitoring social media use.

In addition, in clinic I will always try to say 'let me see how you are growing' rather than 'let me check your weight' to avoid unhelpful preoccupations in this area.

> Charlotte was 12 when I met her. She had been diagnosed with ADHD and we were meeting to try to stabilise her on medication. When checking her height and weight, it became obvious that Charlotte was anxious about getting on the scales. When she was seen by herself, she admitted to feeling uncomfortable about her body and that she was trying to lose weight. She had gone through puberty earlier than her peers and was quite self-conscious about her body shape. Her older brother had teased her a few times about her weight. She was starting to ask for diet foods and to cut down on her portion sizes. Reassurance that she was the right weight for her height, advice to the family to avoid any teasing about weight, some input from Mum about body changes and some education around the importance of eating regularly was enough to nip this in the bud. In clinic we were careful to talk about 'healthy growing' rather than focusing on weight.

Although eating disorders are rare, there are some studies suggesting a link between having ADHD and being vulnerable to a range of eating disorders which might increase the risk of developing one (Brewerton and Duncan 2016). There is some evidence that some people (both men and women) with ADHD are more likely to have binge eating disorder than those without ADHD. This is where someone has episodes of bingeing, feeling out of control with eating, along with feelings of guilt and shame. Usually, someone with this eating disorder will be normal weight or overweight. It is thought the link may be related to poor impulse control.

For women with ADHD, there is also an association with both bulimia and anorexia nervosa and some question as to whether having ADHD could be a risk factor for these conditions (Brewerton and Duncan 2016). Bulimia is thought to be more common in ADHD than anorexia nervosa due to issues with impulse control.

Bulimia is an eating disorder where people have periods when they restrict what they eat, followed by binges of food where they feel out of control, feel guilt and shame, but then try to get rid of the food by vomiting or using other methods. Anorexia nervosa is an eating disorder characterised by having a distorted view of your own body, where you see it as fat even when it is clear to everyone else that you are underweight. People with anorexia nervosa will try to control and limit what they are eating and will often over-exercise or run to lose weight in other ways. Both of these eating disorders are linked with low self-esteem, anxiety and fears of not being in control, often when life feels overwhelming. It is quite possible that the link between ADHD and eating disorders is due to the fact that young women with ADHD often struggle with self-esteem and anxiety and so may be more vulnerable to eating disorders.

☀TIPS: What can you do to encourage a healthy body image?

- Make sure that any difficulties with sleep, confidence and self-esteem are addressed as described above.

- Model 'body confidence' at home. Avoid making comments about your own body in a negative way and avoid talking about food in a negative way such as 'I shouldn't have that; it is bad for me.' Be quick to stamp on any teasing about weight at home from family members.

- For younger children, monitor social media use, and limit exposure to negative role models with unrealistic and unachievable bodies. Teach them about how social media models use digitally altered images to change how they look. For older young people, have conversations about social media use and who they are following and why.

- If you are worried that your child has an eating disorder, do seek help. See your GP and discuss your concerns. If you are seeing a medical professional to manage ADHD medication, then discussing this with them will also be helpful. Do monitor ADHD medication carefully so it cannot be misused as some young people with eating disorders may intentionally increase their dose to increase the loss of appetite side effect.

BIPOLAR DISORDER AND PSYCHOSIS

Psychosis is extremely rare. So rare that you could debate that it isn't worth including in this book. However, it is something that parents will often ask about. In popular culture there are lots of misunderstandings about psychosis; that it is a 'split personality' or that rapid mood swings must mean you have schizophrenia or bipolar disorder. When young people with ADHD often present with rapid mood swings, or there are times when their behaviour seems completely random and illogical, it is not surprising that this can be raised as a question.

Psychosis is when someone is so unwell that they experience hallucinations (they see/hear/feel/smell things that are not there in real life). An example of a hallucination would be hearing voices when there is no one there. Having hallucinations of voices is different from having negative thoughts, but for some younger children it can be hard to describe their own thoughts and they will sometimes say 'the voices told me...'. Hallucinations would typically be voices that you hear outside of your head as if they are in the real world and feel different to your own thoughts. People with psychosis also often experience delusions (a fixed, false belief that has nothing to do with cultural or religious backgrounds). An example of a delusion would be believing that aliens were reading your mind and could only be stopped by wearing a tinfoil hat. In psychosis, there is often a disturbed sense of reality, and often young people with psychosis, start losing skills that they had before, and their speech can become confused and jumbled. There are lots of different types of psychosis, such as bipolar disorder, schizophrenia or psychosis caused by drug use. It is exceedingly rare. Only 0.7% of the population experiences psychosis, and it is even rarer for anyone under the age of 18 years, and extraordinarily rare for anyone under the age of 13 years (Public Health England 2016).

Bipolar affective disorder is where someone has extreme mood swings. Someone with bipolar disorder is likely to experience extreme episodes of depression lasting for weeks, or episodes of mania, extreme highs in their mood, which last at least a couple of weeks. There are some extremely rare situations where someone will have much more rapid mood swings, but these are very much the exception. The mood swings with bipolar disorder are different from the mood swings that you see in young people with ADHD and mood lability. In ADHD you will often see rapid shifts in mood. One moment they are happy and laughing, the next they are angry and shouting. With ADHD there is usually a trigger that has caused the shift in mood. Their response may not be proportionate to the trigger, but there is usually a reason why their mood has changed. With ADHD there will be many changes in mood during the day and at times it can feel a bit like a roller coaster. In bipolar disorder there is often no reason or trigger, their mood just changes, but once it has changed it tends to stay the same for a while. With bipolar disorder there will often be psychotic symptoms, such as hallucinations or delusions, and these psychotic symptoms tend to reflect the person's current mood. So for example, if someone is feeling manic, or over-happy, their delusions and hallucinations might be expansive or extremely grand (often termed grandiose). They may start believing that they are royalty or the saviour of the human race, or their voices tell them that they have superpowers. If someone is low, their delusions can be self-critical or self-blaming, such as believing that they have caused a war or illness, or their voices may tell them that they are a terrible person.

Confusingly, there is a difference in how bipolar disorder is diagnosed in America compared with Europe, Australia and Asia (Clacey, Goldacre and James 2015). The American diagnosis of paediatric bipolar disorder allows for a child who has irritability, mood instability and no symptoms of mania or psychosis to get a diagnosis of bipolar disorder. This means that an irritable child with ADHD with emotional mood swings may be diagnosed as bipolar disorder in America, whereas they would not be given a bipolar disorder diagnosis in Europe, Australia or Asia. The diagnosis rates of bipolar disorder in America are significantly higher than in the latter countries. There have been various suggestions as to why there is such a big difference in how America diagnoses bipolar disorder in children, such as the insurance-based health system (which, it has been argued, prioritises medication over psychological treatments) and different training practices. Whatever the reasons, I would urge a lot of caution in the diagnosis unless there was clear evidence of prolonged mood swings or psychosis; but I would say that, as a doctor trained in the UK.

If a young person with ADHD does develop a psychosis, your doctor is very likely to stop their ADHD medication. There is some debate about this as the research is mixed, (Hollis *et al.*, 2019, and Gough *et al.* 2016) but the overall consensus is that stimulant ADHD medication can make psychosis worse if you have developed it, and the recovery is usually easier without ADHD medication. Once the psychosis is controlled, it is sometimes necessary to try introducing a non-stimulant ADHD medication, or to cautiously reintroduce stimulant ADHD medication if this is agreed as the best option. This can be very challenging.

> Stephanie was 16 years old when she developed psychosis. She had been on ADHD medication for several years and had been doing well at school. However, during the weekends, when she was not on medication, she had started using cannabis regularly. Over a few months she developed a lot of paranoid ideas that she was being followed and started to hear people talking to her, telling her she was unsafe, when there was no one there. Immediately, we stopped her ADHD medication, started her on antipsychotic medication and arranged for some support from the local child and adolescent substance misuse team. She did stop her cannabis use. Relatively quickly, over a few months, her voices and paranoid ideas subsided. However, she was really struggling academically and was finding it very hard to manage without her ADHD medication.

We were able to cautiously reduce her antipsychotic medication and reintroduce her ADHD medication with a lot of close monitoring, and she was able to get back on track without issue. She has not had any psychotic symptoms since.

PHYSICAL HEALTH

Although this is a chapter on mental health and well-being, I will briefly mention accidents, hormonal issues and teenage pregnancy as there is a close interplay between these issues, ADHD and mental health.

Accidents

Young people with ADHD are more likely to have accidents (Fleming *et al.* 2017). This ranges from the commonest minor injuries (knocks, scrapes and strains) to more serious accidents (broken bones, and bike and car accidents). Usually, this is because of their inattention and poor impulse control. They are not paying attention to the world around them and they don't always think whether a situation is safe before jumping straight in. The commonest, minor accidents of sprains and twisted ankles rarely seem to cause any ongoing distress other than that of missing out. However, young people with ADHD are less patient with their recovery and more likely to ignore the advice of doctors, which can lead to a longer time needed in recovery. Bigger injuries can be associated with anxiety disorders such as an adjustment reaction or post-traumatic stress disorder (PTSD), although this is rare. PTSD is where someone develops anxiety after a frightening event. They will often have bad dreams, intrusive memories of the event that pop into their head uninvited, and feel jumpy and jittery. Younger children may show this through repeatedly playing about the event or through a change in their behaviour. As with anxiety, the main treatment for PTSD is therapy, but for severe cases in older children, anxiety medication may be suggested.

There is an important group of accidents that young people

with ADHD are more likely to experience, and that is accidental poisoning (Ruiz-Goikoetxea *et al.* 2018). The poor impulse control, particularly of younger children with ADHD, makes them more likely to eat and drink things that they shouldn't. Older children with ADHD, particularly those experimenting with drugs or struggling with depression and suicidal thoughts, are vulnerable to impulsivity as described above and more likely to take risks with tablets if they are not safely stored away.

Hormones

Girls with ADHD can struggle more during adolescence. The onset of puberty and the start of periods has an effect on ADHD symptoms with a worsening of attention in the last half of the menstrual cycle (Roberts, Eisenlohr-Moul and Martel 2018). This can be confusing for a young person as their performance can appear to randomly change before the pattern is identified. If there is a component of premenstrual syndrome as well, this can lead to additional difficulties with irritability, impulsivity and changeable mood adding to the labile (up and down) mood of ADHD. Some young women do find it helpful to be on the oral contraceptive pill as this can help to even out the mood swings associated with hormonal changes, but it is always important to be aware that the contraceptive pill can also worsen depression for some individuals and does not suit everyone.

Teenage pregnancy

Adolescence is often a time of self-discovery, and for some sexual experimentation. We do know that young people with ADHD have issues with impulse control, and for both young men and women with ADHD, this can lead to not thinking about consequences and not planning ahead. In terms of sexual activity, not thinking about consequences and not planning ahead has obvious risks in terms of teenage pregnancy. A study by Meinzer and colleagues (2017) found that young people with ADHD had twice the risk of teenage pregnancy as peers without ADHD. Those young people with ADHD who also had behavioural disorders and a substance misuse problem showed a higher risk, whereas those young people with ADHD who were engaged with school had less risk. Although conversations about safe sex and contraception can be awkward, they are particularly important for young people with ADHD.

☀ TIPS: What can you do to reduce the risk of accidents?

- Ensure adult supervision for younger children with ADHD when they are involved in activities where injuries are more likely, such as climbing or swimming.

- Make sure the child wears a helmet when riding a bike. Pay particular attention to teaching road safety and remind children as often as is needed.

- Young adults with ADHD are less likely to have accidents if they drive while on their ADHD medication. Arrange driving lessons and allow driving when the medication is active. Advise them on reducing distractions, such as switching phones to silent while driving.

- Ensure the house is safe in terms of household cleaning products being locked away and household medications being safely stored where only adults can access them.

☀ TIPS: What can you do to help a child or young person manage the impact of hormones on their ADHD?

- An ADHD diary can be helpful, where you and the child or young person rate the level of inattention, impulsivity and labile mood over several months. This can highlight whether there is a clear pattern related to their cycle. Bear in mind that these conversations can be extremely embarrassing for young teenagers, so normalising this as much as possible can be helpful, for example by saying things like, 'This is a really common thing' or 'A lot of young women find this helpful'; or if you have your own hormonal cycle, even doing this exercise for yourself and sharing how you found it helpful.

- Supporting young women to plan work ahead of time where possible to avoid times in their cycle they are more likely to struggle.

- Discussing with your family doctor whether a contraceptive pill may be helpful if a young woman experiences a lot of difficult mood swings associated with her cycle (but be aware that for some young people, hormonal treatments can worsen depression).

- You may wish to discuss ADHD medication with your specialist as sometimes during puberty ADHD symptoms can be more difficult and it can be helpful to review the treatment.

🤚 KEY POINTS

» Eating disorders in girls with ADHD are not common; more usually, there are concerns around body shape.

» The mood swings with bipolar disorder are different from the mood swings that you see in young people with ADHD and mood lability.

CONCLUSION

Although it is not unusual for young women with ADHD to have other mental health conditions, it is still the case that most girls with ADHD do not. Although with the various mental health difficulties we have been talking about there is an increased risk, this is not the same as saying everyone will experience difficulties. However, as it is frequent enough, it is definitely worth keeping an eye out for the common difficulties, such as low self-esteem, anxiety and depression. There are a lot of early interventions that can help, such as ensuring a good night's sleep, building activities that make them feel confident and good about themselves, and structuring social activities so there are fewer chances for these to go wrong.

If a young woman with ADHD does struggle with other mental health difficulties, it is important to get these addressed. Your GP is likely to know what resources are available locally, from local counselling services all the way to CAMHS. If a child or young person is already seeing someone in CAMHS for ADHD, then it would be helpful to raise any concerns with your clinician.

As always, if you are concerned about the well-being of a young person, make an urgent appointment with your GP. If it is extremely urgent and you are concerned about their safety in terms of self-harm or suicidal ideas, then most areas can provide an urgent assessment through Accident and Emergency, and then refer you on to the appropriate services.

RESOURCES

- Childline.org.uk: a UK-based counselling charity for young people that has a lot of online resources to support young people.

- Samaritans.org: a UK-based charity supporting people in crisis.

- Youngminds.org.uk: a UK-based charity supporting young people's mental health.

REFERENCES

Brewerton, T.D. and Duncan, A.E. (2016) 'Associations between attention deficit hyperactivity disorder and eating disorders by gender: Results from the National Comorbidity Survey Replication.' *European Eating Disorders Review 24*, 6, 536–540.

Clacey, J., Goldacre, M. and James, A. (2015) 'Paediatric bipolar disorder: International comparisons of hospital discharge rates 2000–2010.' *British Journal of Psychiatry 1*, 2, 166–171.

Fitzgerald, C., Dalsgaard, S., Nordentoft, M. and Erlangsen, A. (2019) 'Suicidal behaviour among persons with attention-deficit hyperactivity disorder.' *British Journal of Psychiatry 215*, 615–620.

Fleming, M., Fitton, C.A., Steiner, M.F.C., McLay, J.S. *et al.* (2017) 'Educational and health outcomes of children treated for attention deficit/ hyperactivity disorder.' *JAMA Pediatrics 171*, 7, e170691. DOI: 10.1001/ jamapediatrics.2017.0691.

Gough, A. and Morrison, J. (2016) 'Managing the comorbidity of schizophrenia and ADHD.' *Journal of Psychiatry and Neuroscience 41*, 5, 79–80.

Hollis, C., Chen, Q., Chang, Z., Quinn, P.D., Viktorin, A. and Lichtenstein, P. (2019) 'Methylphenidate and the risk of psychosis in adolescents and young adults: A population-based cohort study.' *The Lancet 6*, 8, 651–658.

Masi, L. and Gignac, M. (2015) 'ADHD and comorbid disorders in childhood psychiatric problems, medical problems, learning disorders and developmental coordination disorder.' *Clinical Psychology 11*, 1. DOI: 10.21767/2471-9854.100005.

Meinzer, M.C., LeMoine, K.A., Howard, A.L., Stehli, A. *et al.* (2017) 'Childhood ADHD and involvement in early pregnancy: Mechanisms of risk.' *Journal of Attention Disorders*. DOI: 10.1177/1087054717730610.

National Institute for Health and Care Excellence (2017) *Antisocial Behaviour and Conduct Disorders in Children and Young People: Recognition and Management (NICE Guideline CG158)*. Accessed on 27 July 2020 at https:// www.nice.org.uk/guidance/cg158/chapter/2-Research-recommendations.

Public Health England (2016) *Psychosis Data Report: Describing Variation in Numbers of People with Psychosis and Their Access to Care in England*. London: Public Health England.

Ramtekkar, U.P., Reirson, A.M., Todorov, A.A. and Todd, R.D. (2010) 'Sex and age differences in attention-deficit/hyperactivity disorder symptoms and diagnosis: Implications for DSM-V and ICD-11.' *Journal of the American Academy of Child & Adolescent Psychiatry 49*, 3, 217–228.

Roberts, B., Eisenlohr-Moul, T. and Martel, M.M. (2018) 'Reproductive steroids and ADHD symptoms across the menstrual cycle.' *Psychoneuroendocrinology 88*, 105–114.

Ruiz-Goikoetxea, M., Cortese, S., Magallón, S., Aznárez-Sanado, M. *et al.* (2018) 'Risk of poisoning in children and adolescents with ADHD: A systematic review and meta-analysis.' *Scientific Reports 8*, 1, 7584.

Tung, I., Li, J.J., Meza, J.I., Jezior, K.L. *et al.* (2016) 'Patterns of comorbidity among girls with ADHD: A meta-analysis.' *Pediatrics 138*, 4, e20160430. DOI: 10.1542/peds.2016-0430.

Chapter 5

Navigating the Education System with an ADHD Girl

How to Square the Circle

— EVA AKINS —

Figure 5.1 The problem with trying to fit a square peg into a round hole is not that the hammering is hard work. It's that you're destroying the peg!

INTRODUCTION: FROM EXCLUSION TO EDUCATION LAWYER – A TREE-CLIMBING FISH

Asking a girl with attention deficit hyperactivity disorder (ADHD) to line up, sit still, concentrate, start and persist with her work, remember kit, hand in homework, be quiet, wait her turn, think before she acts, be calm and considerate, be punctual and organised, be tidy, be prepared, remember and follow instructions, abide by the rules of friendship and control her temper – all appears perfectly reasonable. After all, that is what we ask of all our pupils. It is what we reward with star charts, certificates, praise, teacher recognition, peer acceptance, exam results and inclusion, and it can't be one rule for her and another for everyone else. The absurdity of this model for girls with ADHD is aptly encapsulated by the quote commonly attributed to Einstein: 'If you judge a fish by its ability to climb tree, it will live its whole life believing that it is stupid' (Figure 5.1). Applying these expectations to girls with ADHD in education is akin to requiring a fish to climb a tree; it is requiring them to spend the majority of their day functioning outside their area of competence (Figure 5.2).

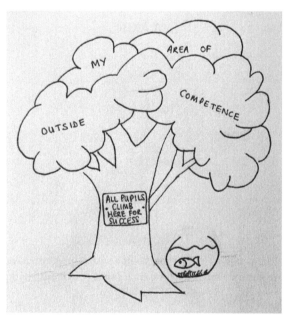

Figure 5.2 *Tree of Incompetence* (reproduced with permission of Ché Dyson-Holland)

A girl with ADHD is often of average or above-average intelligence. However, she is typically inattentive, impulsive and hyperactive with executive functioning that impedes all of the key skills required in formal education. This includes organising, prioritising and initiating work; focusing, sustaining and shifting attention to task; regulating alertness, sustaining effort and processing speed; managing frustration, modulating emotions, utilising working memory, accessing recall, monitoring and self-regulating action (Brown 2014). This is of course compounded if, as is commonly the case, she is also contending with the cumulative effect of co-occurring conditions such as dyslexia, obsessive–compulsive disorder, sensory processing disorder, autism spectrum disorder or rejection sensitive dysphoria, or is simply a teenager contending with puberty and a strong desire for social acceptance.

It is a crying shame that the experience of so many girls with ADHD is of underachievement, bullying, victim blaming, lacking friendship, knowing they are clever but feeling stupid, wanting to do well but failing to get started, failing to hand in homework (including work they've done), failing to attend appointments that are important to them, and appearing not to care because they are late or forgot. Labelled as trouble or troubled, eventually deciding at some level not to care and to stop trying because it's hopeless. Adopting a carefree exterior beneath which their self-esteem plummets, anxiety rises, sleep becomes evasive and school refusal, school exclusion and self-sabotage intrude.

As an education lawyer, my focus is on children and young people receiving education provision and placements that enable them to thrive and reach their potential with their self-esteem and self-efficacy intact. My aim is to empower parents who are often consumed by caring, campaigning and coping to overcome challenges they and their children face navigating the education system, and to raise awareness and upskill professionals to promote best practice and compliance thereby reducing risk. My method is solution focused and, where necessary, robust legal problem solving. My work comprises special educational needs and disability (SEND) including Tribunal appeals, Equality Act claims, admissions, exclusions, child protection and complaints. I work in cross-departmental specialist teams in claims involving negligence or breach of contract occurring in education. As a result of my personal experience and associated voluntary work, much of my practice is comprised of representing parents of neurodiverse children, in particular ADHD.

There is a huge irony in my being an education lawyer as my first contact with the education law system came at the age of 11 when I was first permanently excluded from an Inner London comprehensive school. I spent brief periods at another failing school and at a centre for conduct disordered children, which I recall as a cross between today's pupil referral units (PRUs) and a young offenders institution. However, most of my secondary years were spent exploring the educational wilderness, primarily with other NEETS (not in education employment or training) who were mainly risk-taking older boys. I also spent time with my older sisters who, despite their intelligence, had also failed to thrive in education. They internalised their mental health distress through anorexia and self-mutilation and would later attract serious mental health diagnoses and be institutionalised. I externalised my frustration, exhibited challenging-to-manage behaviour and an anti-authority 'attitude problem', and found a sense of belonging in a sub-culture operating an alternative hierarchy, one I could succeed in. My younger sister school refused. Our mother, at the end of her tether, developed alcoholism and suffered a nervous breakdown requiring hospitalisation.

I was underdeveloped for and overexposed to a variety of societal ills including substance misuse, the criminal justice system, homelessness and sexual exploitation. Some of my best gifts come wrapped in sandpaper and I learnt many transferable skills. It was becoming pregnant with my daughter at 16 years old that motivated a change in this trajectory and prompted my enrolment at further education college. As a 17-year-old teenage mum, I lived with my 23-year-old 'jail bird' boyfriend in a cockroach- and mice-infested block of flats. Our high-intensity, tempestuous relationship had an addictive quality to it. Despite it resulting in broken bones, including my right arm, the one I needed to write with shortly before my first-year university exams, it was hard to give up.

Living in hostels and working part-time, I completed a law degree, graduating with first class honours. I then completed law school and a training contract, purchased my council flat and qualified as a criminal lawyer aged 25. Experientially, I had by then learnt how to learn, and recognised that I could focus well only on things I was intrinsically interested in or when there was a powerful enough gun to my head. I struggled to work to others' agendas, but I could harness my 2am hyperfocus. In my zone of genius, I managed to write my final dissertation in a 48-hour period with no sleep. Unfortunately, I then fell asleep and failed to collect my daughter from school. My mum's and sisters' support with childcare during these years was invaluable.

I realised that my authority-challenging tendencies and transferable skills from the educational wilderness could be put to good use. I was not afraid to stand up to judges. I frequently succeeded in advancing novel arguments at trial. I was not socially in tune enough to be anxious about many of the things my peers were. I was independent of other people's opinions. Being nocturnal, arguing with police officers about my clients' rights at 3am down the 'cop shop' felt more like sport than a job.

It was over a decade later, by necessity born of exasperation, following my third child's exclusion from primary school aged 6 and prep school aged 9, that I transitioned into education law. Fighting for the rights of my son with ADHD and against the 'toxic identity' assigned to him caused the earlier challenge of achievement 'against the odds' to pale into insignificance. It was an isolating parenting experience consuming every ounce of my resilience and often all of my time, such that it seemed fairer for my comparatively neglected older son to take up a foundation place at boarding school.

I was determined not to allow my very bright and sporty youngest son's educational experience to end in failure, so I upskilled. Despite everything that could go wrong doing so in the first half of his education, knowledge really is power and in the second half, I was able to secure him a Statement of SEN (now an Education, Health and Care Plan, or EHCP), high-quality school placements and special educational provision. Reasonable adjustments were made to mitigate the disadvantages he faced academically and socially. When necessary, I utilised the Equality Act to fend off unfavourable treatment such as trip bans, excessive sanctioning and exclusion from school, usually following episodes of emotional dysregulation. I was by then able to 'speak softly but carry a big stick'. I am proud to say that he completed GCSEs at a selective independent school named in his EHCP with excellent results and is now completing four A levels at sixth form. More importantly, he has good friends, is confident and embraces his quirks.

GIRLS PRESENTING DIFFERENTLY: WHY I SAVED MY SON BUT LET MY DAUGHTER DROWN

I am distinctly less proud to say that whilst as an older, better resourced and more aware parent, I was able to save my son, during the course of my social climb out of deprivation, I let my daughter drown. I was extremely conscious of the importance of education, as a student myself, during her early education. I embraced a 'growth mindset', creative visualisation and a strong work ethic. I read her books, filled our hostel room with educational toys and sent her to drama and swimming lessons, and we recited timetables on the walk to school. However, there were few signs of academic progress.

Whereas my son's expression of combined type ADHD was such a crowd-control issue that it commanded everyone's attention, my daughter who was well-behaved failed quietly. No alarm was raised by her educators when she did not learn to read, and I am ashamed to say I was frustrated with her for not trying harder. I took her for a dyslexia assessment in Year 6 and the assessor reported, without elaboration, that there appeared to be something else alongside dyslexia going on to explain the disparity between her average cognitive ability and lack of academic progress. My guilt inferred she must mean the emotional trauma of secondary domestic violence, our moving around so much. Unfortunately, the assessor did not mention precisely what she suspected, and I did not know to ask.

Back then I had never heard of ADHD let alone inattentive subtype. I did not know that the education system operated within a legal framework. I did not know that what my daughter's rights and entitlements were or how to advocate for them effectively. I did not recognise her vastly different manifestation to mine of a highly hereditary condition. I had no idea that I could request a neurodevelopmental assessment through the NHS or pay for one privately. When she eventually got a Statement of SEN in secondary school, I did not know it was inadequate, less still that I could and should have challenged its contents. Indeed, it was only working backwards from my son's diagnosis and my subsequent immersion in ADHD that the penny finally dropped in relation to my daughter's, my own and my sisters' neurodiversity. Back then, I trusted professionals. I did not realise that many well-intentioned educators are either unaware or misinformed. Others seem unsure if they should say what they suspect in the context of scarce resources and sensitive parents. I took what my daughter was given without challenge, oblivious to the conflict of interest between service users and providers. I was unaware of the legal obligations on schools and local authorities (LAs) to intervene, provide appropriate support, protect from harm and promote welfare.

There are many girls with ADHD out there, just like my daughter, conventionally inattentive, silently suffering whilst their self-esteem and self-efficacy are eroded and replaced with a sense of inadequacy and self-loathing, fish tested on their tree-climbing skills, feeling stupid. In private practice, their parents typically seek help shortly after transfer to secondary school when, in response to increased academic, organisational and social demands, their worlds fall apart. There are others like my teenage self, raging against authority, unable to articulate in words why they are so angry and frustrated, often out of education due to exclusion or school refusal, impulsively risk-taking and finding the recognition they crave in an alternative social hierarchy. I owe it to girls just like us, their parents, of whom super SEND parenting skills are required, and those very special, way too rare professionals who care enough not to be complicit bystanders, to information share – mindful that for many, engaging an educational lawyer is a luxury they can ill afford and should not need to.

Much of the information I share below is factual and practical, intended to equip you with the tools to capacity build, promote self-efficacy, and empower you to square the circle of a disabling education system that was not designed with a girl with ADHD in mind.

✋ KEY POINTS

> » Symptoms of ADHD impact on all the key skills required in formal education.

> » The experience of many girls with ADHD in school is that of failing.

> » Against the odds, girls with ADHD can be successful in education and beyond.

> » Awareness, early intervention and knowledge of the SEND framework can protect girls with ADHD from educational failure.

THE POLITICAL CONTEXT: KNOW THE HISTORY AND YOU WILL UNDERSTAND WHERE THEY ARE COMING FROM

At the time of writing, in early 2020, a much-needed ambitious overhaul of the SEND system has been implemented following the SEND reforms of 2014 (Children and Families Act 2014). The catalyst for this change was the Lamb Inquiry of 2009 (Lamb 2009) and overwhelming evidence that the system was not working for the children it sought to protect and empower. Analysis of the effectiveness of the reforms was the subject of reports published in October 2019 by a cross-party Education Select Committee and the Local Government and Social Care Ombudsman (LGSCO) (King 2019). The Committee described that children and young people with SEND had been 'let down'. The reforms had resulted in 'confusion and at times unlawful practice, bureaucratic nightmares, buck-passing...a lack of accountability, strained resources and adversarial experiences'. In terms of the reforms themselves, it found they were 'the right ones' but that there is 'too much of a tension between the child's needs and the provision available' due to 'significant funding shortfall'. Concerningly, it also found 'a general lack of accountability within the system…the absence of a rigorous inspection regime…those required, or enabled, to "police" the system limited by unwillingness to grapple with unlawful practice, while others are limited by the narrowness of their remit'.

Its overarching view, which is entirely consistent with my own observations in private practice, is that 'children who receive SEN Support are being let down by schools failing to meet their needs at this level... Parents and carers have to wade through a treacle of bureaucracy, full of conflict, missed appointments and despair... The Department for Education set local authorities up to fail.' The Committee was 'surprised that Ofsted and the Care Quality Commission (CQC) told [them] that it was not in their remit to report on compliance with the law'. Finally, it concluded that it did 'not think that the Department for Education is taking enough responsibility for ensuring that its reforms are overseen, that practice in local authorities is lawful, that statutory timescales are adhered to, and that children's needs are being met'.

The LGSCO report (King 2019) focusing on the introduction of Education, Health and Care Plans makes for equally alarming reading, painting a dismal picture of serious problems, including: 'Severe delays of up to 90 weeks... Poor planning and anticipation of needs – such as council areas simply without any specialist provision available to them; Poor communication and preparation for meetings...no, or insufficient, paperwork... EHC plans regularly issued without advice from health or social care services...attempts to farm out responsibilities to parents.' Of particular concern to the LGSCO is the development of 'councils putting up additional barriers to services in efforts to ration scarce resources', and it concludes that 'While sympathetic to the severe financial constraints... Always on the receiving end of these problems are children missing out on the support to which they are entitled, and families left to pick up the pieces...we often see parents having to fight the system that was established to support them. It is not uncommon to hear the SEND process described as a battleground'.

Parents caught up in this quagmire face a minefield of myths and half-truths, typically peddled by often well-meaning but ill-informed Special Educational Needs Co-ordinators (SENCOs) and LA caseworkers or treating professionals who appear to be operating in a knowledge vacuum. It never becomes less shocking to hear of parents seeking support being told support cannot be provided for their daughter without an EHCP, but then that ADHD isn't enough for an EHCP. Further, that there is no point applying as their daughter is too bright, not far enough behind, or her problem's just poor behaviour or academic irresponsibility. Common misinformation includes that the school must support an application for it to be successful. Schools themselves can believe that they need to complete endless cycles of SEN support with no meaningful progress before an application is made. Alarming, others report being told (unlawfully) of blanket LA policies requiring a reduction in EHCPs. To add insult to injury, when placements fail and the girls is are out of school, words appear to lose their ordinary meaning, with LAs maintaining that 'suitable full-time education' actually means between two and ten hours of tuition per week. The pervasive and dissuasive message is that this is going to be really hard, too hard, nigh impossible. The reality is that it will take effort and persistence, but the far harsher reality is that failure to take action now will result in her life becoming progressively harder, perhaps too hard, even impossible.

Typically, well-resourced parents with pre-existing expectations that public services will be fit for purpose eventually seek professional support and are emboldened, albeit counterintuitively, to challenge the system. This will not, of course, relieve them of the profound anxiety, distress and frustration experienced in the process whilst simultaneously meeting their daughter's complex needs. However, many parents less well equipped, perhaps in the habit of 'taking what they're given', accept the position, and their daughter's needs go unmet during important windows of opportunity. Until, that is, they reach crisis point, with their daughter experiencing a mental health crisis, self-harming, or feeling depressed and even suicidal. Now that she is entrenched in victimhood or even criminality, the journey back, whilst not impossible, is a tough one. It is these children I worry about the most often, those from the poorest and most marginalised sections of our society and triply disadvantaged by poverty, institutional discrimination and inequality of opportunity.

THE LEGAL FRAMEWORK: OH, WHAT A TANGLED WEB – WHERE IS SHE WITHIN IT?

There is a comprehensive and, in many respects, complex legal framework within which education exists. It permeates every aspect of school life from admissions to exclusions, nursery to university, maintained and independent schools, and all things in-between such as curriculum, child protection, behaviour and relationship education. There are countless regulatory bodies and interested parties including the Department for Education (DfE), Ofsted, Independent Schools Inspectorate (ISI), Information Commissioner's Office (ICO), Charity Commission, LGSO, Secretary of State for Education, MPs, local councillors, Children's Commissioner, Parliamentary and Health Service Ombudsman, the Chief Inspector, Education and Skills Funding Agency, and Office of the Independent Adjudicator.

The legal framework is made up of statutes, case law, regulations, statutory guidance and advice, which are too voluminous to detail in their entirety here. For a girl with ADHD as a child with SEND, the most relevant include: Part 3 of the Children and Families Act 2014; SEND Regulations 2014; and the SEND Code of Practice 2015. These set out the legal framework for identifying, assessing and supporting children and young people with SEND. Equally important is the Equality Act 2010, protecting her from disability discrimination and requiring reasonable adjustments to mitigate disadvantage; and the Education Act 1996 and Human Rights Act 1988, enshrining a right to effective education, a fair trial and freedom from inhumane and degrading treatment. Also pertinent is the Children Act 1989, setting out a duty to promote and safeguard welfare and to assess and provide social care services for children in need by virtue of disability. Overall, it is important to be aware that in any specific situation she encounters, there are legal duties to which professional decision makers are accountable.

✋ KEY POINTS

» There is a complex legal framework within which education exists.

» The SEND system creates legal rights to support.

» Education Select Committee (2019) and LGSCO reports (King 2019) highlight many failings in the operation of the SEND system.

» Decision makers in education must operate within the law.

» The Equality Act 2010 protects girls with ADHD from discrimination and requires reasonable adjustments to be made.

SEN SUPPORT: WHAT SHOULD MY CHILD WITH ADHD WITH NO EHCP BE RECEIVING?

For the avoidance of doubt, if your child has a diagnosis of ADHD, she meets the legal definition of having special educational needs and requires special educational provision (section 20(1), Children and Families Act 2014). ADHD is a disability within the meaning of the Equality Act 2010 (section 6(1)). It is useful to accept this in the context of advocating for your child's needs in education, whether or not you see beyond the challenge of ADHD, tell her it's a 'superpower' or subscribe to the social model of disability. Put simply, disability attracts rights and entitlements.

If she does not have an EHCP, that is, a formal legal document issued to you directly by the local authority, she is entitled to appropriate support at 'SEN Support' level, which was formerly known as 'School Action' (extra help) or 'School Action Plus' (with external professionals involved).

Schools must use their 'best endeavours' (section 66, Children and Families Act 2014) and do 'all they can' (section 34, Children and Families Act 2014) to secure the special educational provision called for. Schools receive notional funds up to a nationally prescribed threshold per pupil (currently £6000); however, this is not ring fenced, unlike an EHCP. The SEND Code of Practice requires schools to perform a cycle of Assess → Plan → Do → Review. This should be holistic, including communication and interaction, cognition and learning, social, emotional and mental health, and sensory and physical needs. Parents should be informed, and a SEN Support Record kept and made available to them with three meetings arranged annually. All staff (vitally, including playground supervisors and supply teachers) should be made aware of the needs, support and teaching strategies required for your child. External specialists can be involved at any stage. Your girl with ADHD has a right to a mainstream education and to be educated with her typically developing peers with very limited exceptions.

ORDINARY ADMISSIONS: SOCIAL, MEDICAL AND GOOD REASONS

For a girl with ADHD without an EHCP, applications to maintained (state-funded) schools, including academies and free schools, can be made at conventional entry points or any other time by way of 'in-year' admission application. Most admissions arrangements include oversubscription criteria relating to social and medical reasons for seeking the particular school. ADHD is a medical condition and if it is demonstrated that for associated reasons this is the only appropriate school, it is worth including that in the application.

If your child is refused a place, an admission appeal can be made. Save for infant class size and grammar schools, the panel must follow a two-stage process. First, it must consider whether:

1. the admission arrangements complied with the mandatory requirements; and

2. admission arrangements were correctly and impartially applied; then

3. whether the admission of an additional child/ren (if a group

appeal) would prejudice the provision of efficient education of those with whom she would be educated or the efficient use of resources. The burden of proof is on the admission authority to demonstrate incompatibility beyond simply exceeding the published admission number (PAN).

The second stage, if reached, involves 'balancing the arguments'. The panel must balance the prejudice to the school against the parent's case for her to be admitted. If the panel considers that the parent's reasons outweigh the prejudice to the school, it must uphold the appeal. Influencing the outcome here involves collating evidence from the GP, treating therapists, current school, extra-curricular activities and academic ability where relevant. Ultimately, your aim is to attach a narrative to the facts that is more compelling than the competing version advanced by the admission authority. It is often helpful to request information from the school relevant to prejudice, for example around planned expansion.

APPLICATION FOR AN EHCA: WHEN, HOW, WHY?

When school is unlikely to be able to meet a child's needs because it does not have the expertise or funding to identify needs or provision required, or it knows what the child's needs are and provision is but cannot make that provision, application should be made to the child's home LA for an Education, Health and Care Assessment (EHCA). It is important to emphasise here that there is a remarkably simple legal test in relation to which the bar is low for triggering an assessment. That test is:

The LA must secure an EHC needs assessment…if,

a. the child or young person has or **may** have special educational needs, and

b. it **may** be necessary for special educational provision to be made for the child or young person in accordance with an EHC plan.

(section 36, Children and Families Act 2014; emphasis added)

May simply means it is possible. 'Provision in accordance with a plan' means broadly the amount of provision that maintained mainstream schools nationally should be able to provide from their own resources. This may be around ten hours of a teaching assistant weekly or two lots of direct therapy weekly. It may also be necessary as the only means of ensuring the child's needs are met. There are way too many myths around suggesting the test is quite different, such as the school must already be spending over £6000 or the child must be two years behind. These are nonsense. It is true that LAs may want to see schools demonstrate meaningful intervention, but whilst this may strengthen the application, it is not a requirement. An application should not be delayed if the actual legal test appears to be met. Myths appear to be perpetuated by schools receiving their advice and information from LAs. As the Education Select Committee (2019) and LGSCO (King 2019) identify, the inherent risk in this is that the LA holding the purse strings has a conflict of interest with the children and young people they are obliged to support. Budget protection and gate-keeping resources are at odds with agreement to fund assessments, provision and placements. Schools should avail themselves of independent sources of advice and information. Local authority policy explicitly and culturally embedded is often at odds with the law; where such a conflict exists, law trumps policy. Parents or the young person can initiate the EHCA application themselves. Most LAs have a form to complete (downloadable from their Local Offer websites); alternatively, a letter can be sent (template EHCA letters are available online on SEND charity websites). Anyone else, including professionals, can bring a child who has or may have SEND to the LA's attention, especially if an EHCA may be needed (section 24, Children and Families Act).

It is very common for deserving applications with plenty of merit to be refused. For this reason, although supporting evidence available at the outset is helpful, it is best to apply straight away even without any evidence, to start the statutory clock ticking. Expert and other evidence can be collated simultaneously and used either to inform the assessment or for an appeal against a refusal to assess (see below). Two main sources of evidence include expert and school/LA records. Expert evidence comes from the diagnosing or treating professionals or independent experts, typically an educational psychologist (EP), occupational therapist (OT), speech and language therapist (SALT), physiotherapist, clinical psychologist (CP) or independent social worker (ISW). It is essential that experts have relevant SEND Tribunal experience, to ensure the fitness for purpose of their reports and the ability of the authors to give persuasive evidence at any appeal hearing. Subject access requests to current or past schools and the LA should be made under the Data Protection Act 2018 and General Data Protection Regulation to access documents beyond the school file. This includes internal emails, minutes of meetings, provision maps, and incident reports and risk assessments that may capture information beyond that intended for parental consumption.

EHCA AND REQUIREMENT OF AN EHCP: HOW TO INFLUENCE THE OUTCOME

The purpose of an EHCA is to assess the child's needs and provision required. An EHCP is the means through which long-term additional funding can be secured for provision at her current school, a specially resourced provision unit, or a more expensive type of school setting. Alternatives often sought for girls with ADHD are ordinary independent schools with smaller class sizes, specialist schools for cognitively able neurodiverse pupils, or therapeutic schools where the primary need is social, emotional and mental health. Named unconditionally in an EHCP, the LA then funds placement inclusive of school fees and SEND provision.

Key points in the 20-week process (Figure 5.3) are week 6: decision to assess; weeks 6–12 assessments; week 14 draft due; week 16 refusal to issue decision and week 20 final plan. As noted by the LGSO deadlines are frequently missed. Should the statutory timeframe be breached, action should be taken. At the time of writing, during the coronavirus outbreak in 2020, the Secretary of State has issued a notice relaxing some absolute duties on LAs and replacing these with 'best endeavours' requirements. This should be temporary, and it is important to note 'best endeavours' does not mean doing nothing.

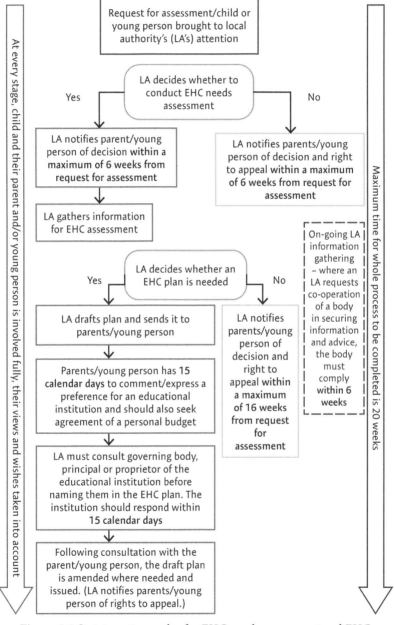

Figure 5.3 Statutory timescales for EHC needs assessment and EHC plan development (reproduced from Department for Education 2015)

During the assessment the LA must seek advice and information from:

1. the child's parents and/or the child or young person

2. the head teacher, usually, for educational advice; or if she is not in education, another person experienced in teaching pupils with SEND

3. the secretary of state for defence, if a parent is in the armed forces

4. a healthcare professional identified by the responsible commissioning body

5. an educational psychologist

6. social care

7. any other person the LA thinks is appropriate

8. any person the child's parents or young person reasonably request that the LA seek advice from

9. a qualified specialist visual and/or hearing impairment teacher, where the child appears visually and/or hearing impaired.

When a child or young person is in Year 9 or above, the advice obtained must also include the provision required in preparation for adulthood e.g. independent living skills.

Previously obtained advice can be relied upon where all parties including the author of that advice, parents/young person and LA are satisfied it is current and sufficient to inform the assessment.

Parents must be offered the opportunity to meet with an LA officer during the EHCA to discuss identified need, usually after assessments. The LA must then decide whether to issue an EHCP. If so, it must issue a draft by week 14 (to allow adequate time for the remaining steps); if not, it must issue a decision letter confirming the refusal to issue and informing of the associated right of appeal.

REQUIREMENTS OF AN EHCP

The preparation process and the contents of the EHCP must reflect four key statutory principles:

a. The wishes and feelings of the child/young person and her parents.

b. The importance of the child/young person and her parents participating as fully as possible in decision making.

c. The importance of the child/young person and her parents being provided with information and support necessary to enable participation in those decisions.

d. The need to support the child/young person and her parents in order to facilitate the development of the child and to help her **achieve the best possible educational and other outcomes**.

(section 19, Children and Families Act 2014; emphasis added)

The EHCP should be clear, concise, understandable and accessible to parents, children, young people, providers and practitioners. The provision within the plan must be detailed and specific (Department for Education 2015). The LA must first issue this in draft form. The LA must allow parents 15 days to respond to a draft EHCP, including proposing amendments. It is almost always appropriate to make amendments because plans are often written in unlawfully vague terms or will result in under-provision. The method for doing so is to request an editable electronic copy and then to insert amendments (additions or deletions). It is preferable, where available, to insert a footnote referencing the evidential basis (e.g. 'from p.5 of SALT report') for ease of reference.

Leaving no room for doubt in terms of what is required means provision must be specified and usually quantified, that is, the plan must specify the frequency and duration of the provision and by whom, in terms of qualification or experience, it should be devised and delivered (e.g. '1 x 1:1 direct OT for 45 mins weekly delivered by an OT with sensory integration certification at level 2'). Upon returning the draft, parents should also make a request for or indicate their school preference, which the LA must then consult with alongside any others it considers appropriate.

Typical deficiencies

The following are typical deficiencies in plans issued by the LA to watch out for.

Section A (Personal details and child/young person's and parents' views, interests and aspirations)

Deficient if basic information is missing such as contact details for parents or the need for an interpreter; or if it does not contain parents' and child's views or appropriate attribution.

Section B (All of her identified special educational needs)

Deficient if it does not include each of their identified needs across all areas of functioning; and for children in Year 9 or above, also those relating to independence and self-help skills in preparation for adulthood.

Section C (All health needs identified which relate to her SEN)

Deficient if all health needs are not described here, and vague and or inaccurate wording is used such as 'None reported'.

Section D (All social care needs identified that relate to their SEN or require provision under s.2, Chronically Sick and Disabled Persons Act 1970)

Deficient if it does not specify any needs, for example 'None reported' or 'Not known to service', which typically indicates that there has been an unlawful EHCA as no social care assessment has been carried out to provide the required information and advice. A child is in need if disabled (section 17, Children Act 1989). There is a duty to assess a child appearing to be in need and to identify needs, provision and outcomes (section 6, Children Act 1989) and determine eligibility for services (section 58, Children Act 1989). Common problems include LAs acknowledging a child is disabled but denying she is in need.

Section E (A range of outcomes sought for her over varying timescales including for adult life covering education, health and social care and steps towards meeting them should be included)
Deficient if the outcomes are not specific, measurable, achievable, realistic and time-bound (SMART).

Section F (Special educational provision specified for each and every need identified in Section B)
Deficient if it does not include provision for each of her identified needs and/or the provision that is included is under-provision, for example anxiety is identified but no therapeutic provision to address it is included. Or, provision included is not adequately specified or quantified, for example 'A high degree of adult support' does not meet specificity requirements whereas '32.5 hours of 1:1 teaching assistant support trained and experienced in meeting the needs of a child with ADHD' leaves no room for doubt. Required equipment that the child needs, such as a tablet or adaptive seat cushion or stationery, should also be included.

Section G (Health provision reasonably required by the learning difficulty or disability which results in the child having SEN)
Almost all therapeutic provision a girl with ADHD is likely to need (OT, SALT, cognitive behavioural therapy) 'educates and trains' so should appear in Section F, which the LA must then secure. Section G is deficient if it omits other ongoing medical provision, such as regular appointments with CAHMS, and the frequency of review visits or required medication prescribed. Provision in this section is funded by the NHS, not the LA SEN team, and therefore requires the clinical commissioning group (CCG) consent to include. It is worth noting there should be a separate Individual Health Plan detailing arrangements for safe administration and storage if ADHD or other medication is required during the school day (see statutory guidance: Department for Education 2014).

Section H1 (Social care provision which she has
been assessed to need under Section 2 of the
Chronically Sick and Disabled Persons Act 1970)
This may include: practical assistance in the home; provision or
assistance in obtaining recreational and educational facilities at home
and outside the home; assistance in travelling to facilities; adaptations
to the home; facilitating the taking of holidays; provision of meals at
home or elsewhere; provision or assistance in obtaining a telephone
and any special equipment necessary; non-residential short breaks.

Deficient if no assessment, or if provision is not included for
needs identified in Section D at all or at an inadequate level or
hourly rate. Examples of provision could include a support worker
to access leisure or community activities, or non-means tested direct
payments for care or respite hours. Additionally, any provision
required following a parent/carers assessment, for example gym
membership to relieve stress, help with housework or family
strengthening programmes.

Section H2 (Any other social care provision reasonably
required by the learning difficulties or disabilities which
result in the child or young person having SEN)
Deficient if other provision, early help or safeguarding assessment
information or adult social care provision for a young person aged
18 years and over under the Care Act 2014 has not been included.

Section I (Must include the type of school and, if one
has been identified, the name of the school)
Deficient if it does not name a type of placement (but note this
should be left blank at draft plan stage).

Section J (Detailed information on any personal budget
including arrangements for direct payments that will
be used to secure provision detailed in the plan)
Deficient if it *inaccurately* says 'None requested' or if a personal
budget and direct payment have been agreed and are not fully and
accurately specified.

Section K (Appendix: must set out the advice and
information gathered during the EHC assessment)
Deficient if it does not include all advice obtained during assessment
including that obtained by parents from independent experts. Also,
a useful indication of whether all required advice for the assessment
has been obtained.

✋ KEY POINTS

» All children with a diagnosis of ADHD meet the legal
definition of having special educational needs and require
special educational provision.

» If a child's needs are not being met at SEN Support level
(whether or not she is keeping up academically), a request
can be made for an EHCA, including by parents.

» An EHCP must contain the wishes and feelings of the child
or young person and her parents.

» An EHCP must identify all of the child or young person's
needs and contain specific and quantified provision to
meet each of them.

ANNUAL AND EMERGENCY
REVIEWS: CHANGE OF PLAN?

Once issued, an EHCP must be reviewed annually either within
12 months of issue or within 12 months of the last review. It must
also be reviewed when the child is approaching phase transfer. For
example, transition from primary to secondary school, the plan
must be amended to specify the new type of placement and where
identified the specific placement to be attended. This includes where
the current school attended delivers both primary and secondary
education.

A review requires consultation with the child or young person
and her parent, and the LA must take account of their views, wishes

and feelings; consider progress towards achieving the outcomes specified; and consider whether these outcomes and the provision remain appropriate. The LA must consult the school or other institution attended by the child or young person and ensure a meeting is held to review the plan. The school typically is required to arrange and hold that meeting and must invite the following to attend:

- the child's parent or the young person

- the provider of the relevant early years education or the head teacher or principal of the school, post-16 or other institution attended

- an officer of the LA SEND team

- a healthcare professional identified by the responsible commissioning body

- an officer of the LA's social care team.

At least two weeks' notice of the date of the meeting must be given. The person arranging the review meeting (usually the SENCO) must obtain advice and information about the child or young person from the persons included above and must circulate this at least two weeks in advance of the review meeting. When the child or young person is in or beyond Year 9, the review meeting must consider what provision is required to assist the child or young person in preparation for adulthood and independent living.

Where she attends a school or other institution, the LA must ask the head teacher or principal to prepare a written report setting out their recommendations on any amendments to be made to the EHC plan, and referring to any difference between those recommendations and the recommendations of others attending the meeting. The report must then be sent within two weeks of the meeting to the LA and everyone referred to above who is invited to the review.

The LA must then decide within four weeks of the meeting whether it proposes to:

1. continue to maintain the EHC plan in its current form

2. amend it, or

3. cease to maintain it.

It must notify the child's parent and those invited of its decision.

If the decision is not to amend, there is right of appeal upon receipt of that decision letter. If there is a decision to amend, the LA must give notice of the proposed amendments, usually by way of issue of a draft plan, and it must then issue a final amended plan as soon as practicable and in any event within eight weeks. There is a right of appeal against the contents of the amended plan issued.

As with other parts of the process, influencing the outcome is most effectively done by way of the provision of up-to-date evidence of needs, required provision and progress or lack thereof. This may also include the appropriateness of the child remaining at their current school. Expert and other evidence obtained to inform the annual review can then serve the dual purpose of informing a subsequent appeal.

SEN APPEAL: FAVOURABLE ODDS

An appeal can be made to the First Tier Tribunal, also known as the SEN Tribunal or SENDIST, in respect of Sections B (needs), F (provision) and I (placement) of an EHCP. In accordance with a National Trial, since April 2018 and currently extended to August 2021 the SEN Tribunal is also now able to include sections C, D, G, H1 and H2 (health and social care) in the appeal, providing this is alongside an appeal of the education sections. Their powers in respect of the National Trial sections differ in currently having the power to make only recommendations on health and social care rather than binding orders. However, it is anticipated that LAs and CCGs will in most instances follow those recommendations, drawing parallel with complaints upheld by and powers of the LGSO. Pre-existing remedies, including mediation, internal complaint, complaint to LGSO and judicial review, remain available for other sections of the plan (A, E, J and K) that cannot be appealed in their own right.

However, these can be considered by the Tribunal where incidental to other aspects of the appeal.

Whilst the prospect of a SEN appeal can appear daunting, the appeal system, at least theoretically, is designed to be used by parents without lawyers. There are also SEND charities offering free or low-cost support with appeal. As around two-thirds of appeals settle in parents' favour without a hearing and 89% of those that proceed to a hearing are upheld (i.e. settled in parents' favour), from a parental perspective it is always worth appealing an unwanted decision. In 2018–19, 6374 appeals were registered, double that of 2016–17; however, this is around a mere 1.6% of potentially appealable decisions (Ministry of Justice 2019).

In order to lodge an appeal, a trigger event giving rise to the right of appeal under the Children and Families Act 2014 is required. Trigger events include a decision by a local authority to:

- refuse to secure an EHC needs assessment

- refuse to issue an EHC plan

- refuse to reassess

- refuse to amend an EHC plan following a review or reassessment

- refuse to amend the contents of an EHC plan following issue

- cease to maintain any EHC plan.

Save for placement-only appeals (which are inadvisable; it is better also to include sections B and F), parents are required to obtain a mediation certificate within two months of the LA decision letter before appealing. There is no obligation to actually engage in mediation. An appeal must be lodged within two months of the LA decision letter or one month from the date of mediation certificate, whichever is later. This requires completion of a notice of appeal form (downloadable from the SEN Tribunal's website). There is a checklist on the form detailing documents that must be attached, for example mediation certificate and LA decision letter.

Within approximately 10–20 working days, the SEND Tribunal

will register the appeal, notifying of the final hearing date (usually within 12 weeks) and timetable of next steps. This includes the LA response, witness attendance forms and final evidence deadline.

During the course of preparation for appeal, the LA must supply a formal response to appeal and a 'working document', which is an electronic copy of the final EHCP, to parents or their representatives. Proposed amendments are then inserted by or on behalf of parents and sent to the LA for it to agree. Unlike at draft plan stage, this document usually passes back and forth between the representatives several times while the issues in the appeal are narrowed down. Similarly to draft plan stage, the basis for proposed amendments is the body of expert evidence obtained during the proceeding EHCA or subsequently by either party in preparation for appeal.

If the issues in the appeal can be narrowed to the point of agreement via negotiation of the working document, the case is settled without the need for a hearing. However, if it is not possible to reach agreement, then the case will proceed to a contested final hearing on the remaining issues in dispute. Typically, the authors of the expert reports will attend as witnesses to answer questions such as on why they recommended the level of provision, or say a particular school may be suitable or unsuitable. It is important to note that staff from maintained schools and NHS- or LA-employed therapists, social workers or educational psychologists usually appear as witnesses for the LA in SEN appeals. Therefore, in order to provide for 'equality of arms' for parents and to challenge the LA evidence where necessary, independent expert evidence is always required.

Typically, appeals last for one day although in National Trial cases involving health and social care they are routinely listed for two days. However, current practice is that the second day is reserved for panel deliberations, and the parties and witnesses do not attend. Judgment is then made by way of a written order, usually within ten days of the final hearing although on occasion, the tribunal judge will direct the parties to serve written closing submissions after the hearing, in which case the final order may be delayed.

If, as is often the case, parents are seeking to challenge the current placement, the prospect of success is typically dependent on expert evidence on the suitability of the respective placements. Evidence is often heard from school representatives about the provision they can offer including, for example, an appropriate peer group. In the event they are both suitable, the respective costs and any additional educational or other benefit will be considered to determine whether naming the parents' preference (which is the starting point) would be incompatible with either the efficient education of other children the child is to be educated with or the use of resources or reasonable public expenditure.

SEN appeals are currently heard at the Royal Courts of Justice for almost all cases originating in London and the Home Counties, or within two hours' travelling distance from the child or young person's home address. Initiating this process as soon as possible is now imperative, with around 75% of listed hearings being postponed, often due to lack of available court time, although this appears to have reduced since the coronavirus pandemic with more hearings being carried out by video.

WHEN THINGS GO WRONG: KNOW HER RIGHTS

I being a girl with ADHD have rights…

United Nations Convention on the Rights of the Child (UNCRC)

- My best interests shall be a primary consideration in all actions concerning me.

- I should have a full and decent life, in conditions which ensure my dignity and promote self-reliance and facilitate active participation in the community.

- I have a right to education.

United Nations Convention on the Rights of Persons with Disabilities (CRPD)

- Freedom from discrimination, full and effective participation in society, equality of opportunity and accessibility, including between men and women with disabilities.

The Human Rights Act 1988 (incorporating ECHR)

- Freedom from torture, inhumane and degrading treatment.
- A fair trial (including in relation to exclusions).
- An effective education.
- Freedom from discrimination.

The Children Act 1989

- To be safeguarded from harm and my well-being promoted by preventing impairment of my health or development in circumstances consistent with the provision of safe and effective care to enable me to have the best outcomes.

The Equality Act 2010

- Protection from direct and indirect discrimination.
- Protection from unfavourable treatment because of something arising in consequence of my ADHD that is not a proportionate means of achieving a legitimate aim.
- To have reasonable adjustments made to mitigate any substantial disadvantage I face in relation to, for example, admissions, exclusions, provision of education, or access to benefit or service or equipment.

The Act permits more favourable treatment for disabled people

It is a myth that everyone must be treated equally. We can have one rule for her and one for everybody else. There are at least 101 reasonable adjustments that can be made for girls with ADHD (Figure 5.4).

Reasonable adjustments for ADHD

Schools have a statutory duty under the Equality Act 2010 to take such steps as is reasonable to have to take to avoid substantial disadvantage to a disabled child caused by a provision, criterion or practice applied by or on behalf of a school. Most if not all children with ADHD will be deemed disabled under the Act. This is an anticipatory duty and the school is required to take positive steps to ensure that disabled pupils can fully participate in the education provided by the school. The Act permits more favourable treatment of disabled pupils. The requirement applies irrespective of whether a child has an EHCP or not. What is 'reasonable' varies according to the circumstances. The variables to be considered in assessing this include but are not limited to:

1. Existing provision being made under the SEN framework
2. School's resources including financial and others
3. Financial cost of making the adjustment
4. The likely effectiveness of adjustment in overcoming the disadvantage
5. Practicability of the adjustment
6. Effect of the disability on the individual
7. Health and safety requirements
8. Need to maintain academic, musical, sporting and other standards
9. Interests of other pupils and prospective pupils

Further useful guidance is available from the EHRC: www.equality humanrights.com/publication/reasonable-adjustments-disabled-pupils
Here are some examples of adjustments that have proved helpful with ADHD children. They are grouped under general headings, albeit there is plenty of cross-over.

Cognition and learning

1. Classroom positioning (front to avoid distraction or back to avoid need to look around or to be close to peer role models)
2. Break larger tasks down into chunks in class and for homework
3. Accept less or no homework
4. Provide facility for homework to be done at school
5. Provide sample work to model what is required
6. Reduce length of assignments required

7. Provide list of steps to complete task
8. Adult to check early in lesson that entire instruction understood and give prompt to make start on task
9. Use private signal to return pupil to task in the event of loss of focus, or 'zoning out'
10. Half-termly 1:1 meeting with subject teachers to monitor progress
11. Provide reader
12. Provide scribe
13. Provide prompter
14. Allow extra time for exams/testing
15. Allow rest breaks
16. Allow use of lined answer sections
17. Allow peers to share notes
18. Allow use of ear defenders to reduce distractions
19. Allow testing in separate, distraction-free room
20. Allow extra time in class and in exams
21. Use timers
22. Give single-step instructions
23. Teach specific memory techniques
24. Provide memory aids
25. Provide white noise
26. Provide headphones
27. Provide individual specialist teaching
28. Providing specialist computer programs
29. Provide privacy partition
30. Personalise work topics to increase pupil's level of intrinsic interest

Physical and sensory

1. Provide with fidgeter
2. Provide with stress ball
3. Provide with wobble cushion
4. Provide with weighted lap or shoulder 'hug' or blanket
5. Allow regular movement breaks
6. Allow touch typing instead of writing (handwriting/fine motor skills difficulties)
7. Provide with sloping board
8. Allow dictation
9. Allow photos with phone/tablet of written work instead of copying from board
10. Provide with copy of PowerPoint notes
11. Relax uniform requirements
12. Allow high-calorie snacks if appetite issues
13. Provide adult support for eating and hydration if needed
14. Allow oral presentation of work
15. Provide additional adult support during less structured time
16. Provide pencil grip

17. Use a foot fidget
18. Incorporate motor component to tasks, e.g. highlight important points/quotes when reading
19. Administer top-up medication
20. Allow gum chewing for hyperactivity in place of fidgeter so hands available to work
21. Provide occupational therapy
22. Provide sensory diet

Social, emotional and mental health

1. Provide ADHD and equality training to staff
2. Plan to catch student doing the right thing and reinforce
3. Seek out opportunities for child to show strengths
4. Provide opportunities for pupil to have positions of responsibility
5. Provide opportunity for pupil to develop relationship with those with responsibility for discipline. This should be separate from and ideally prior to first contact to address a behavioural issue
6. Provide counselling
7. Arrange structured activities during break time
8. Provide adult support for predictable trigger situations
9. Provide social skills training
10. Provide problem solving training
11. Provide conflict resolution training
12. Administer top-up medication
13. Depart from standard rewards policy to specifically reinforce progress in areas of difficulty
14. Depart from standard sanctions policy and apply different sanctions
15. Disregard some behaviours
16. Teach emotional literacy one to one and in small groups
17. Have calm space
18. Have nominated key worker
19. Be allowed to observe new social situations before joining in
20. Give child opportunities to be responsible
21. Use individualised reward system
22. Provide quiet place for lunchtimes
23. Pair with role model buddy
24. Provide extra support for changes (e.g. trips, plays, supply teachers)
25. Agree secret communication for behaviour feedback
26. Agree/plan alternative to calling out
27. Extra warnings for transitions between activities
28. Provide additional adult support for transition times
29. Provide anger management therapy
30. Raise peer awareness of ADHD
31. Provide play therapy
32. Provide nurture groups
33. Provide structured behaviour management programme

Language and communication

1. Actively teach social skills
2. Teach child active listening skills
3. Directly teach non-verbal cues
4. Provide speech and language therapy

Self-help and independence

1. Teacher/teaching assistant check homework diary or provide written homework slips or emails
2. Provide reminders regarding work completion or organisation
3. Arrange homework handing-in buddy
4. Arrange study buddy with contact details
5. Provide email access to subject teachers
6. Do not penalise for executive function related difficulties (e.g. organisation, forgetting things)
7. Provide organisational skills training
8. Provide with reading material with important points already highlighted
9. Copy parents into work/organisation/trip emails/team sheets
10. Provide spare set of books, equipment
11. Provide visual timetable
12. Provide visual checklists

Adapted from a list collated by Eva Akins for ADHD Richmond and Kingston (www.adhdrichmond.org)

Figure 5.4 Reasonable adjustments for ADHD

EXCLUSION AND EXCLUSION APPEALS: WE ARE A VERY TOLERANT SOCIETY BUT...

Children with ADHD face much higher rates of sanctions and exclusion than their typically developing peers. They are frequently punished for executive function deficits, such as failure to have the right equipment and kit or failure to hand in homework on time, and for impulsive behaviour from low-level calling out or chatting in class to defiance or more serious breaches of behaviour policy. They are frequently internally excluded, informally excluded (sent home early without a formal exclusion letter – which is unlawful), and formally fixed term and permanently excluded. They are also regularly the subject of manged moves which facilitate exclusion from school without the safeguards of external scrutiny afforded by formal exclusion.

Permanent exclusion in particular often has many observed negative long-term consequences for young people, including poor educational attainment, prolonged periods out of employment and subsequent scarring effects, as well as poor mental and physical health.

For all maintained (state-funded) schools and PRUs, statutory guidance on exclusion sets out how head teachers, governors and independent review panels must act when contemplating or reviewing exclusion (Department for Education 2017). The decision to exclude a girl with ADHD is often unlawful because it is contrary to these most pertinent aspects of this guidance:

> Permanent exclusion should only be used as a last resort, in response to a serious breach, or persistent breaches, of the school's behaviour policy; and where allowing the pupil to remain in school would seriously harm the education or welfare of the pupil or others in the school.

> Disruptive behaviour can be an indication of unmet needs…

> Any decision of a school, including exclusion, must be made in line with the principles of administrative law, i.e. that it is: lawful…; rational; reasonable; fair; and proportionate.

> Under the Equality Act 2010 ('the Equality Act') schools must not discriminate against, harass or victimise pupils because of their:…; disability… For disabled children, this includes a duty to make reasonable adjustments to policies and practices.

> It is unlawful to exclude or to increase the severity of an exclusion for a non-disciplinary reason. For example, it would be unlawful to exclude a pupil simply because they have additional needs or a disability that the school feels it is unable to meet, or for a reason such as: academic attainment/ability;…

> 'Informal' or 'unofficial' exclusions, such as sending pupils home 'to cool off', are unlawful, regardless of whether they occur with the agreement of parents or carers.

In relation to the proportionality of the decision to exclude, a key question to be considered is whether less intrusive measures have been used (*R(Tigere) v Secretary of State for Business, Innovation & Skills* [2015]). If so, the exclusion is unlikely to be proportionate and likely to be unlawful.

OUT OF EDUCATION: WHAT AM I ENTITLED TO?

A child who is out of education due to illness, or exclusion, or other reasons must be provided with suitable education, that is, the same number of hours as she would be receiving if she was at school, the only exception being if she is too unwell. As a result of exclusion, or life at school becoming untenable, or because of anxiety and mental health distress, girls with ADHD are too often out of school. If she does not have an EHCP, the LA inclusion or exclusion officer should be contacted. If she does have an EHCP, an emergency review of the EHCP should be held by the LA SEND team. It has a duty to ensure not just suitable full-time education, but that any provision detailed in the EHCP (e.g. therapies) is secured. Again, the Secretary of State has issued notice under the Coronavirus Act 2020, which should be temporary, relaxing some requirements from an absolute duty to a 'best endeavours' requirement. This does not mean doing nothing.

COMPLAINTS

Complaints may be used by parents or professionals with a view to seeking resolution when things go wrong before escalating to proceedings. Often this will be in relation to unfavourable treatment, lack of support or child protection concerns. This can be internal; for example, schools typically have a three-stage process complaint to head teacher, to governors and to appeal panel. LAs typically have a complaints team with three stages up to director level, after which complaint can be made to the LGSCO. It is important when complaining to be factual (not emotional or personally critical of individuals) and most importantly to be clear about what resolution you seek.

Depending on the type of school and nature of the complaint, you can also complain to others including DfE, Ofsted, ISI, ICO and the Charity Commission. For some, you will need to have exhausted the internal complaints procedure first; for others, this can be done simultaneously to increase the impetus for resolution and especially when the complaints process is not being progressed appropriately, or a child is missing education or is at risk.

JUDICIAL REVIEW

Judicial review is a court process through which senior judges examine public bodies' acts, omissions and decision making for consistency with the law and public law principles. It is often a last resort where other remedies are unavailable or have been exhausted, or the matter is time sensitive. Grounds include illegality, irrationality/proportionality and procedural unfairness. Strict time limits apply, usually three months. If the school or LA is in breach of its statutory duties, a pre-action protocol letter before commencing proceedings can be sent. Often this is sufficient to bring about resolution; if not, application for permission can be made to the Administrative Court.

For girls with ADHD, this is most likely to be considered in relation to failure by the LA to comply with its statutory duties relating to the provision of education for a child out of school, enforcing the delivery of provision detailed in the EHCP (which it is primarily the LA's rather than the school's duty to secure), school transport disputes and granting interim relief, for example to maintain the ongoing school provision pending the outcome of a SEN appeal. The advice of a lawyer or a SEND charity that provides independent advice should be taken before any action is commenced as this is a potentially very costly and complex process. Legal aid may be available.

EQUALITY ACT CLAIMS
(DISABILITY DISCRIMINATION)

A child is disabled within the meaning of the Equality Act 2010 (section 6) if:

- they have a physical or mental impairment

- that impairment has a substantial (more than minor or trivial) and long-term (has lasted or is likely to last 12 months or more) impact on their ability to carry out normal day-to-day activities.

A child can be disabled within the meaning of the Equality Act and therefore attract the protection of it without having a diagnosis. Where a claim is brought under the Equality Act, to establish disability, it is the underlying impairment (e.g. persistent difficulties with inattention, hyperactivity, impulsivity and/or executive functioning in the case of undiagnosed ADHD) that is relevant, not the label attached to it. A school which, either whilst working with the child or when responding to an Equality Act claim, is aware of a child's impairment is not relieved of its obligations because the child does not have a diagnosis or the school did not realise that the impairment amounted to a disability.

Claims typically for unfavourable treatment exclusion from school, trip bans and sanctions or failure to make reasonable adjustments (e.g. to academic requirements or the behaviour code) can be made against a school both independent and maintained. Intention to discriminate is not necessary. Claims for disability discrimination against schools are heard in the SEND Tribunal and follow a similar timetable in terms of preparation before hearing as a SEND appeal. Although typically heard in 20 rather than 12 weeks, they can follow a 6-week expedited timetable when reinstatement following permanent exclusion is sought. They are, however, much more contentious and so expert legal advice should be sought where possible in advance of filing a claim. Available remedies include a declaration of discrimination, reinstatement following exclusion, removal of exclusion from the pupil's record, an apology and the school being ordered to undertake training or a policy review.

Where discrimination relates to a child's other 'protected char-acteristics' such as race, sex, gender reassignment, sexual orientation, pregnancy and/or the claim is not being made against a school, it is dealt with via a different procedure, usually in the County Court.

Where discrimination relates to a child or young person being trans or non-binary (e.g. relating to access to appropriate toilets, 'dead-naming' or refusal to use gender neutral pronouns), it is likely to be strategically advantageous to bring a disability claim based on 'gender dysphoria' rather than gender reassignment.

✋ KEY POINTS

- » EHCPs should be reviewed annually in consultation with the child or young person, her parents and her school.

- » Girls with ADHD have rights; these are legal rights.

- » Children with ADHD face higher rates of sanction and exclusion than their peers.

☀ TIPS:

I recognise that a chapter cannot do justice to this vast subject matter. However, I hope to have provided some insight and highlighted sources of further information. Reflecting, I consider that many of the core skills required to navigate the education system with an ADHD girl have little to do with the law and so leave you with some practical top tips:

- – Know your core values, aims and objectives – let this guide your actions, what you focus on and what you let go of.

- – Anxiety usually means you do not have enough information yet – the antidote is action.

- – Focus on the 'micro-win' and overcoming the barrier to the step – not the entire mountain to climb.

- – Never ask permission to promote the rights, entitlements and welfare of your girl with ADHD – give notice that, respectfully, that is precisely what you will be doing.

- Before attending meetings, identify the specific objective(s) you intend to achieve.

- Evidence is everything – create a paper trail of phone calls and meetings by follow-up email.

- Emails should be factual and concise – no shouting, CAPITAL LETTER rants. Unless it's genuinely urgent, draft it then sleep on it.

- Free advice and support are available – from independent and pan-disability and ADHD-specific charities, support groups and coaches and, subject to means testing, legal aid education lawyers.

- Avoid conspiracy theories – if you being right makes others wrong, they are unlikely to agree with you. Instead, use 'appreciative inquiry' and focus on lack of awareness/ resources, underdeveloped skills and lessons learned.

- Work smarter – support her intrinsic interests, find her area of competence and build upon that (arguing – politics; hyperactivity – sport; creativity – fashion and make-up).

- Be in charge – demonstrate this through routine and consistent firm, fair boundaries. Mean what you say; girls with ADHD need to know the world can contain them and that you can be trusted. One supporter is enough but a village is preferable.

- Self-care – apply your own oxygen mask first; others are best fed from the overflow of your full cup. It is when you have the least time, money, energy and enthusiasm that you most need nurture. Make a non-negotiable self-care plan.

- There is no magic bullet – approach the challenge of her being 'wired differently' from a number of different angles. Girls with ADHD can be innovative, enigmatic, entertaining and successful. There is life beyond school where the need to be a tree-climbing fish is redundant; she can be comfortable in her own skin, and dance to the beat of her own drum knowing 'it's not what you call me but what I answer to' that matters.

REFERENCES

Brown, T.E. (2014) *Smart but Stuck: Emotions in Teens and Adults with ADHD.* San Francisco, CA: Jossey-Bass.

Children and Families Act (2014) London: HMSO.

Department for Education (2014) *Supporting Pupils at School with Medical Conditions.* Accessed on 27 July 2020 at https://www.gov.uk/government/publications/supporting-pupils-at-school-with-medical-conditions.

Department for Education (2015) *Special Educational Needs and Disability Code of Practice: 0 to 25 Years. Statutory Guidance for Organisations which Work with and Support Children and Young People Who Have Special Educational Needs or Disabilities.* Accessed on 27 July 2020 at https://www.gov.uk/government/publications/send-code-of-practice-0-to-25.

Department for Education (2017) *Exclusion from Maintained Schools, Academies and Pupil Referral Units in England.* Accessed on 10 October 2020 at https://assets.publishing.service.gov.uk/government/uploads/system/uploads/attachment_data/file/921405/20170831_Exclusion_Stat_guidance_Web_version.pdf.

Education Select Committee (2019) *Special Educational Needs and Disability Enquiry.* Accessed on 27 July 2020 at https://www.parliament.uk/business/committees/committees-a-z/commons-select/education-committee/inquiries/parliament-2017/special-educational-needs-and-disability-inquiry-17-19.

Equality Act (2010) London: The National Archives.

King, M. (2019) *Not Going to Plan? Education, Health and Care Plans Two Years On. Focus Report: Learning Lessons from Complaints.* Coventry: Local Government and Social Care Ombudsman.

Lamb, B. (2009) *Special Educational Needs and Parental Confidence. Report to the Secretary of State on the Lamb Inquiry Review of SEN and Disability Information.* London: Department for Education.

Ministry of Justice (2019) *Tribunal Statistics Quarterly: July to September 2019.* Accessed on 27 July 2020 at www.gov.uk/government/statistics/tribunal-statistics-quarterly-july-to-september-2019.

R(Tigere) v Secretary of State for Business, Innovation and Skills [2015] UKSC 57.

Chapter 6

Too Little Too Late?

Coaching Girls with ADHD

— VALERIE IVENS —

Figure 6.1 *ADHD and Me* (reproduced by permission of Brooke Griffith)

LEARNING THE HARD WAY: MY COACHING JOURNEY WITH JEMMA

Overflowing with misplaced confidence – as a result of my professional training, qualifications, extensive academic research and at that stage having worked with families of children with attention deficit hyperactivity disorder (ADHD) for 15 years – I approached my first teenage student, Jemma, with a spring in my step, 'Fear not, support is on its way!'

I had recently completed training as a REACH ADHD coach with Jan Assheton, one of the trailblazers for ADHD coaching in the UK. Jan worked in association with the Institute for the Advancement of ADHD Coaching in the USA to develop training for those wishing to coach in this country. The definition of ADHD coaching is:

> a designed partnership that combines coaching skills with knowledge of Attention Deficit Hyperactivity Disorder. The coaching process enhances quality of life, improves performance and supports growth and change. The purpose of ADHD coaching is to provide support, structure and accountability. Coach and client collaboratively explore strengths, talents, tools and new learning to increase self-awareness and personal empowerment. Together they design strategies and actions and monitor progress by creating accountability in line with goals and aspirations. (Assheton 2009)

This chapter covers why I believe there are so many benefits to coaching girls like Jemma. I will cover what coaching is, what sessions actually look like, the evidence, and the factors in our society which impact these girls so significantly.

Jemma: an introduction to coaching

My first client, Jemma, aged 14 years, was a school refuser, recently diagnosed with ADHD and a regular user of cannabis. She battled with social anxiety and dyslexia. Unquestionably clever, she had become increasingly oppositional and recalcitrant following numerous exclusions and detentions for incomplete work and talking in class. Jemma had argued with teachers about the unjust nature of these punishments. Recently, Jemma had failed to show up for classes; she had also failed to show up for the detentions she received for failing to show up for detentions. For four weeks Jemma had refused to engage at all, putting herself at the risk of permanent exclusion and transfer to a pupil referral unit. Her anxiety and emotional distress had brought her to the attention of health services, where she had received a diagnosis of ADHD which had been sitting below the anxiety and depression. This was not an unusual story, and neither is it an appropriate solution for these very vulnerable, often very bright girls. Her behaviour was telling us something; we simply weren't listening and understanding.

I was naively confident I could reach through the stress and anxiety and connect in a way which was fresh and would enable Jemma to re-engage with the system. Using strategies to encourage engagement through clear consequences, I was confident she would respond. The 'three strikes and you are out' approach was one of the tools we had been using. What could possibly go wrong, I thought? Short, clear instructions, no emotional content, and immediate consequences; a perfect strategy for someone with ADHD and delays in their executive functions (EFs).

Through Jan's extensive and rigorous training programme, coaching skills are developed using face-to-face sessions, case studies, pilot cases and role play over a period of six months. I trained alongside a group of other enthusiastic recruits: clinical nurse specialists, speech and language therapists, psychologists and social workers. Jan has run supervised courses for many years for those wishing to extend their coaching or other professional skills with ADHD, and provided supervision, too. She recently retired from her training business.

As you will have predicted, three sessions later Jemma remained doggedly in bed, refusing contact, rebuffing all attempts at engagement, inert and unwilling to be the subject of unwanted attention. She had no interest or motivation to meet another professional sent to encourage her back into a system which simply made her feel a failure. I needed to understand life through her eyes. In truth, I forgot my common sense and with it I forgot the most important lesson: the first task.

Skip forward ten years and I regularly thank Jemma for teaching me more about coaching than any training or qualification has done. Whilst a recognized coaching qualification is essential, using common sense is essential, too. Alongside developing an understanding of what coaching can be, Jemma also taught me what coaching *is not*. I didn't tear up the rule book, but I did start to apply a lot more insight using my pre-existing knowledge of the real ADHD.

Jemma now has eight solid GCSEs, including two A* and an award for academic achievement. She has workplace qualifications, as well as being clear of substances for 18 months. Her (and with it my) coaching journey has been a turbulent one, but ultimately incredibly satisfying. There is little she hasn't tried, there are few poor choices she hasn't made and few risks she hasn't taken. Many happened when I thought things were going well, and many times she accepts she had a fantastic ability to deceive; but threading through this journey has been enough scaffolding, discussion, determination and trust to enable her to tilt the balance of her journey back from negative to positive. She is clearer about why things are difficult and she's clearer about the strengths and creativity she can use to overcome the challenges. As her coach, I'll definitely take that.

THE COACHING TOUCH: WHAT DOES IT ADD?

I like to describe coaching as more of a walk alongside someone. Assheton (2009) suggests, 'It's about offering a focused opportunity to move forward and engage (with a client) using their own skills in their own way.' It felt as though it might have been too late on numerous occasions with Jemma, but in the end it rarely was. She went back to school using an extremely graduated approach after thinking through how it would feel and look if it could work for her using 'the miracle question'. She was met by a new and preferred mentor for her first session, and then joined classes after registration once her social anxiety had calmed. The school was fantastic at providing focused teaching support in those lessons where she really struggled. It offered one-to-one intensive teacher tutoring/ over-learning opportunities for missed work. Jemma left school for the lunch break, and the entire process was repeated in the afternoon. Through coaching, and by working with the school to provide exceptionally well-adjusted teaching, she became more able to discuss her struggles directly and what could help, and she was more able to understand and verbalize her fears.

Coaches are agents for change. Coaching is designed to be a partnership which combines coaching skills with a knowledge of ADHD. It has the potential to enhance the quality of life and improve targeted performance areas by supporting and encouraging a growth mindset, in effect providing support, structure and accountability. The coaching relationship enables the coach and client to explore strengths, talents, tools and new learning. This is delivered collaboratively in order to increase the client's self-awareness and personal empowerment. In many cases, young people arrive believing they have no control over their environment. By working together, the object is to design short-term strategies towards a chosen goal. Together, the steps are planned, actioned and monitored. Progress is discussed regularly. Ultimately, the client is accountable for her actions, but barriers and challenges are identified and discussed and a new route around them is created.

Coaching can add so much. It can encourage you to be your best and remind you of what is important to you. It can keep you on track when things challenge your persistence. The relationship encourages and supports changes and provides an open and honest place for rehearsal of ideas and thoughts. From a psychoeducation perspective, coaching can teach young people about the condition and can magnify strengths as well as supporting an understanding of weaknesses. It encourages a solution-focused approach to barriers: 'What has worked before when you have had a similar problem?' It can also offer a space to challenge false beliefs and raise self-esteem and resilience. Using a neurolinguistic approach, young people can, with practice, learn to self-regulate through externalizing positive self-talk: 'I can do this', 'I'm OK.' So why didn't Jemma engage and what was the first task which I failed to do?

HOW DOES COACHING WORK?

Typically, parents who call are at the end of their tether: 'My daughter is causing us so much angst, she's rude, insolent, falling behind at school and her friends, well, I don't even want to tell you what time she gets in at the weekend. Help her.' So I often ask, 'Is your daughter interested in coming to coaching, or is this something you think might fix the problem?' In truth, everyone must be ready for coaching and that's the first task. The task I failed to do with Jemma. Had I even considered that Jemma might not want to be coached? No, I hadn't. I had listened to the head teacher, I had listened to educational psychologists, to Mum, to Dad, to almost everyone except Jemma. Nor had I listened to the person who knew her best, a teaching assistant who had taken her under his wing and really got to know her, offering little more than time and understanding.

Coaching steps

Assessing a 'readiness for coaching' is an imperative, and this together with setting the scene for a trusting relationship through coaching is the initial priority. At which motivational stage for change does the young person find themselves, and is that something they are willing to discuss with support? Once this is established, the second task is to identify the areas where the client is keen to see change:

- 'What are your goals?' It might be that she wants to be invited round to a friend's house, or it might be that she wants to be able to manage homework without feeling overwhelmed.

- 'What are your strengths? Let us look at some examples.'

- 'Which methods shall we use to track change? Shall we meet face-to-face, over the phone, by video link?' Then set goals which are realistic, achievable, meaningful and motivating. They need to be goal focused, not time focused. They need to be small steps which are likely to guarantee success, not lifetime projects.

- Monitoring the process is key. Young people tend to have a habit of getting lost in a mind-wandering or adrenalin-grabbing activity…they dive into a rabbit hole of pleasurable and rather delicious procrastination. A thought stream or a video game, each a sumptuously and riotously unproductive hassle-free zone, but something which occupies their entire attention nevertheless. So, the role of a coach is to parachute into that space and haul them out. This could be by using texts, WhatsApp or other easy message means.

- Feedback needs to be relevant and regular. In this way, we can start to identify barriers to success such as the temptation of going on a tablet as homework is due to start; feeling hungry or thirsty; feeling tired or fractious after a challenging day at school; a favourite TV programme interrupting study time. There are any number of reasons why you can't sit down and do homework and most are far more attractive propositions than that history project you just can't seem to start.

A coaching relationship can help to identify and negotiate ways around these barriers and create new goals to overcome them. If the point of performance is homework, then that is the focus; if, however, the point of performance is starting homework, then that's where action is needed. Coaching should be a motivational experience, inspiring the young person to take action; a seismic nudge for the frontal lobe to wake up, sit up and pay attention (Figure 6.2).

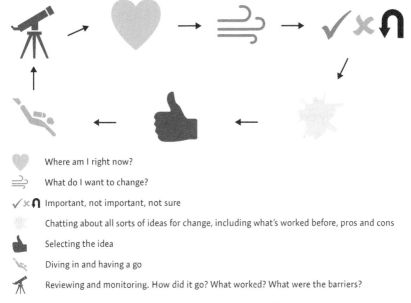

Where am I right now?

What do I want to change?

Important, not important, not sure

Chatting about all sorts of ideas for change, including what's worked before, pros and cons

Selecting the idea

Diving in and having a go

Reviewing and monitoring. How did it go? What worked? What were the barriers?

Figure 6.2 The coaching cycle

Working through this coaching cycle, we can use various established means to discuss obstacles, plans and role plays. The Social Stories tool by Carol Gray, originally written for children with autism spectrum disorder (ASD), is equally useful for ADHD (https://carolgraysocialstories.com). Hand-drawn timetables and visual journey planners, comic strip conversations, as well as role play and comic strip situation problem solving can all be used to add humour and real-life planning. Dr Susan Young's STAR Detective problem solving model (Young 2017) is great for helping younger children to look at problems in a systematic way.

🤚 KEY POINTS

» Coaching offers a unique support system for girls with ADHD, encouraging a strength-based engagement.

» To be an ADHD coach, an in-depth understanding of ADHD is imperative.

» Establishing a bond of trust is the essential first step in a successful coaching relationship.

THE COACHING FUNDAMENTALS: A POSITIVE OUTLOOK BUT BEWARE OF BLACK ICE – JEMMA'S STORY

From this early experience, I learnt quickly not to make an assumption about a young person I was about to meet. This is not easy when the diagnosis is well understood and in front of you sit reports from parents, teachers and other professionals from whom a referral may have originated. My advice is to forget them all and just listen.

I made an assumption that Jemma would engage willingly and be grateful for my support to overcome her struggles. I forgot the most important task: to connect and listen. In fact, what happened next involved six hours simply walking with Jemma and my dog Roxy. She gave Jemma an excuse to come out. We walked side by side, encouraging a trusting relationship and creating a space where she eventually felt safe enough to begin to introduce me to her world. I simply listened, reflected, reassured and asked the occasional question for clarity. So this, for me, is the start point for any coaching relationship. It absolutely must be about gaining trust, and perhaps even more importantly, simply getting along. Without it, sessions go nowhere. Every client is unique, every conversation is bespoke, and the focus must be based on exactly where that client is on their journey and where they wish to be.

One of the first things we changed for Jemma was the mentor with whom she worked. Although this isn't always possible, if it is, just do it and don't take it personally. With a young person with ADHD, a trusting relationship based on a genuine liking for the other person is a most effective and simple intervention. Change the class, change the assistant, make it work; it will be repaid tenfold. In Jemma's case, it was the catalyst that enabled her return to school. Now she buys me a coffee and sends me her latest running figures as the pillars of strength in her life continue to build. She laughs at the times she's pulled the wool over my eyes and blagged her way through a session, but the remarkable thing is, ten years on, she still takes the time to stay in touch and check through her thinking in a tricky situation. The strategies she developed work for her.

Coaching for ADHD is a concept which has been around for 20 years. The aim is not only to support the development of strategies which empower an individual to identify and manage daily tasks themselves, but to achieve those goals deliberately. Through supported, step-by-step, 'solution-focused' thinking, student and coach move forward by identifying the steps to reach those goals in a sustainable way. The client has a growing sense of personal well-being, reduced emotional overload and an increasing sense of control over their ability to bring about change in their world. There is also a clear opportunity to discuss difficulties in a way which is rarely covered by other professionals. This is a powerful tool to enhance self-esteem and self-worth. More importantly, it plots a route to successful task completion in individuals who have more experience of failure than success.

ADHD COACHING: THE NEED TO SUPPORT EXECUTIVE FUNCTIONING IN SCHOOL AND AT HOME

The path to diagnosis has been explained by others in this book, with impulsivity, inattention, poor emotional control, and physical and mental hyperactivity being key components. As a further complication, young people with ADHD tend to exhibit delays in their EFs. Described earlier in this book by Peter Hill, the EFs are the cognitive processes which reside in the prefrontal cortex of the brain and direct activity in a timely and focused manner. For students, this equates to an ability for timely commencement of homework, organization of materials, planning work, starting a task and sticking with it even when it gets difficult or just dull; and all this in a timely, calm manner. The completed work then needs to be packed in a bag, taken to school and handed in on time. Having flexibility in approach and an ability to re-sequence or reprioritize when information changes underpins an ability to switch flexibly between competing demands without incurring undue anxiety or feeling overwhelmed.

Russell A. Barkley (2018) compares well-functioning EFs to a 'Swiss-army knife of mind tools' ready to support someone to navigate everyday challenges well. With optimal EFs, an individual can throttle back on an impulsive thought or emotion, employing the brain's 'stop and think' control system before blurting out an impulsive response. They also allow students to switch from a pleasant daydream into focused concentration in order to pay attention to a lesson. The same cognitive functions are used to override a mild hunger or boredom response to stay focused until the end of class, or manage in a socially acceptable way an emotion which threatens to overwhelm. These are powerful cognitive processes which allow us to engage appropriately with our personal goal, whether that is managing the academic demands of the day or managing unruly emotions with friends. We all struggle with these skills some of the time, but for those with ADHD, they are persistent and impact their lives in a negative way. As a predominantly hereditable condition, ADHD in parents can cause additional family stress. Home life may well lack the organization, routine, structure and role modelling that can help the development of these important life skills. It could also mean family flash points as areas of weak emotional control in child and adult add to an already tense family dynamic.

Everyone with the diagnosis, and hence every client, will have a unique ADHD signature, or fingerprint. For many teenagers, the challenges faced would not present as a difficulty if there was a different approach in their education. These young people are keen and eager to learn. Academic settings which encourage learning through practical exploration, and a 'hands-on, big picture' approach support and encourage these learners. Yet the range and diversity of presentation of ADHD, and with it EFs, is immense. In 20 years, I have met only two children who seem to have similar strengths and weaknesses with a similar outlook on life. So, there is no template which fits everyone; each and every person has a different EF skillset and it is the task of the coach to sift through the challenges faced by the individual with the individual. By getting to grips with this, the client's own EF skillset can often support the areas which need to be strengthened. A weak working memory may be supported by strong verbal rehearsal skills, or poor time management may be supported by stronger organizational skills (e.g. by setting timers).

It is important to recognize that in a secondary school, college or university, the EFs are the platform upon which these young people are judged. A high IQ can be tripped by weak EFs: a teen may have the knowledge but they just can't get it down on paper. Children who achieve early success in primary school can have that snatched away in the transition to secondary school. For example, a student who is highly verbally able but unable to process information efficiently will present as bright in history class but will struggle to start an essay on the very same topic alone, and may be labelled as 'lazy' as a result. This despite being a passionate historian. The challenge is to harness what is in their head in a way which allows them to achieve the required goal (Figure 6.3). That could be an essay, revision for an exam, an extended art project, a Design Technology assignment or any other task requiring sustained and focused attention. In fact, to summarize, these children and young people are at a natural disadvantage in precisely the areas where they are assessed and graded in school.

Figure 6.3 Understanding and harnessing unruly thoughts

For all these reasons, an ADHD coach must be deeply acquainted with the condition as it presents in their client, in order to address the various areas of life impacted and start to reduce the feeling of helplessness.

COACHING NEEDS FOR TEENAGE GIRLS WITH ADHD

So, how do students end up like Jemma, when ADHD brings with it delightful, bright, inventive, energetic and inquisitive learners? Surely these traits offer a perfect precondition and prerequisite for learning?

I would argue that the characteristics associated with ADHD are managed in primary schools, where scaffolding and controlling the flow of information and engagement with the task are micromanaged by teachers. Friendships too are one-dimensional, free from the teenage emotions. Children sit at the same desk every day, which contains all of their books and equipment. The teachers move around the students, their books are in one place, and instructions are generally single, small, stepped and repetitive. There are lots of opportunities to play, paint and be creative as well as colourful interludes like story time and games involving hand–eye coordination. Children are less formally examined, and homework is light, allowing for home time to be home time. In essence, teachers and parents play the role of the EFs, managing the pace and degree of engagement. With an engaging teacher, and there are many, there is an opportunity for exploration and learning on the go. Girls, societally driven to conform, tend to copy and follow, and it's not so hard for these bright girls to manage well in this environment, often showing real talent.

Things start to unravel in secondary school as the EF support systems present in primary schools are effectively simply removed. Added to that, the demands on the EF increase as pupils are now required to navigate themselves around new classrooms, and manage the differing teaching styles and an ever-increasing academic load of increasing complexity. These often pubescent girls are now required to operate in this system with a set of EFs which are not matched to that of their peers or to the cognitive and social load they are required to carry. It is no surprise that we often see a slow slide between the ages of 13 and 16 years. Supporting these girls through transition needs to be a far more robust exercise, with coaching summer schools and coaching support through the first two years of secondary helping them to build the EF skillset they need to navigate a far more complex academic day.

The strengths displayed by girls with ADHD can be different to those valued by secondary school, and they may not be the strengths which assist in efficient task engagement or task completion. Contrary to popular opinion, hyperfocus, a well-documented feature of ADHD, cannot be switched on and off by choice. Whilst a girl may become super absorbed in studying an intrinsically fascinating period of history, and know all the dates, characters and personalities, this is irrelevant if the history essay is on a different time period in which she has no natural interest. It does, however, offer an opportunity for coaching. It's a question of helping the girls to see that the skillset is the same even though it *feels* different; it's the *emotional engagement* with the task that has changed and that, with ADHD, is crucial to task engagement. If we can find a way to engage with the characters in the new task (give them a backstory and colour and purpose so that they become more emotionally engaging), then suddenly there is a way to see the task differently.

It will be harder, but practising this means strategies start to be developed. A similar approach can be used for organizing material and planning out an essay. Using templates such as the Hero's Journey for an essay can bring the historical period and characters to life so the task becomes a far more interesting one. (The Hero's Journey is a very common template used for stories. It usually involves a central character, 'the hero', who is called away on an adventure. Normally, there is at least one crisis which has to be overcome and the hero returns victorious, having grown in personality. *The Hobbit* and *Star Wars* adventures all use this template.) The route to task completion may be different and may take longer; but once they know how to get there, it reduces the emotional and cognitive load, and that is an important step in managing anxiety. Yes, school needs to be on board with this approach – and be willing to shift expectations, by differentiating tasks and making reasonable adjustments as required under the Equality Act 2010 and SEND Code of Practice 2015 (see Chapter 5 for more details). In this case, they would need to simply request an outline plan for the essay by the next day and require separate paragraphs over the following days. With this tailored support, the results can be pleasantly surprising for both teachers and students.

I have worked with brilliant Oxbridge mathematicians, magically abundant storytellers, inspired musicians and poets, inventors, philosophers and so many original thinkers. Enabling them to express their struggles or their joys through a different medium, but one which feels more natural, is certainly empowering and allows a much better display of intelligence. These are the novelists, inventors, musicians, academics, athletes, journalists and politicians of tomorrow. These young women are so full of potential, but so weighed down by a system that struggles to recognize their version of 'difference'. My task as a coach is to help them to navigate this system, which tends to focus on their weaknesses and unintentionally pushes them backwards into a corner from which they struggle to escape. Coaching can help them find their own way through the tough landscape of the years when they believe their education grades and social media persona define who they are.

Without intervention, or diagnosis, by early to mid-teens many have been judged, assessed and classified into sets. They may also have been unwittingly characterized by parents, friends and often most harshly, by themselves, their opinion of who they are often predominantly reflecting the opinions and values of others. They usually know they are bright; they know they understand the work, but *they just can't do it*. Over time, the emotional impact of this growing realization can be overwhelming and internalized. Layers of self-defence can build up to protect them from daily struggles; ultimately, simply not engaging can be the safest option. It certainly was for Jemma.

Yet I am always struck by how bright, funny, mischievous and enquiring these girls are when you catch them off guard despite feeling ground down by a system that requires them to be a certain way. They express feeling 'outsiders' in a society which celebrates diversity in a non-diverse way; they express their frustration that the world expects them to be someone they are not and is not understanding or supportive of their difference. Yes, they are different, and they know it, but that difference needs to be valued and nurtured.

'Just do it': a teacher's opinion

Jemma gave me an example of the type of repeated experience which had led her to just give up. She hadn't understood some work as it had been removed from the board before she could write it down and there had been too much noise for her to concentrate. She wanted to ask the teacher for help. She had stayed behind at the end of class and then tried to explain the problem. The experience was not a happy one.

'What can't you understand now? The instructions were clear, and we have been over this so many times before,' she reported the teacher as saying. 'If you still have a problem, make an appointment to see me at another time and explain. Teachers are busy people and can't spend time discussing every student's struggles.' I shuddered silently; let's just take a moment to look at the EFs involved in the solution this teacher proposed (Figure 6.4).

Making an email appointment with a strict teacher to discuss struggles	Executive function involved	What you see
manage feelings	emotional regulation	anxiety, task avoidance
find email	organization, time management	anxiety, task avoidance, frustration
decide what to say	emotional regulation, goal-directed persistence	anxiety, task avoidance
work out why I can't do my work	emotional regulation, metacognition	anxiety, task avoidance, procrastination
start the email	task initiation	procrastination, failed attempts
work out availability	organization, working memory, time management	stress builds as next lesson approaches
complete the email and send	goal-directed persistence, emotional regulation, task completion	anxiety, task avoidance
check for reply	organization, emotional regulation	anxiety, task avoidance
respond and agree date	organization, time management, emotional regulation	anxiety, task avoidance

Figure 6.4 Outcomes when the executive functions are overwhelmed

This approach was rather disappointing. I think we need to put the student at the centre of the learning experience and listen to work out how to support the development of her skillset. It could have been such a great learning opportunity; instead, Jemma didn't complete the work, received a detention and felt a failure.

BUILD-UP OF TOXIC EXPERIENCES: PEELING BACK THE LAYERS

In most cases girls arrive at their session rather husk-like. Hoodie, head down, guard up. It is a fact that our culture and society still expects girls to internalize a narrative which requires accommodating the needs of others, compliance, neatness and timeliness, to name a few. In addition, they are expected to be calm. We know these skills call on the very areas which are likely to be developmentally delayed in ADHD. It is understood and accepted that boys with ADHD can and will 'act out'; but many girls tend to 'act in', as I like to describe their restless minds, and so tend to turn the confusion, anger, frustration and anxiety in on themselves. Initially, this can appear as a reluctance to engage. Girls can become obsessive in an attempt to control an area of their life. They may stay up all night to try to complete a piece of work they struggled to start and end up destroying it as 'just not good enough', rather than verbalising their difficulties. They are rarely troublemakers and often go unobserved until too late.

The changes in the brain during the teenage years also drive a need for acceptance within a social group. Yet friendships are notoriously difficult for girls with ADHD. Social acceptance is a powerful indicator of self-worth, particularly for girls seeking social groups. ADHD makes conforming to the rules of social engagement unfathomably difficult. Traditional friendships are not always instinctive, and girls will often try to change who they are to conform. More worrying, others act out to gain popularity amongst girls who applaud their risky behaviour. This can lead vulnerable girls to be exposed to unsafe activities and relationships. It has been said that the drive to be socially accepted during the teenage years is as strong as the drive for a toddler to walk. Giving up is not an option: despite how many times you are rejected, you will try again. Girls can be routinely rejected from social gatherings and friendship groups at school as a result of poorly regulated emotions, over-verbalization and poor listening skills. It is difficult to describe the hurt they relate when they finally talk.

I believe these increasing pressures can result in a toxicity that gets to a point where some fail to function altogether. Those worse affected can become school refusers, prone to self-harm, eating disorders, anxiety and depression. I like to present this build-up of toxic ingredients by way of the diagram in Figure 6.5.

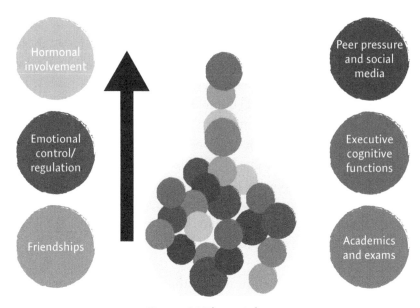

Figure 6.5 The toxic brew

✋ KEY POINTS

> » Establishing a trusting bond is the first task in any coaching relationship.

> » An understanding of the executive functions and the role they play in secondary school is the basis for teasing out areas where support might be needed.

> » Teenage girls are under particular pressure to behave in a socially acceptable way, which challenges their core deficits.

THE COACHING SESSION: GETTING IT RIGHT FIRST TIME

Coaching is an unregulated industry in the UK, so you need to be sure a coach has the requisite skills and clinic hours, membership of a professional coaching body as well as professional supervision. One of the most important factors for clients is to be supported in a regular and predictable way, and what drives those feelings of security in a coaching environment can be listed as:

- trusted person (qualifications, experience, references)
- trusted, safe and comfortable environment (membership of professional body, supervision, professional insurance)
- consistency of approach (available references)
- consistency of session structure (session template).

A session should include the following phases:

- getting comfortable and reflecting on the time since last session
- feedback from previous tasks and identifying the successes and struggles
- adjusting approach to take account of experience
- goal setting or revision and problem solving
- reviewing new targets and identifying successes.

When a young person has made the decision to come to see you as a professional coach, you get one shot. Success during the first session means you may get a second shot. They quickly have to feel like they have entered a safe and reliable space, and they have to believe you are on their side. In fact, the very essence of coaching is to create that oasis away from the external pressures. The first task is to listen. Creating a comfortable, calm and predictable environment where the client can feel secure enough to talk requires homework. So, find out if are there any sensory or physical issues, any fears or dislikes; most important, what is their favourite snack?

Settling in and settling down is important. Clients have often had a full day at school or college replete with the social, emotional and academic baggage that accompanies every day. Their first session has probably been forced or coerced upon them by their parents, and they may be less than keen to engage. The pressure is on you to make it work. They need in that first session to believe a burden has been lifted and shared, they need to know you understand, and they need to believe that together you can really make a difference. You have to encourage them to open up and discuss whether they are ready and willing to have a go at some of these struggles – where they are in their motivation for change.

The setting

Setting up the room and ensuring it is welcoming, calm, distraction free and comfortable is important. This starts with human basics: a drink, some snacks, warmth, light, a comfortable place to sit, blankets for security, blinds for privacy and at least five minutes to allow for scanning. Allowing these focused five minutes to have a good look around means we don't spend the next 15 minutes trying to do the same thing. Girls are exceptionally observant and enquiring and will scan the room extensively when given the opportunity. Opportunities to move around, sit on the floor and a choice from two fidget toys all sets the scene.

In my sessions, after a brief introduction to who I am and why they might find the sessions different, I listen. In fact, the first session, and the first ten minutes of every session, is all about listening. This means active listening: checking understanding, reflecting and adding education about the diagnosis where that might help illuminate particular struggles. Most girls have only a sketchy idea of what the diagnosis really means, and exploring the strengths and the challenges the diagnosis presents (and why EF skills are so important) is a really worthwhile task. We also look at the quite brilliant and innovative ways in which this incredible brain can flourish, but we are honest about the challenges it presents. We discuss people who have the diagnosis and how they have honed their passion to succeed. I can't teach others how to have a brain like theirs, but as a coach I can help girls with ADHD navigate the world in which they must engage.

Typically, once you ask the right questions, stories pour forth with ease and fluidity. The challenge is to stop. I capture these words and feelings as a pictogram and as I reflect this to the client, I use the drawing to check the accuracy of my understanding. Once we have a real-time representation of how they are feeling and how much they would like to see change, it is possible to highlight the areas of most pressing need. The miracle question is used at this point: 'If you woke up tomorrow morning and it all felt better, what would have changed?'

With their struggles represented on paper, it's easier to review core difficulties (Figure 6.6). Next, we take the first step to settle the 'snowstorm' in their head and crystallize the thoughts and feelings. Sometimes this is the first time that the thoughts and feelings have been externalized enough to allow them to be approached rationally, and often this can be immensely reassuring. I use free-hand drawings so I can demonstrate an individual and organic understanding – and, as my drawing is so very poor, there is a great opportunity for a very good laugh.

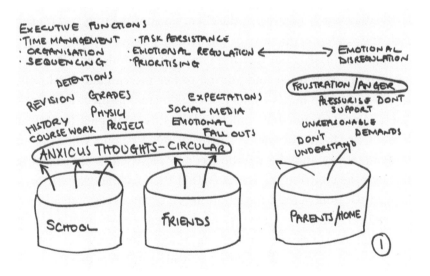

Figure 6.6 Example of session one: diagrammatic representation of the client's story

The session will continue with the young person reviewing the drawing and amending or prioritizing the various strands of her thinking (Figure 6.7).

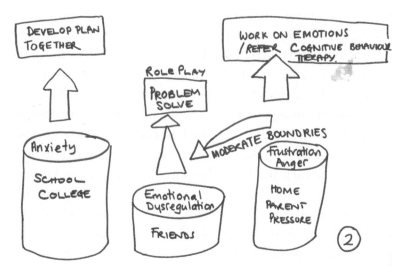

Figure 6.7 When reviewing the drawing, the client amends and reprioritizes her concerns and agrees areas for work focus

In the diagram in Figure 6.7, the client's own weighting suggest she feels the academic pressure of the history project and revision are driving the anxiety, but that the family and friendship difficulties are driving each other and adding to her increased stress levels. In her view, she needs to sort out the history project and work out a revision timetable, which will positively impact her stress levels. Once these are started, she believes her parents will be more understanding and she will be freer to see friends. By thinking through the contributing issues (rather than feeling overwhelmed by the toxic pool of resulting emotions), it becomes easier to address the matters one at a time. As we proceed, so we interleave an understanding of elements which may be contributing to her current situation; for example, the following all add a different dynamic and every young person weights these very differently:

- how they feel about ADHD

- EF strengths and weaknesses

- friends

- family strengths and flash points

- academic pressures.

The discussion allows the coach to cluster the streams of thought, ensuring a better focus on the principle concerns and maybe seeing other issues as 'mental clutter' clouding thinking. This is the first step in identifying where coaching will focus. When asking what ADHD means for them, girls particularly are often keen to represent this through their own artistic representation (Figures 6.8 and 6.9).

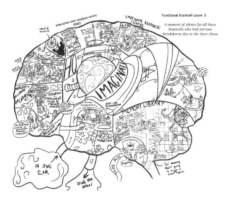

Figure 6.8 A client's representation of how her head can be both organized and chaotic (reproduced by kind permission of Anne Mundt)

Figure 6.9 (reproduced by permission of Brooke Griffith)

By the end of session one, it is imperative to have achieved five goals. These are that the client:

- feels comfortable and safe

- feels heard and understood

- feels calmer

- feels valued

- believes things can change.

Finally, it is important to crystallize the areas where work will focus during the next few sessions and how we will stay in touch and find out how things are going – texts or WhatsApp work best.

✋ KEY POINTS

» Settling in and settling down are a key starting point to coaching success.

» Capturing thoughts and feelings organically on paper can help the client reflect on their situation.

» Identify and work with their version of ADHD.

» Us a step-by-step analysis of the problem and baby steps to achieve success.

SUBSEQUENT COACHING SESSIONS

I fundamentally believe that girls have the requisite knowledge and ideas to bring about the changes they need if these are presented in a way with which they can engage. To do that, there needs to be a deep understanding of the condition.

Charlotte, aged 14 years, describes her struggles to write an essay:

'Sometimes there's so much information, particularly if it's something which inspires me, it's just a wild snowstorm in my head. I mean, how do I choose the right bits in the right order to answer the question? I don't even know where to start and it's really stressful, I have so much I want to say.'

In this case a coaching session might proceed as follows:

- We discuss the essay title and capture her verbal knowledge onto a mind map (task initiation and organization of material).

- Together we work to identify the key themes which answer the question (sequencing and organization of material).

- We prioritize the points she has made in the mind map into an essay plan (prioritization and sequencing).

- We use a template to organize the plan into an introduction, supporting paragraphs and conclusion (planning, organization task persistence, task completion).

- We then identify barriers to completion of these tasks and set out a timetable (time management, emotional regulation and motivation).

Supporting students in this way encourages a growth mindset where they start to see a way through their blocks and can begin to use new strategies themselves. More steps are needed than for most neurotypical students, but once that is understood, it is possible to see a way through.

By identifying the areas of weakness and using the strengths to manage the task in a different way, coaching can support the client to develop alternative systems to reach the goal. As one of the Year 10 girls I coach commented, 'You help me build the bottom of a pyramid, which helps me climb the steps to reach the top.' Figure 6.10 aims to reflect the concept she describes.

Every single school task demands varying degrees of EF skills. Coaching sessions will map onto this pyramid the study tasks which are needed to prepare, write and submit the work on time. The EF inputs can be understood by the client in a task-related way, bolstering their strengths and supporting weaknesses through identification and structured practice. Determining exactly what steps the client will take is central to the session and needs to be assessed in terms of the realistic chance of success When this is presented in a digestible way, clients are capable of developing their own strategies and solutions.

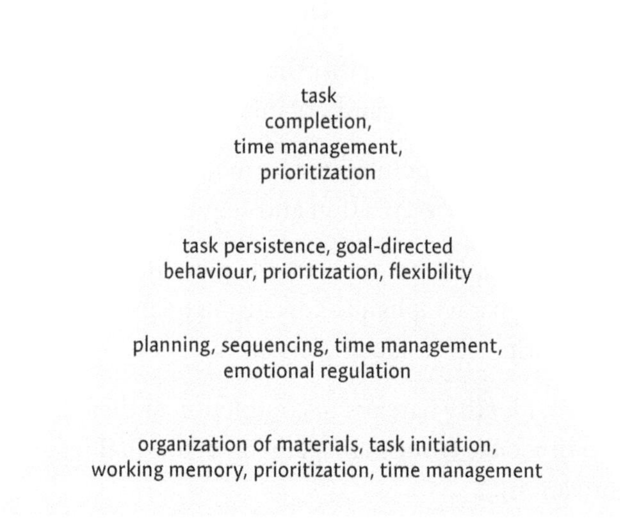

task
completion,
time management,
prioritization

task persistence, goal-directed
behaviour, prioritization, flexibility

planning, sequencing, time management,
emotional regulation

organization of materials, task initiation,
working memory, prioritization, time management

Figure 6.10 EFs deployed in planning and writing an essay

Sessions take place in a safe and predictable setting so the burden of anxiety is removed, which in turn frees up working memory space to focus on the work at hand.

Amy, aged 16, reflects:

'Coaching gives me a wonderful place to explore my difficulties in a calm way. I can focus more easily on the stuff I need to work on and not be overrun by stuff in my head.'

Pippa, a 16-year-old student, describes it as:

'...a place where I can focus and believe in the areas where I am strong, as well as looking at the things which hold me back. It just suddenly all feels ok rather than all too much. I go away with the ideas clear in my head, and even if I become muddled again, my drawing and plan give me direction.'

It seems that what really works with girls with ADHD – once they have reached this point of despair – is for them to have a high-level, short-term intervention which generates a feeling of success. More flexible systems can then be introduced for follow-on sessions as new challenges arise. In this way, students are able to deal with similar obstacles using their own resources, but knowing support is available should it become necessary to address a new challenge.

To have experienced success in a task, and to have new and relevant skills to call on, means they are more able to manage stressful situations, with greater kindness to themselves. In my view, a task- and goal-focused timeframe seems to work better. In fact, it is the stories from the girls themselves which makes me inclined to this approach. ADHD does not disappear, and one of the most frequent complaints is that just as they are starting to make progress towards a goal, support disappears. This can actually cause a feeling of further failure to these sensitive girls, often making them disinclined to engage further. I feel it is therefore appropriate to choose as the goal of the sessions a new skill. Once that has been mastered, that is the time to step back until a new goal is needed.

THE EVIDENCE: A SHORT REVIEW OF ADHD COACHING

Downey (2003, p.21) described coaching as 'the art of facilitating the performance, learning and development of another', and Whitmore (1992) proposed that it assisted with the 'unlocking of a person's potential to maximise their own performance'. I like to think that it is 'a catalyst for sustained cognitive emotional and behavioural changes that facilitate goal attainment, and support the student to reach their goal, whether personal or professional', as found by Grant and Stober (2006). This certainly follows the qualification training model I studied through REACH ADHD coaching.

If, as Ramsay and Rostain conjectured in 2016, 'ADHD is a problem of implementation', then it follows that the goal of ADHD coaching is the development of skills and strategies to manage practical challenges faced in achieving one's goals. To be able to connect a challenge to its neurobiological origins has key advantages, the most important of which is that students stop feeling 'stupid', 'ignorant', 'slow' or 'just lazy' – all ways that clients have been described by their teachers.

In the video 'An Introduction to ADHD', I worked with teenage girls with ADHD to give feedback to their teachers. I have given permission for ADHD Richmond and Kingston to host the video, which is very enlightening (https://www.youtube.com/channel/ UCZ6G2NcMz4MbloVhL0quUfA?app=desktop).

Within the research literature, coaching has been recognized as a 'useful and important component of a multifaceted treatment approach for individuals with ADHD' (Ahmann 2019). In their review of the literature, Ahmann, Saviet and Tuttle (2017) analysed all the available publications and research on the efficacy of ADHD coaching as part of a multimodal package of treatment. Acknowledging that emerging adults with ADHD 'experience a decreased quality of life across many domains' (Ahmann *et al.* 2018), academic difficulties were highlighted by DuPaul *et al.* (2009) and Weyandt and DuPaul (2013), as were 'difficulties with self-esteem and social adjustment' by Blase *et al.* (2009). Students with ADHD have 'less effective study habits, lower academic performance, lower test scores and higher rates of class withdrawal' (Advokat, Lane and Luo 2011).

We know that evidence supports a multimodal approach to ADHD (Hinshaw and Arnold 2015; Knouse *et al.* 2008) but whilst medication remains the first line treatment for those diagnosed with moderate to severe ADHD, in 1994 Hallowell and Ratey introduced the idea of coaching individuals with ADHD in their book Driven to Distraction. Since that time, there has been an ever increasing and ever more persuasive body of research recognizing coaching as an important part of that multimodal treatment approach.

In 1995, Favorite found that the primary focus of coaching, as well as being self-awareness, insight and emotional self-regulation, is to 'take action to get things done' (Favorite 1995).

Reflecting the feedback from clients, researchers have also found that the findings in literature led to an understanding that students with ADHD participating in coaching found it to be 'a unique partnership meeting needs not adequately addressed by other personal or professional relationships, including academic advisors, tutors and therapy' (Kubik 2010; see also Parker *et al.* 2013).

The descriptive review by Ahmann *et al.* (2017) finds that 'ADHD coaching may be an effective approach for improving motivation, academic skills, self-efficacy, achievement, persistence, and, ultimately retention among college students with ADHD' (see also Robbins *et al.* 2003; Tinto 1975, 1993). This review of the impressive literature in this fast-emerging field does offer some illumination, and suggests that ADHD coaching supports improved outcomes in the various areas of ADHD and improves both EFs and well-being.

✋ KEY POINTS

» Coaching assists girls with ADHD to quieten the noise in their heads and see things more clearly.

» Coaching offers a safe and predictable space to explore their struggles and develop solutions.

» Evidence supports coaching as a unique partnership meeting needs not adequately addressed by other personal or professional relationships, including academic advisors, tutors and therapy.

GIRLS WITH ADHD IN AN AGE OF SOCIAL MEDIA AND HIGH-OCTANE EDUCATIONAL DEMANDS

Whilst we have a clear idea of what ADHD is, and how it can impact girls in particular, it is worth setting this within the context of the social whirl in which they must operate today. We live in an age of high-speed, high-octane activity and expectations. Things must be done now; apps and computer games fuel instant gratification. An idealized social media presence is essential, making tasks which require sustained attention and persistence an increasing struggle in the general population. Girls report a serious strain to retain their sense of who they are through their teen years with competing demands from school friends and family. The following feedback given by neurotypical teenage girls to a standard set of questions highlights this.

On self-esteem:

'It has always impacted me. I've never felt intelligent enough or good enough from an academic perspective.'

'I expected rejection when I applied for university because I was never the best at anything.'

'At university I was very average and even now, despite doing a good job, I'm waiting for me to do something wrong. In fact, a total lack of self-belief.'

On body image:

'I think it affects most young girls. My friend was tall and slim but would eat what she wanted. I was envious of her appearance and the attention it would get her. I would therefore avoid certain foods (typical of our generation) mostly carbohydrates or fats.'
(This girl subsequently developed an eating disorder.)

'I absolutely loved going to an all-girls school, but there were drawbacks. We were so competitive, and it definitely affected my body image as I would constantly compare myself with my friends.'

'We seemed to all suffer from eating disorders and many of my friends still struggle with a difficult relationship with food today.'

On academic pressures:

'I didn't get into university because my grades weren't good enough. My mum regrets being so hard on me, when actually not getting in was a great thing. I grew up a lot and in hindsight it's such a minor part of my life when I was made to feel that my world had fallen apart.'

'My worth was judged only by my grades.'

'My goals weren't my goals; they were my parents'. What I wanted was considered unimportant after all the expense that they invested in me. They seemed to forget that was their choice, not mine. I wanted to study computer design, but they insisted on politics.'

On social media:

'It's huge for our generation, we've grown up being made to feel that certain foods shouldn't be eaten, that size zero is something we should all be trying to attain in order to look our best on social media.'

'We are constantly striving for more likes or more friends or more clicks and that meant making sure how we looked was all important; it's emotionally exhausting. I made terrible mistakes and lost good friends in an effort to be more popular.'

On anxiety:

'There was no day that wasn't filled with anxious thoughts. Am I working hard enough, how will I finish this work, will I get the grades, I need to get a new outfit for Friday, will I be thin enough, will I get an invite to the party. It was endless and sometimes all too much, and I'd sit in my room and just cry.'

'There was no one I could tell the truth to about how I was feeling who didn't expect something from me or who I could trust to not tell others.'

If we add the neurodevelopmental delays which characterize ADHD to this mix, and understand the emotional, social and executive challenges faced by these girls, we should not be surprised that so many turn in on themselves and end up with significant mental health issues. Eating disorders, self-harm, depression and considerable anxiety are not at all uncommon. I do not think that these issues are well enough understood or that there is a positive intervention early enough to support these teens through these challenging years. Many of those I work with are now using ADHD medication, but also medication for anxiety and depression, or attending a clinic for other serious mental health conditions, obsessive–compulsive disorder, eating disorders or addiction.

So, when they walk through my door, they can be full of doubt in addition to typical teenage angst. They are also stressed about terrorism, the coronavirus, climate change, the rise of nationalism, animal welfare and looking good. Many have become vegan, often exacerbating pre-existing complex relationships with food. Many simply do not possess the coping mechanisms of the neurotypical teens who, although struggling, fare better with their more developed cognitive toolkit and ability to gain support from friends. These girls tend instead to internalize their struggles in order to stay afloat, often removing themselves from situations where they feel exposed or anxious and in so doing exacerbating their difficulties. We need to take great care of these girls who are caught in the crossfire of a need for social acceptance and academic pressure and thrown by hormonal involvement complicating their ADHD. These external demands also call on the very skills where they are at a developmental disadvantage. So, should we consider coaching as a realistic support system for them? Can the rigours of the world they face really be made more manageable through this intervention? The evidence would suggest that there is a real advantage.

KEY POINTS

» Today's focus on body image, social hierarchy and friendships exacerbates the challenges faced by girls with ADHD.

» Isolation and social rejection lead to other secondary and more debilitating mental health conditions.

» Girls with ADHD tend to internalize their struggles, 'hibernate' in their rooms or take unnecessary risks to win friends, thereby increasing their vulnerability.

CONCLUSION

I decided the best way to conclude this chapter was to ask the girls, how have the coaching sessions helped and supported them and what is it that coaching brings? The answer seems to be close to that espoused by Kubik (2010) and Parker *et al.* (2013) in their reviews of the benefits of ADHD coaching, that *coaching provides a unique partnership which meets needs not addressed by other personal or professional relationships.* Too little, too late? *Absolutely not!* Over to the girls.

Elle, aged 16 years:

'I have always been sceptical about receiving help, having seen more therapists than the average kid; however, I would not be in the place I am today without the dedicated coaching support and guidance I have received.'

Alicia, aged 17 years:

'I struggled massively during my education and it proved very difficult for others to comprehend why I struggled. The coaching sessions were my sanity, the only space to explore my own mind and develop my own solutions. I learnt that I didn't need to do things the way others did. It was OK to go my own way to reach the goal. I feel so much better.'

Grace, aged 14 years:

'We were able to draw out, literally draw a picture, of what was happening in my head, and by seeing it laid out before me, I could focus on the various parts without being overwhelmed by the total chaos.'

Lily, aged 16 years:

'I have three characters in my head, three voices. The first is my natural self-voice, pretty chaotic and apt to go off into a dream world at the slightest opportunity; I call this Lily's Brain. The second voice is my sensible voice, which sometimes gains control, and gets me to stay on task and focus on my work, or tells me not to get too wound up about what people feel about me, or what I imagine people feel about me. The third, which only recently I have come to realize is anxiety, is the most troublesome of all, over-analysing everything in minute detail until every sort of apocalypse seems like the only plausible scenario and disaster is imminent. With patience and an IT specialist (coach) you can cancel the subscription or at least bring it back to a more balanced podcast. I only learnt that anxiety was this troublesome character through coaching, and I found a way to keep it in check by treating it as a character and rewriting his lines.'

Harriet, aged 15 years:

'Some days were so bad, we just wrote a poem or went for a walk or composed a tune on the piano, which really helped me to process those awful feelings, and I always leave feeling lighter, understood and with a couple of new ideas in my pocket. Also, I know I can manage those feelings better now when I'm on my own.'

Lucy, aged 15 years:

'I was never doubted, always respected, always listened to. It was so refreshing. I started telling lies about everything and coaching ended up being the only place where I could be honest and not fear blame. I learnt why I found stuff so hard and I stopped thinking I was an idiot. I don't like being told how to do something, so over time I learnt to come up with my own ideas, some of which actually worked.'

Bea, aged 18 years:

'My personal growth can be directly attributed to my coaching.'

Jade, aged 13 years:

'Sessions help me to understand why I do the things I do, and that it's actually pretty normal for kids with ADHD to do them, so I don't need to feel like I'm a total loser when I mess up. We usually manage to find something positive to take from the situation and I'm really good at coming up with different things to try to make it better. I think I will be able to get better at not doing them in the first place sometime soon, but at least now I can try and sort it out.'

Katrina, aged 18 years:

'We talk through things that are bothering me. I am still coming to terms with the diagnosis having struggled all the way through school and teachers' thinking I was just lazy. We talk about the diagnosis and then spend time coming up with what I want to work on. I'm now working out my own solutions. Sometimes I just bring my work and we plan how to do it and how long each section is going to take me. I always underestimate time, which means my work is always late, or I cram at the last minute, which makes me so scared, but I'm getting better at planning that now.'

Zara, aged 14 years:

'It really helps me to get organized, and sometimes I even help to organize my sisters with a chart I have made. Next, I'm going to work on starting my homework, but I'll have to think about how to do that as I'm really bad at it!'

☀ TIPS:

If you are considering having coaching, here are a few tips and questions that may be helpful:

- Interview two or three coaches before you decide (or as many as needed).
- Look for a coach with an accurate breadth and depth of knowledge about adult ADHD.
- Ask the coach if they have received specific ADHD training.
- Ask the coach about their level of experience (how many delivered hours of coaching, how many coaching clients).
- Ask questions about their coaching techniques and tools

(look for a coach with a flexible approach rather than a 'one-size fits all' approach).

- Ask the coach for details about their formal training, accreditation and continuing professional development (what their training covered, the length of the training programme, whether they are keeping their skills up to date, whether they are being supervised, whether they are a member of a coaching body such as the International Coach Federation, the Association for Coaching, the Special Group in Coaching Psychology or the European Mentoring and Coaching Council).

- Ask the coach about any other training or work/life experiences they may have incorporated into their coaching style (e.g. psychology, creative arts, law or counselling).

- Look for someone who is a good listener and is also asking you the right questions (questions that will help you see the direction in which you wish to move).

- Ask if they subscribe to a coaching code of ethics and ask to see that code.

- Ask the coach for at least two references and then contact them. Do not rely upon testimonials.

- Make sure that their contract for services includes a schedule of coaching sessions, all costs including any extra expenses/fees, payment terms, outcomes and deliverables, a confidentiality clause and termination of the service.

- And finally, don't forget that coaching is an important relationship so you should feel that the connection between yourself and a coach is right and appropriate. If in doubt, don't select!

REFERENCES

Advokat, C., Lane, S.M. and Luo, C. (2011) 'College students with and without ADHD: Comparison of self-report of medication usage, study habits, and academic achievement.' *Journal of Attention Disorders 15*, 656–666.

Ahmann, E. (2019) 'Communication modalities and their perceived effectiveness in coaching for individuals with attention-deficit/hyperactivity disorder (ADHD).' *International Journal of Evidence Based Coaching and Mentoring 17*, 2, 93–107.

Ahmann, E., Saviet, M. and Tuttle, L.J. (2017) 'Interventions for ADHD in children and teens: A focus on ADHD coaching.' *Pediatric Nursing 43*, 3, 121–131.

Ahmann, E., Tuttle, L.J., Saviet, M. and Wright, S.D. (2018) 'A descriptive review of ADHD coaching research: Implications for college students.' *Journal of Postsecondary Education and Disability 31*, 1, 17–39.

Assheton, J. (2009) 'Coaching clients with ADHD.' *ADHD in Practice 1*, 2, 15–17.

Blase, S.L., Gilbert, A.N., Anastopoulos, A.D., Costello, E.J. *et al.* (2009) 'Self-reported ADHD and adjustment in college: Cross-sectional and longitudinal findings.' *Journal of Attention Disorders 13*, 297–309.

Downey, M. (2003) *Effective Coaching*. London: Texere Publishing.

DuPaul, G.J., Weyandt, L.L., O'Dell, S.M. and Varejao, M. (2009) 'College students with ADHD: Current status and future directions.' *Journal of Attention Disorders 13*, 234–250.

Favorite, B. (1995) 'Coaching for adults with ADHD: The missing link between the desire for change and achievement of success.' *ADHD Report 3*, 11–12.

Grant, A.M. and Stober, D.R. (2006) 'Introduction.' In D.R. Stober and A.M. Grant (eds) *Evidence Based Coaching Handbook*. Hoboken, NJ: John Wiley & Sons.

Hallowell, E.N. and Ratey, J.J. (1994) *Driven to Distraction: Recognizing and Coping with Attention Deficit Disorder from Childhood through Adulthood*. New York, NY: Pantheon.

Hinshaw, S.P. and Arnold, L.E. (2015) 'Attention-deficit hyperactivity disorder, multimodal treatment, and longitudinal outcome: Evidence, paradox, and challenge.' *Wiley Interdisciplinary Reviews – Cognitive Science 6*, 1, 39–52.

Knouse, L.E., Cooper-Vince, C., Sprich, S. and Safren, S.A. (2008) 'Recent developments in the psychosocial treatment of adult ADHD.' *Expert Review of Neurotherapeutics 8*, 1537–1548.

Kubik, J.A. (2010) 'Efficacy of ADHD coaching for adults with ADHD.' *Journal of Attention Disorders 13*, 442–453.

Parker, D.R., Field, S., Sawilowsky, S. and Rolands, L. (2013) 'Self-control in postsecondary settings: Students' perceptions of ADHD college coaching.' *Journal of Attention Disorders 17*, 3, 215–232.

Ramsay, J.R. and Rostain, A.L. (2016) 'Adult attention-deficit/hyperactivity disorder as an implementation problem: Clinical significance, underlying mechanism, and psychosocial treatment.' *Practice Innovations 1*, 1, 36–52.

Robbins, S.B., Davenport, M., Anderson, J., Kliewer, W., Ingram, K. and Smith, N. (2003) 'The Role of Motivation and Self-Regulatory Behaviors on First-Year College Adjustment.' Unpublished manuscript. Iowa City, IA: ACT. Cited in V.A. Lotowski, S.B. Robbins and R.J. Noeth (2004) *The Role of Academic and Non-academic Student Factors in Improving College Retention: ACT Policy Report*. Iowa City, IA: ACT.

Tinto, V. (1975) 'Dropout from higher education: A theoretical synthesis of recent research.' *Review of Educational Research 45*, 89–125.

Tinto, V. (1993) *Leaving College: Rethinking the Cause and Cures of Student Attrition*, 2nd edn. Chicago: University of Chicago Press.

Weyandt, L.L. and DuPaul, G.J. (2013) *College Students with ADHD: Current Issues and Future Directions*. New York, NY: Springer.

Whitmore, J. (1992) *Coaching for Performance*. London: Nicholas Brealey.

Young, S. (2017) *The STAR Detective Facilitator Manual: A Cognitive Behavioral Group Intervention to Develop Skilled Thinking and Reasoning for Children with Cognitive, Behavioral, Emotional and Social Problems*. London and Philadelphia: Jessica Kingsley Publishers.

Chapter 7

Assessment of ADHD in Women

—— DR SALLY CUBBIN AND DR ALLYSON PARRY ——

'Thank you from the bottom of my heart …I have been diagnosed with ADHD! It is a relief to finally be taken seriously…'

'I am able to move on and believe that I can make something of myself, which I was giving up on. I have gone from rock bottom to believing that I do have a future.'

INTRODUCTION

Women with attention deficit hyperactivity disorder (ADHD) experience a sobering array of adverse outcomes throughout their life. Treatment is highly effective, yet only a minority of affected women ever obtain a diagnosis and treatment.

The aim of this chapter is to provide an overview of the clinical assessment process. The prevalence of ADHD, a brief overview of the key symptom manifestations in women and the possible reasons for the frequently observed delayed diagnosis in women are first discussed. This is followed by an outline of the essential components of a comprehensive clinical assessment.

ADHD in women is commonly comorbid with other psychiatric conditions and this may, at least in part, account for the frequent delay in the diagnosis of ADHD. The pitfalls of a potential psychiatric misdiagnosis are briefly discussed. Women with ADHD often suffer impairments in multiple domains, such as in their relationships, education, occupation and social life. A description of how these impairments can manifest is provided, alongside an important reminder that women with ADHD are more likely to experience intimate partner violence.

The information provided in the previous sections is then brought together to provide some useful tips and insights for the diagnosis of ADHD in women. Although emotional symptoms are currently not listed as core diagnostic features of ADHD, a brief description of the emotional symptoms commonly seen in women with ADHD is given. A summary of some of the more common associations between certain somatic conditions and ADHD is also provided.

PREVALENCE AND KEY SYMPTOM MANIFESTATIONS
What is the prevalence of ADHD?

Whilst noting significant variability in prevalence estimates (most likely due to methodological differences between studies), a large meta-analysis of the worldwide prevalence of ADHD in individuals aged *18 or younger* estimated a pooled prevalence of 5.3% (Polanczyk *et al.* 2007). It is now recognized that ADHD can occur across the lifespan in both females and males with most cases continuing to be symptomatic into adulthood.

The prevalence of any disorder is dictated by the diagnostic criteria used to define it. The diagnostic criteria are therefore critically important, because they decide who is eligible for treatment and other support, and influence what research is carried out to further understand the disorder.

ADHD runs in families. The high heritability (70–80%) observed *both in children and in adults* indicates that having ADHD is *highly influenced by genetic (inherited) factors*. If the presence of ADHD is largely driven by genetic factors, the individual will not 'grow out' of that intrinsic neurobiological difference. However, the individual may well 'grow out' of the diagnostic criteria for ADHD, which were designed to capture features of ADHD which occur in childhood and adolescence.

For many individuals, how their symptoms manifest will change with increasing age. An adult may realize that it is not appropriate for them to repeatedly get up and down from their chair when in a meeting. The visible hyperactivity previously seen in the classroom may instead manifest as a feeling of internal restlessness and a sense of always being 'on the go', or unable to 'switch off'. The adult with ADHD may no longer differ from an adolescent without ADHD, but nevertheless, continue to remain a *relative* distance from other similarly aged adults in terms of ADHD symptoms and their associated impairments. Indeed, older adults (over 55 years) with ADHD have been shown to have a similar profile of difficulties (such as mood disturbance, poorer general health, rate of divorce and lower income) to those in younger age groups (Kooij *et al.* 2016).

To fulfil the criteria for a diagnosis of ADHD given in the latest version of the *Diagnostic and Statistical Manual of Mental Disorders* (DSM-5) (American Psychiatric Association 2013), several symptoms should have been present before the age of 12 years (NB no impairment is required before this age) and at least five symptoms with impairment in either the inattentive or hyperactive/impulsive domains should be present as an adult. For individuals presenting in adulthood, there are several potential barriers to meeting the criteria required for diagnosis. First, the adult may fail to recall the precise age of symptom onset, especially if they did not experience significant academic or social problems during early adolescence. Protective factors in adolescence, such as high intelligence, living in a structured and supportive environment or presenting with predominantly inattentive problems (which in childhood may not cause problems for others around them), may diminish the accurate recall of symptom onset. Second, adults may 'compensate' for their difficulties to minimize impairments in certain settings. Finally, having 'always been like this', an individual may not make the connection between symptoms and their associated impairments (Kooij *et al.* 2019).

Women with ADHD have many significant adverse outcomes across the lifespan when compared with women without ADHD.

They are less likely to stay in education and more likely to suffer poverty, be divorced, have a teenage pregnancy, suffer intimate partner violence, and to experience childhood abuse, alongside having an increased risk of substance abuse. They are more likely to have comorbid psychiatric disorders and symptoms such as depression, anxiety, suicidal ideation and post-traumatic stress disorder (PTSD). Women with ADHD are also more likely to suffer with chronic pain and sleep disorders and to suffer a loss of self-esteem.

Treatment with stimulant medication is effective. About 7 out of 10 people will get a good response; more when both types of stimulant medications (methylphenidate or dexamfetamine) are separately tried in series, (in order to find the optimal stimulant type for that individual). However, only around 5% of adults with ADHD are receiving treatment, mainly due to under-diagnosis of ADHD.. This is a particularly concerning statistic when the benefits of treatment are appreciated. Large registry studies have demonstrated that treatment is associated with a significant reduction in many adverse outcomes, such as serious road traffic accidents, depression, suicide, substance abuse and criminality.

Why are more males than females diagnosed with ADHD?

'ADHD? ...me? That's just boys bouncing off the walls and misbehaving, isn't it? I just probably need some discipline, more fitness and stuff.'

In clinical practice, the male to female ratio of children diagnosed with ADHD ranges from 1:5 to 1.9:1. In paediatric epidemiological studies, the sex ratio is closer to 1:3, whilst the sex ratio in adulthood is closer to being equal. This discrepancy suggests that girls with ADHD are not being recognized in paediatric clinics. A possible explanation is that girls and women with ADHD present with more 'internalizing' (depression and anxiety), than 'externalizing' (disruptive behaviour or overt aggression) symptoms and are therefore more likely to cause problems for themselves, rather than for others (the latter being more likely to trigger a referral from school). In our experience, even when a brother has a diagnosis of ADHD, the introverted teenage girl with anxiety, depression and self-harm who daydreams at the back of the class and is not disruptive is often not even screened for a possible diagnosis of ADHD. Clinicians see what they are trained to see. Our experience is that ADHD is largely ignored in medical education and consequently, the diagnosis is usually not even thought of. ADHD is commonly both a misdiagnosis and a missed diagnosis.

Key symptoms in women

Females with ADHD are more likely to be diagnosed with a mood disorder prior to their diagnosis of ADHD. This may be due to mood disorders occurring more often as independent events in women with ADHD, the development of a mood disorder secondary to the impairment and distress caused by a delayed ADHD diagnosis, the fact that women are more likely to seek medical help for their low mood compared with men, and the fact that the clinician is more likely to interpret the presenting symptoms of a woman as a mood disorder rather than a manifestation of ADHD.

The core diagnostic features of ADHD are inattention, impulsivity and hyperactivity. The DSM-5 (American Psychiatric Association 2013) presentations of ADHD are sub-classified as (i) inattentive, (ii) hyperactive-impulsive and (iii) a combined type. Women with ADHD who have the inattentive sub-type are even easier to overlook than individuals with hyperactive-impulsive types. In addition, hyperactivity may be experienced more as internal restlessness and sleep disturbance, rather than overt visible hyperactivity (although fiddling with nails or jewellery, or being 'on the go' is common).

It must be emphasized that these features are derived from the childhood criteria that are largely based on overt, hyperaroused, countable behaviours that may not be commonly seen in women. Therefore, the clinician must have a high index of suspicion and make an extra effort to look for features and history that would suggest the lifelong impairment of ADHD.

Women with ADHD may present with impairing emotional symptoms (temper, mood instability and emotional over-reactivity). Importantly, these symptoms are qualitatively *different* to a mood disorder. Emotional symptoms are currently recognized as associated, but not core diagnostic features of ADHD in DSM-5, although research supports their importance in ADHD symptomology and impairment. Figure 7.1 highlights the three main symptom groups seen in ADHD.

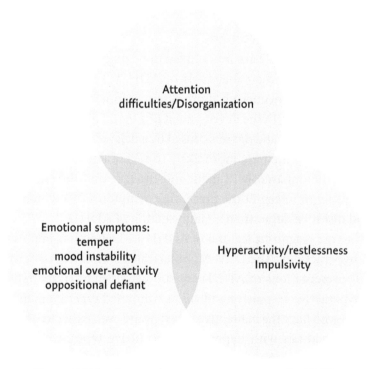

Figure 7.1 The three main symptom groups seen in ADHD

A recent study has provided further evidence supporting the validity of two alternative presentations of ADHD, differentiated by the presence or absence of a significant burden of emotional symptoms. As the patients with more emotional dysregulation represented a more impaired group of individuals, the authors suggested that this categorization offered a more clinically relevant approach to diagnosis than using the DSM-5 criteria. The authors stated that emotional symptoms generate interpersonal conflict, and that this can be a key reason why someone may seek help (Reimherr *et al.* 2020). However, if emotional symptoms are not officially recognized as being intrinsic to ADHD, it is possible that patients will be misdiagnosed, for example with a personality disorder or bipolar disorder.

Females often compensate for their difficulties

A second probable explanation for a delayed diagnosis in women is that females are often good at compensating for their difficulties, although usually there is ultimately a significant detrimental cost to their mental or physical well-being. Ironically, working hard can work against women with ADHD (especially when interviewed by an inexperienced clinician who is unable to see beyond the woman's 'external' achievements).

Women commonly deal with the fear and potential emotional distress of 'messing up again' by becoming 'people pleasers'. They closely attend to the needs of others and often forget their own needs. Alternatively, they aim to be beyond criticism, relentlessly working extra hours in the drive for perfectionism, often driven by harsh self-criticism. However, even this approach can trip them up as increasing success often requires pushing compensation strategies to their limit.

It is therefore not unusual for women to present after a promotion at work, or after the birth of their children, when life becomes even more demanding. The loss of structure and support from parents and from structured education can also cause problems and trigger a referral for assessment. Many women also present after the diagnosis has been made in their children. As they are completing diagnostic questionnaires and interviews for their children's diagnosis, they realise that they have had many of the same symptoms throughout their own lives. Alternatively, women present after having read an article about ADHD and identifying with the clinical features.

Women with undiagnosed ADHD usually have low self-esteem

'I feel like a disappointment. Everything I have committed myself to over the years has ended abruptly. Countless further education courses, over 20 jobs and relationships. I have found it so hard to study, hit brick walls and zero focus. Then I'd realize that I'm still not good enough, or lazy and just bound to disappoint. So, I would stop. I felt like a quitter, weak with no determination.'

The trajectory for many women diagnosed with ADHD in childhood makes sober reading. Further work is needed to determine to what extent early treatment in childhood mitigates the accumulation of these potentially devastating associated impairments and comorbidities.

For the woman who presents in adulthood, there is usually a lifetime of underachievement *relative to ability*, adverse outcomes, low self-esteem and the shame of being 'less than' when compared with their peers. It is crucial to appreciate that high intelligence, academic achievement or apparent high functioning within one domain (e.g. at work) does not exclude a diagnosis of ADHD.

🤚 KEY POINTS

» Treatment for ADHD is highly effective, yet only a minority of affected women ever obtain a diagnosis and treatment.

» ADHD is commonly comorbid with other psychiatric conditions such as a mood disorder, anxiety or substance misuse and this may contribute to the frequent delay in the diagnosis of ADHD.

» Women with ADHD often suffer impairments in multiple domains, such as in their relationships, education, occupation and social life.

» Hyperactivity may manifest as a feeling of internal restlessness and a sense of always being on the go, or unable to switch off, often contributing to sleep disturbance.

» Women may compensate for inattentive symptoms, for example by working harder than their peers, ultimately at a detrimental cost to their mental or physical well-being.

» Women with ADHD may present with impairing emotional symptoms (temper, mood instability and emotional over-reactivity). As these are often not recognized as being intrinsic to ADHD, some patients may be misdiagnosed, for example with a personality disorder or bipolar disorder.

AN OVERVIEW OF THE CLINICAL ASSESSMENT
Components of the assessment

A comprehensive assessment should accurately assess for the key ADHD symptoms, associated symptoms, resulting functional impairments and for the presence of any other psychiatric disorders. A clinical interview should obtain examples of how difficulties interfere in the person's functioning and development at home and in education/work and social environments.

Since the majority of individuals with ADHD will have at least one other common psychiatric diagnosis (e.g. a mood, eating or substance misuse disorder), it is *essential* to look for the presence of other psychiatric disorders. This is a critical part of the assessment and the commonest cause of misdiagnosis.

A developmental history is essential, including a history of neurodevelopmental disorders (e.g. dyslexia or autism). A history of past or present medical disorders should also be obtained, with additional attention being given to enquiring about the common somatic comorbidities in women with ADHD (e.g. obesity, sleep disorders, chronic pain or fatigue), or conditions which may influence options for treatment (e.g. symptomatic cardiovascular disease). Alongside this, a history of medicines used, including the use of illegal drugs, alcohol, caffeine and nicotine, is needed.

A family history should be obtained. A history of allergies and previous drug side effects alongside current medication should be noted. The key elements that should be included in an ADHD assessment are summarized in Figure 7.2.

Figure 7.2 Key elements of an ADHD assessment

The influence of female hormones on ADHD symptoms

It is important to note that many women with ADHD are affected by changes in hormone levels both within the menstrual cycle (with a seemingly high frequency of significant premenstrual dysphoria syndrome) and in the perimenopause period, with an apparent worsening of both the core and associated features of ADHD. It is therefore worth enquiring about the relationship of symptom severity to the menstrual cycle or to the onset of menopausal symptoms and, if present, enquiring whether the woman has any medical contraindications to the use of hormonal contraceptives or hormone replacement therapy (HRT).

Risk assessment

A risk assessment should enquire into suicidal ideation, the use of illicit substances and alcohol, antisocial attitudes and behaviours, harm to self and others, bullying and assault, excessive internet use, unsafe sexual practices, and whether the patient is being exploited in a sexual, financial or social nature. In some cases, a referral for a physical health assessment may be warranted, particularly if there are cardiac concerns that may affect future treatment choices.

Not all compensation strategies are constructive. Drinking alcohol or using cannabis and other substances may be used to cope with inner restlessness, emotional turmoil, social isolation and feelings of rejection. Some may seek to obtain a social network by forming damaging relationships (e.g. joining a gang, engaging in promiscuous and unsafe sexual practices, or being used by others for criminal activities) and a risk assessment needs to seek to identify this.

ADHD and driving

Unfortunately, adults with ADHD experience higher rates of motor vehicle crashes. ADHD medication reduces impulsivity and carelessness, improves attention and makes driving safer. An enquiry should be made as to whether a patient has a driving licence, if they have points on their licence, and about their history of accidents. In the UK, the Driver and Vehicle Licensing Agency (DVLA) provides guidance (Driver and Vehicle Licensing Agency n.d.). The DVLA states that car and motorcycle drivers 'may be able to drive but must notify the DVLA if [their ADHD] affects the ability to drive safely'. All learner drivers with a provisional licence who discover that they have ADHD should notify the DVLA as their ability to drive has not been established. Bus and lorry drivers 'may be able to drive but must notify the DVLA'.

The core diagnostic features and associated impairments

For a diagnosis of ADHD, the individual must have sufficient core symptoms, of sufficient severity, and which are impairing in more than one domain of life (e.g. work, social functioning). A detailed history of symptom onset is required to demonstrate that symptoms (even if there was no associated impairment) were present prior to the age of 12 years. However, as stated earlier, the diagnostic criteria were designed for children and it is crucial that the clinician has a high index of suspicion and makes an extra effort to look for features and history that would suggest the lifelong impairment of ADHD. Figure 7.3 highlights the core diagnostic features of ADHD outlined in DSM-5.

Semi-structured clinical diagnostic interviews are helpful as they guide a less experienced healthcare practitioner through a comprehensive ADHD interview. A commonly used and freely available interview is the Diagnostic Interview of Adult ADHD (DIVA). The most recent edition is the DIVA-5 (Diva Foundation n.d.). Alternatives include the copyrighted Conners' Adult ADHD Interview for DSM-IV (CAADID) and the ADHD Evaluation for Adults (ACE+, Young n.d.), the latter being, like the DIVA, free to download and available in multiple languages.

The use of the Wender–Reimherr Adult Attention Deficit Disorder Scale (WRAADDS, Wender 1995) is recommended to adequately identify the emotional symptoms commonly associated with ADHD. It is available as a self-report scale (which could be sent to a patient in advance), and is also designed as an interviewer-administered scale assessing adult ADHD symptoms grouped into seven domains: attention difficulties, hyperactive/restlessness, temper, affective lability, emotional over-reactivity, disorganization and impulsivity.

Diagnostic features of ADHD (DSM-5)	
Inattentive symptoms are where the patient *often*:	• fails to give close attention to details or makes careless mistakes in schoolwork, at work, or with other activities. • has trouble holding attention on tasks or play activities. • does not seem to listen when spoken to directly. • does not follow through on instructions and fails to finish schoolwork, chores, or duties in the workplace (e.g. loses focus, side-tracked). • has trouble organizing tasks and activities. • avoids, dislikes, or is reluctant to do tasks that require mental effort over a long period of time (such as schoolwork or homework). • loses things necessary for tasks and activities (e.g. school materials, pencils, books, tools, wallets, keys, paperwork, eyeglasses, mobile telephones). • is easily distracted • is forgetful in daily activities.
Symptoms of hyperactivity-impulsivity are where the patient *often*:	• fidgets or taps with hands or feet, or squirms in seat. • leaves seat in situations when remaining seated is expected. • feels restless. • is unable to engage in leisure activities quietly. • is 'on the go' or acting 'as if driven by a motor' • talks excessively. • blurts out an answer before a question has been completed. • has difficulty waiting his or her turn. • interrupts or intrudes on others .

In adults, diagnosis requires five symptoms (six for children) of either inattention or hyperactivity/impulsivity (or both for the diagnosis of 'combined type' ADHD).

Impairment must be at least moderate and present in more than one domain (domestic, social, academic or occupational), and the onset of 'several' symptoms (but not necessarily impairment) should precede age 12 years.

Figure 7.3 Diagnostic features of ADHD (adapted from American Psychiatric Association 2013)

It is important to recognize that many women compensate for their symptoms or hide them as they are ashamed of their difficulties. In addition, the prominence of the symptoms may vary between the home and work environment. The assessor must be aware of these confounding factors and ensure that questions are asked in such a way as to elicit these symptoms. Practical tips to help address this are provided in a following section.

Further detailed information on how to conduct a diagnostic interview is outside the remit of this chapter. For further information on how to diagnose adults with ADHD, and for more information on treatment approaches, the UK Adult ADHD Network (www. ukaan.org) provides training for healthcare professionals.

Collateral information from an informant

Ideally, the clinical assessment should include an interview with someone who knew the patient well as a child. If a reliable informant who knew (and can recall) the individual well during their early childhood cannot be identified, it may be helpful to obtain information from an informant who currently knows the individual well. As ADHD is highly heritable, it is important to be mindful that informants who are family members may also have ADHD, which may affect their judgement of 'typical' behaviour. If there is no informant available, this does not necessarily prevent a diagnosis from being made. Studies have shown that adults with ADHD are often adequate historians themselves and, if anything, they tend to underestimate their symptoms and impairments.

School reports can provide collateral information

School reports may comment on previous behaviours arising from attentional problems (e.g. 'daydreaming', 'careless mistakes', 'distracted', 'unwilling' or 'lacking in confidence to contribute to class discussion'), disorganization with respect to homework and coursework, and regarding a lack of motivation and effort. The *inconsistency* of attention typical of ADHD is particularly problematic if the child has previously demonstrated ability. The inability to score well on the next test is then attributed entirely to a lack of effort on the child's part, with typical comments such as 'she must try harder...she can do it if she really wants to'. Hyperactive or impulsive symptoms are reflected by comments about being too talkative or 'chatty', 'blurting out' answers in class and interrupting. However, a set of school reports with no relevant comments, whilst unusual, does not exclude ADHD.

Sadly, the change in environment, teaching methods and expectations that come with higher education and young adulthood may trip up these young women. The enthusiastic young girl (who always has their hand up, willing to answer questions) may subsequently be viewed as an opinionated adolescent whom the teacher wishes would be quiet. Similarly, the gentle and creative daydreamer becomes an introverted teenager who struggles to keep up and is chastised for being unfocused and disorganized. Although early school reports may be unremarkable, later reports often contain many directives which leave the child in no doubt as to where the fault lies: 'she must try...', 'she must learn to...', 'she should...', 'with a bit more organization and effort she could...', 'come on, Jane – we know you can do it!!!!'

> 'I was always made to feel as if I was stupid or like it was my fault, and despite asking for additional help, I rarely received any. I honestly tried my best, even attending an after-school maths club (after trying to concentrate all day, this was a mammoth task for me), but I never really got better. After a while, I would get frustrated, which resulted in me either walking out of the class or disrupting the other students. It was only when I started college at 16 that a teacher there told me that I may have dyscalculia.'

Some girls get through school without 'causing trouble'. Girls with high intelligence can get by with work done at the last minute and still do well, whilst the tendency in females to 'people please' or strive for perfection can result in excessive working to keep up. Previous educational psychology reports or assessments for difficulties such as dyslexia may be helpful, even if no learning difficulty was diagnosed.

The importance of the family history

'My mother – who is very sceptical about behavioural and psychological conditions, despite showing a lot of symptoms herself – always told me that it was "mind over matter". She never considered that there could be anything inherently wrong with me because she herself had just gotten through life as best she could, grinning and bearing it.'

ADHD is highly genetic; monozygotic twin concordance is around 76% and first-degree relatives have approximately a five-fold increased risk of having ADHD when compared with the general population (Kooij *et al.* 2019). Environmental adversity (such as poverty or a parent with substance abuse or a history of other mental illness) can exacerbate difficulties. Frequently, a careful family history will reveal other family members with ADHD or features possibly suggestive of ADHD.

Neuropsychological tests

Sometimes an objective computerized continuous attention performance test (CPT) is used. However, they are not specific to ADHD and are not essential to make a diagnosis. The QBtech and Test of the Variables of Attention (TOVA) are examples of CPTs. The QBtech have gender-specific normative data for ages from 9 to 60 years. A patient's performance is compared against patients of the same age and gender without ADHD and is represented graphically in an easy to understand format so that they can see if this result reinforces a clinical suspicion of ADHD. Computerized CPTs can be useful for demonstrating impairments in functioning. In our experience, women with ADHD tend to underestimate their symptoms and sometimes worry that they may be over-reporting ('but I suppose everyone has problems like this and it's probably just me making a fuss…'), despite clearly meeting the diagnostic criteria and having a good response to treatment. Objective CPTs may be another way in which to demonstrate 'abnormality' or impairment, although it is possible for some patients with ADHD to hyperfocus and perform relatively well during the task.

Screening for adult ADHD

The WHO Adult ADHD Self-Report Scale (ASRS v1.1) examines *current* ADHD symptoms (Kessler *et al.* 2005). It is a widely used tool and is free to download (https://www.caddra.ca/wp-content/uploads/ASRS.pdf). However, although it is a useful tool, rigid adherence to cut-offs may lead to a relatively high proportion of false negative cases. It takes only 90 seconds longer to do the entire 18-item scale instead of just the 6-item screening version, and the added information is extremely helpful.

Some adult ADHD services demand informant-rated childhood ADHD questionnaires (i.e. scored retrospectively by a parent or other informant looking back at childhood symptoms) as part of their referral process. This may obstruct appropriate referrals because DSM-5 adult diagnostic criteria just require 'some symptoms' of ADHD but not impairment by age 12 years. Furthermore, informants' recall of childhood symptoms has been shown to be unreliable and considerably less reliable than the patient's recollection during a detailed interview. *Insisting on a certain score on an informant-rated childhood ADHD symptom scale is therefore likely to lead to many cases of adult ADHD being missed.*

Rating scales

Alternative rating scales to the ASRS are the Barkley rating scales (Barkley Adult ADHD Rating Scale-IV or BAARS-IV). These assess current ADHD symptoms as well as recollections of childhood symptoms. Directly linked to DSM-IV diagnostic criteria, the scales include both self-report and informant-report forms (e.g. spouse, parent or sibling). A freely available ADHD questionnaire designed for the adult recalling his or her *childhood* behaviour is the Wender Utah Rating Scale (WURS) (http://neurosciencecme.com/library/rating_scales/adhd_wender.pdf). The 25-item version has been validated for use in adults to aid a retrospective diagnosis of ADHD and is designed to be self-rated by the adult patient (Ward, Wender and Reimherr 1993).

Another freely available tool, taking a different approach, is the

Weiss Functional Impairment Rating Scale (WFIRS, Weiss n.d.). A completed WFIRS provides useful prompts to facilitate a thorough exploration of the difficulties and risks associated with ADHD during an assessment interview. A parent report is also available, which is useful for girls and teens or young adults still living at home. A useful questionnaire to give to college tutors for young adults still in education is the CADDRA Teacher Assessment Form. Both are freely available from https://www.caddra.ca/etoolkit-forms/.

🖐 KEY POINTS

» A clinical interview should obtain examples of how difficulties interfere in the person's functioning and development at home and in education/work and social environments.

» The ASRS is a widely used, freely available screening tool.

» A developmental history, a history of medical disorders, a family history, and a history of medicines and drugs used is an essential part of an ADHD assessment.

» Collateral information from an informant and/or school reports provide useful background information.

» A driving history is important as, unfortunately, adults with ADHD experience higher rates of motor vehicle crashes and may need to inform the DVLA of their diagnosis.

» Semi-structured diagnostic interviews, for example the DIVA, are helpful as they guide a healthcare practitioner through an ADHD interview.

» CPTs, for example QbTest or QbCheck, are not specific to ADHD and are not essential to make a diagnosis.

» UK Adult ADHD Network (www.ukaan.org) provides ADHD training for healthcare professionals.

PSYCHIATRIC DISORDERS COMORBID WITH ADHD
ADHD is a highly comorbid disorder

The clinical assessment must identify psychiatric and substance abuse disorders comorbid to ADHD, which may impact on diagnosis or management. About 75% of adults with ADHD will have at least one other mental health or neurodevelopmental disorder. Having three or more psychiatric disorders is associated with a ten-fold increase in the chance of having ADHD (Kooij *et al.* 2019). Sometimes these comorbid conditions, such as depression or anxiety, may have contributed to ADHD being missed, as treatment may have been offered for these other symptoms but with no thought given to the possibility that ADHD may also be present and may be fuelling other mental health problems. The ceaseless mental activity of ADHD, for example, drives rumination, which leads to the exacerbation of anxiety, low mood and sometimes even obsessional thoughts.

Symptoms may be misdiagnosed

A further problem arises if the doctor is not aware of the range of *emotional* symptoms associated with ADHD in adult women. If a doctor does not have ADHD in their differential diagnosis, then ADHD will never be diagnosed. Mood instability and emotional over-reactivity are common in females with ADHD in adulthood. If this is not appreciated, patients are likely to be wrongly diagnosed with a mood disorder such as depression, 'cyclothymia' or bipolar disorder. Similarly, patients may be diagnosed with an emotionally unstable or borderline personality disorder (particularly if very emotionally reactive and impulsive). The psychiatric conditions that are commonly comorbid with ADHD are outlined in Figure 7.4.

The hyperactivity of ADHD often manifests as internal hyperarousal or restlessness in adulthood and is often associated with sleep disturbance. If the chronicity of these symptoms is not appreciated, then they may be interpreted as symptoms of anxiety. Substance misuse is common in individuals with ADHD, and the risk of diversion needs to be identified. Many patients use alcohol or cannabis to reduce the unpleasant internal hyperarousal and to facilitate sleep. Subsequent symptoms of ADHD may then be attributed to substance abuse, rather than looking for the lifelong trait that was present well before the onset of substance abuse.

Figure 7.4 Mental health conditions that are commonly comorbid with ADHD

Women with ADHD often have low self-esteem and feel demoralized by their relative underachievement and other impairments. It is important to differentiate between *despondency* due to repeated failure and *depression*. If the correct diagnosis is not reached, treatment will not be optimal. In addition to being given the wrong medication, women are often referred for talking therapy, usually for low mood or anxiety. Whilst psychological strategies can be extremely helpful, they are often not as beneficial in the case of a woman with undiagnosed ADHD as the therapy is not targeting the core problem. Indeed, even if it were targeting symptoms of ADHD, there is no clear evidence of any lasting change to the *core* symptoms from talking therapies alone. Most women say that 'it was helpful…it made sense at the time…but I still feel anxious'. Indeed, the repeated failure to improve after multiple trials of medications (usually antidepressants) or psychological interventions over many years can reinforce to the woman that *she must be the problem, because she has not improved, despite help.*

Other notable comorbidities: eating disorders

The binge eating disorders and bulimia are more common in patients with ADHD. ADHD symptoms have a negative impact on recovery in eating disorders, and screening for ADHD in all loss of control overeating/bingeing/purging eating disorder patients is recommended. Obesity in both children and adults is also associated with ADHD (Cortese *et al.* 2016).

Other notable comorbidities: suicide and self-harm

A longitudinal prospective study demonstrated that young adult women with combined type ADHD diagnosed in childhood had a higher risk of suicide and self-harm when compared with control subjects or women diagnosed with inattentive type ADHD in childhood (Swanson, Owens and Hinshaw 2014).

Childhood trauma and PTSD

The association between ADHD and the development of PTSD following a traumatic experience suggests that patients with ADHD may be particularly vulnerable to developing PTSD after a traumatic experience. A systematic review has shown a bidirectional association between ADHD and PTSD. Patients with ADHD are significantly more likely to suffer with PTSD, both when compared against healthy controls and when compared against traumatized control subjects. Similarly, there is an increased incidence of ADHD in patients with PTSD when compared with traumatized controls (Antshel *et al.* 2016). Adults with self-reported ADHD admitted for alcohol use showed an overall prevalence of PTSD of 20%, with an increased likelihood in younger patients and in women (El Ayoubi *et al.* 2020).

A large longitudinal study of US soldiers demonstrated that those soldiers with a diagnosis of untreated ADHD prior to deployment to Afghanistan had a significantly increased risk of developing PTSD, generalized anxiety disorder or a major depressive episode in the first nine months after their return when compared against their peer group who did not have a diagnosis of ADHD prior to deployment. Given that the management of ADHD and trauma are different, sensitive enquiry about child, adolescent and adult traumatic experiences may help optimize therapeutic interventions.

Further research is needed to determine if early treatment of ADHD is associated with a reduced risk of developing PTSD, anxiety or depression after exposure to trauma.

The association between ADHD and PTSD has significant clinical implications because adults with ADHD are more likely to experience a range of traumatic experiences such as intimate partner violence and road traffic accidents.

A study examining the retrospective report of childhood trauma in adults with ADHD showed that, in addition to being exposed to trauma in adulthood, emotional abuse and neglect were more common in patients with ADHD when compared with controls. Sexual abuse and physical neglect were also more commonly reported retrospectively by adult females with ADHD, with the presence of ADHD being a predictor of poorer psychosocial functioning in adulthood (Rucklidge *et al.* 2006).

A large (n = 140) longitudinal study of females with ADHD evaluated prospectively throughout childhood, adolescence and young adulthood showed that females exposed to maltreatment by adolescence had poorer young adult functioning. Maltreatment (defined as physical abuse, sexual abuse and/or neglect) occurred overall in 23% of the study participants and was associated with a greater risk of suicide attempts, anxiety, depression, eating disorder symptomatology and lower overall self-worth. This data highlights the potential clinical importance of childhood and adolescent trauma experiences in females with ADHD, especially in those presenting with significant comorbid internalizing symptoms (Guendelman *et al.* 2016).

IMPAIRMENTS IN WORK AND SOCIAL FUNCTIONING

Women with ADHD carry a significant burden of impairments across multiple domains and often have poor self-esteem. Educational, occupational and financial difficulties are more common in individuals in ADHD. Relationship difficulties are common, and women diagnosed with ADHD in childhood are at a significantly increased risk of being exposed to intimate partner violence.

Poor self-confidence and feelings of shame

Most women with ADHD lack self-confidence. They feel disorganized, 'hanging on by a thread' and have had a pre-existing or background level of anxiety their entire lives, often anxious about the possibility of yet another unpredictable 'mess-up'.

Sensitivity to criticism (often from themselves) or rejection, which is superimposed upon a lifetime of unexplained failures or relative underachievement, can lead to fear of failure and the reluctance to try new challenges or relationships. Alternatively, to avoid feeling criticized or rejected, women try to compensate for their difficulties either by focusing on the needs of others or by striving for perfection.

Women with ADHD often feel a great sense of shame; they have always felt 'different' to other girls or women and have never been able to make sense of their seemingly irrational ability to do well in some things and poorly in other (often more basic) tasks. Whilst skilful compensation may mask the difficulties beneath, this deep sense of shame coupled with difficult social relationships can make for a lonely and potentially vulnerable existence.

Fulfilment of traditional female role expectations

Whether modern women seek it out or not, society appears to have a much greater list of role expectations for women than it does for men. The impairments from ADHD make it much harder for women to meet those societal demands.

Women are expected to do it all. More than half of women with children work full time outside of the home. They expect themselves to be able to perform a full day at work and then come home and do what is often more than their fair share of the work needed to keep the household running smoothly.

Society ascribes much more of the care of others to women than it does to men. Women tend to be expected to care for and manage the lives of their children in addition to caring for and managing themselves. Many women with untreated ADHD are just getting by with managing themselves and become overwhelmed when they are expected to manage and direct every moment of their young children's lives. Women are expected to be nurturing, to be emotionally available at any time, and to provide the appropriate level of discipline for each child's developmental needs, all while doing much of the shopping, cooking, cleaning and childcare.

This is an almost impossible level of expectations for anyone, whether they have ADHD or not. Women, especially those with untreated ADHD, seem set up to fail and with that failure have an even greater sense of inadequacy and that they are falling short.

Education and work

'I've gone from job to job over the years, and either quit or moved on to something else, because I get angry, struggle to interact with people and can't stand doing the same thing for hours on end.'

ADHD is associated with learning difficulties, fewer years in education, frequent changes in job and underachievement at work. Individuals often find that they are overlooked for promotions at work or that they tire quickly of a workplace. Alternatively, jobs may end following arguments with bosses. Even individuals with high intelligence may be challenged by deficits in executive functioning such as administrative or planning tasks. If individuals are promoted, the tendency for promotion to be associated with more paperwork and the management of others is potentially problematic and can become overwhelming.

Whilst high intelligence can certainly compensate for impairments to a degree, the stress many women experience from chronically compensating often comes at a significant cost (usually to their health and personal/family relationships). They may display symptoms of 'imposter syndrome', or the relentless drive for perfectionism may become difficult to sustain over many years.

Marriage and other sexual relationships

Individuals with ADHD have twice the risk of marital separation and divorce and often have relationship difficulties relating to their symptoms. Unequal partner relationships due to symptoms can lead to resentment within a couple. Women who are successful in the workplace may have disproportionate difficulty organizing their share of the housework and other tasks such as food shopping.

Whilst some women with ADHD may tire quickly of relationships and rush impulsively into new ones, other women lack the confidence to enter such relationships. The tendency to spend money impulsively can also cause difficulties within a relationship.

Many women suffer with low self-esteem and feel ashamed that they cannot fulfil their roles in the home and workplace as other women appear to do. Intense emotional reactions, sensitivity to rejection or criticism, and feelings of low self-worth can lead to loss of intimacy within a relationship, alongside more general social isolation.

Females with ADHD tend to become sexually active earlier than their peers and have an increased number of sexual partners. Rates of contraction of sexually transmitted infections are five-fold higher and rates of teenage unplanned pregnancies are ten-fold higher due mostly to increased impulsivity and a general lack of planning.

Less often discussed, however, is the burden of sexual dysfunction experienced by patients with ADHD. Some women with untreated ADHD find it difficult to concentrate during sexual intercourse, their mind drifting off to other thoughts. Reduced libido may also occur with antidepressant or anti-anxiety medication. A study of 136 outpatients with ADHD showed that 39% of male and 43% of female ADHD patients respectively had symptoms of a sexual dysfunction. This high prevalence suggests that a discussion about sexual function may be a valuable part of the diagnostic assessment (Bijlenga *et al.* 2018).

Intimate partner violence (IPV)

Females with ADHD diagnosed in childhood have a six-fold increased risk of intimate partner violence in young adult relationships. This significant adverse consequence on relationship functioning may have lasting and far-reaching consequences. A longitudinal study of girls followed prospectively into young adulthood showed that girls with a childhood diagnosis of ADHD had a significantly higher risk of experiencing physical IPV by 17–24 years of age compared with those without childhood ADHD. Even after controlling for socio-demographic, cognitive and psychiatric factors, academic achievement measured during adolescence was a significant mediator of the relationship between childhood ADHD and IPV (Guendelman *et al.* 2016).

Social life and recreation

Just as girls with ADHD may find peer relationships difficult in school, women with ADHD may experience conflicts with social contacts due to miscommunications. They may tire of or find it difficult to keep up with social contacts, leading to the accusation that they are uncaring or self-absorbed. Alternatively, low self-worth and the fear of rejection may prevent women from initiating social contacts in the first place.

The hyperarousal associated with untreated ADHD makes it difficult for the woman with ADHD to properly 'switch off' when possible. Many women become 'busy bees', continuously whirling and developing a 'boom or bust' pattern of exhaustion. They often find it difficult to quieten their brain to allow sleep, whilst inattention prevents the enjoyment of books, films or other activities requiring sustained attention.

Many women use sport as a channel for their energy and to maintain their mood. Injuries arising from intense sporting activity are not uncommon. Obstacles that get in the way of their participation in the sport that they have taken part in throughout their adolescence and early 20s (such as the occurrence of injuries, long working hours, or personal commitments such as having a family) can lead to frustration and a downturn in mood or greater irritability.

Impulsive risk-taking behaviour or moderately excessive impulsive spending can cause problems. Individuals with ADHD also have a higher incidence of road traffic accidents. This may be because of reckless driving or may be due to inattention and excessive fatigue. Anecdotally, speeding or parking tickets are much more common; usually because the woman has left the house too late for her appointment and is then in a rush.

Women with ADHD may present with excessive use of their phone or computer and an 'addiction' to social media. ADHD symptoms are associated with increased addictive technological behaviours, including social media use and gaming. Addictive social media use is more common in women with ADHD (Andreassen *et al.* 2016).

TIPS FOR EXPLORING THE DIAGNOSTIC SYMPTOMS AND IMPAIRMENTS OF ADHD DURING THE ASSESSMENT

One needs to identify sufficient core diagnostic symptoms and to demonstrate that these symptoms are consistent, pervasive, persistent and impairing in several domains of life. The core diagnostic features of inattention, impulsivity/hyperactivity are outlined in Figure 7.3 (above). However, simply asking questions which replicate the phrases used in the diagnostic criteria may not always yield a positive response. Women with ADHD may perform variably according to their level of interest in the task; for example, a woman may be able to perform to a high level in the workplace but find it extremely difficult to function in her social and domestic life. She may be disorganized about her own life (e.g. not deal with her bank statements or insurance paperwork) but be able to focus relatively well on the organizational requirements of her children (e.g. completing paperwork for their school trips) or organizing a holiday in her area of interest. If she (or a collateral historian) is simply asked a broad question about her ability to organize, she may therefore 'average' out her abilities in her response, or feel uncomfortable explaining about her inability to run a household whilst working as a seemingly high-functioning woman. It is therefore important to ask questions which allow for this difference in function to be revealed.

The following section aims to provide some helpful tips and insights into eliciting the key features and impairments of ADHD in women. We would also advise the reader to refer to DIVA-5 as an excellent educational and practical tool.

Core features: hyperarousal (and hyperactivity)

ADHD is often characterized by mental restlessness and an inability to relax or 'switch off' rather than visible physical hyperactivity, although 'fiddling' (e.g. with fingers, nails or hair) may be present. These visible physical manifestations may be observed in the clinic or can be asked about specifically. For internal hyperarousal, it is helpful to ask whether there is a sense of internal restlessness or 'jitter'.

> 'Got about 5 hrs sleep and woke up feeling really hyper, it's like my entire body is filled with electricity!!!'

Multiple thoughts, ceaseless mental activity, a lack of inner peace, a busy, uncontrollable mind or mind wandering are commonly described. Asking a patient, 'How many thoughts do you have in your head at any one time?' can be very helpful, with most patients saying that they have at least two or three, or responding that their brain 'is never quiet'. Some patients feel relieved to share this information, having feared that their multiple thoughts or internal voices would be interpreted by a health professional as them experiencing hearing voices.

> 'It has taken me far longer than usual just to write this diary entry, because I had to keep getting up and walking around. I find it very hard to sit still for any length of time, unless I'm genuinely interested in something… Although I'm interested in potentially unlocking the secret to my weird ways, and hopefully making my life better in the future, I'm finding it all overwhelming and I've got about 100,000 thoughts swirling around my brain at once!!!!'

Some patients will give detailed descriptions of their thought processes, or colourful metaphors.

> 'Inside my brain it is like a whirlwind full of words and pictures, but when I try to reach out to grab one thing, I grab handfuls of them, if that makes sense?'

Often patients complain of anxiety. Whilst anxiety is frequently comorbid with ADHD, it is well worth exploring this in more detail, as symptoms described as 'tension' or 'anxiety' may in fact be a presentation of the physical and mental restlessness seen commonly in ADHD.

Intrinsic to the notion of anxiety is that there must be a large element of *fear*. The diagnosis of all anxiety disorders is based on a pervasive sense that, for no reason, something awful is just about to happen. The hyperarousal of ADHD is a fundamentally different experience (although very often people with ADHD will incorrectly use the term 'anxiety' to describe their inner sense of relentless, driven mental activity). They feel 'driven as if by a motor' that they cannot control. Most people with an ADHD nervous system will report (if asked) that they cannot remember any experience in their entire life in which they have been both mentally and physically 'at peace'. This is due not to fear, but to a constant high level of physical and mental restlessness.

In addition, the ceaseless mental activity common in ADHD exacerbates rumination and flitting migratory worries, further distracting the uneducated physician from a diagnosis of ADHD, with a wrong diagnosis of anxiety or obsessional symptoms sometimes being made instead. When these symptoms are coupled with the common report of insomnia and an inability to 'switch off' at night, a diagnosis of anxiety is often made without much further thought.

If the primary problem is hyperarousal of ADHD and not an anxiety disorder, the symptoms of hyperactivity/hyperarousal are likely to be reduced with ADHD treatment (including stimulants). Anxiety may, of course, be comorbid with ADHD and managed with a medication for anxiety alongside treatment for ADHD.

Core features: inattention

'I excelled in some subjects, particularly at primary school, but my academic prowess very much depended on my level of interest in the topic in question. In English, I was totally engrossed in my work, and used writing stories and reading books as a way of escaping reality and putting my overactive imagination to good use. I distinctly remember my head teacher at primary school telling me that she would love to see me publish a book one day, because she felt that my stories were of a higher standard than my peers. I don't want to blow my own trumpet, but yes, my writing was always above average, and my stories were more creative – however, I lack the attention span and willpower to see a story through until the end! I have attempted to write several books, and they never came to fruition, because the entire story I'd concocted inside my head never seemed to make it onto paper past a couple of chapters (which took months to write due to me having to move on to the next activity within 20 minutes or even less!).'

It is a common misconception that individuals with ADHD are

'hyper', impulsive and full of energy. However, the inattentive form of ADHD is characterized by difficulty engaging in tasks (procrastination) and difficulty sustaining attention (leading to failure to complete), particularly for tasks which they find uninteresting.

It is important to note that attention is *inconsistent* rather than *deficient*. It is not that the individual cannot do a task, rather that they are not neurologically able to get engaged and then stay engaged with the tasks of their lives when the situation demands. Engagement comes and goes from near-perfect engagement and attention (called 'hyperfocus') to a complete inability to get started no matter how hard the person tries.

Patients can focus on topics of interest to them, often with initial enthusiasm. For example, a new hobby or subject may result in hours of internet research or participation with intense focus and concentration, sometimes at the cost of time spent on other responsibilities. This may last for a relatively short time until the interest associated with this new subject wears off. In contrast, there is procrastination on tasks that are mundane or uninteresting, until the pressure of a deadline forces completion at the 'last minute', often resulting in the task not being finished very well (although it is well within the capability of the individual to complete the task well). Specific questions asking about procrastination for uninteresting tasks or the failure to complete tasks when the initial 80–90% of the task has been completed usually elicit a positive response. It is not unusual for the woman to reply that she always completes tasks at work or when someone is dependent on her doing so, but not so at home or when the task is something purely for herself.

Many women with ADHD have a dislike of administration. The question 'How are you with paperwork?' often elicits a laugh and an eye roll. Similarly, the question 'Do you open your post and deal with it reasonably promptly?' normally elicits an 'are you a mind reader?' quizzical and embarrassed look and then the following response: 'How did you know?!!...I just pile it up...oh no...this is really embarrassing!!' Bills are often paid on the very last day, just before interest is added. Even though filing one's taxes is important and the penalties may be severe, many people can go years without filing taxes because they cannot engage with the task because it is so boring and tedious.

Paperwork often prevents women with ADHD from progressing with domestic and work goals. Expenses may not be claimed if there is complex paperwork required. The inability to organize paperwork at home leads to the development of 'paper mountains' which collect alongside other paraphernalia. Women often find it difficult to complete decluttering projects because they cannot face the monotony of sorting through paperwork and other items and they feel overwhelmed. Things often get stored in a box, with the promise that they will be sorted at some point. It can therefore be useful to ask, 'Does a lack of time or difficulties with paperwork get in the way of achieving projects at home and in the workplace?'

Core features: impulsivity

'I have been told many times that I am too outspoken – I just say whatever pops into my head, and I honestly cannot understand why people get offended by the things I say.'

Women may not necessarily be impulsive thrill seekers but excessive talking or interrupting conversations may be common. However, many women have learnt to hold back from talking over people for fear of social rejection.

Frequent, small impulsive buying habits due to poor self-control, rather than excessive spending sprees, are common and lead to poor financial management. It can be useful to ask if problems with money stop them from achieving their goals, or if they quickly spend what they earn without much investment in financial planning.

In the workplace, the individual may have an excellent stream of ideas and energy but be unable to progress them in an organized way. They may suddenly develop an idea and then become relentlessly driven to achieve a specific goal. It can be useful to ask, 'When you have an idea, do you find it difficult to let things go?'

Individuals are often intolerant of waiting in line in queues. The question 'What are you like if there is a long queue at the supermarket checkout?' often elicits the response 'Oh, I just put down my basket and go', or 'I hate that, but I'm OK if I'm on my phone.'

Impulsive individuals are usually quite direct in their approach in conversations. They tend to be 'bottom line' types, who want to quickly get to the point of a conversation. They impatiently finish others' sentences. They may say that they are 'quite blunt' or 'I just say what I think.'

'He says I'm so impulsive that I just get up and go with no word to him or anyone else. I can go out in the evening and get back at midnight, and it feels like I've only been out for an hour max! I lose all track of time, and I make decisions without really thinking them through. Sometimes it even scares me when I think of some of the situations I've gotten myself into, but luckily I've always managed to come out on to the other side in one piece.'

Tips for eliciting the key emotional features of ADHD

'I also get angry very easily and have scared my friends and family when in my rages. A friend described me as a "raving lunatic" when I was angry once, but at the time I didn't see it, I just thought I was shouting my opinions. I can't control my anger, it's like molten lava bubbling away under the surface, ready to erupt at any moment, especially when I get frustrated but also even because of the most trivial, insignificant things.'

Individuals with ADHD often have a 'short fuse', being *quick to temper*, although usually regretting their actions subsequently. They are often emotionally intense and reactive, even if they try to hide aspects of this response. They tend to become upset quite easily and 'over-react' to stress, feeling *easily overwhelmed*, 'hassled and wound up'. When in this state, they can quickly 'fall apart', such that even the simplest tasks become impossible for them to tackle. It is useful to ask questions such as 'Do you often blow things out of proportion or often feel hassled and overwhelmed?'

Some patients may have read about the concept of 'rejection sensitive dysphoria (RSD)' (particularly described on patient ADHD websites in the USA), and feel distressed by these features which they see in their own character (Dodson 2020). To our understanding, RSD is a form of emotional over-reactivity and is described as the exquisite sensitivity to teasing, rejection or criticism, or the individual's perception that they have fallen short of what was expected, whether this perception is real or imaginary. Provocation of RSD appears to result in either an attack of rage against the person that has triggered it, or an episode of profound low mood, usually accompanied by the physical sensation of having being wounded (such as a blow to the chest) and *typically* lasts a few hours to a few days.

Although RSD is not a validated diagnosis, it is our common observation in clinic that many individuals with ADHD strongly identify with the description of RSD and are extremely relieved to have a construct for something that they are usually very ashamed of and which is often very impairing. It is our general experience that patients greatly value reading relatable descriptions of the emotional symptoms (and indeed other features) of ADHD. They often become emotional and relieved, commenting, 'I thought that it was just me...that I was mad...'. Consistent with the description of RSD, the DIVA structured interview also lists 'an excessive intense reaction to criticism' as an impairment.

In addition to emotional over-reactivity, many patients suffer with *mood lability*. Like any personality trait, this occurs daily, often with multiple, short-lived changes of mood within a day. If bored, they may become irritable and prickly, gaining a reputation for being 'moody'. Conversely, when interested, they may become over-excitable and excessively enthusiastic. They frequently have relatively short (hours to a few days) periods of feeling discouraged by failures or being sad and low in mood, which can lead to the wrong diagnosis of depression or a rapid cycling mood disorder (particularly when an outside observer does not see a cause for the sudden change in mood).

'My friend said that people 'tread on eggshells' around me, and quite honestly, I do the same thing with myself... I wake up, and my first thought is, "What mood am I in today?" If I know I'm feeling depressed or moody, I try to avoid others, but sometimes I'm not consciously aware of my demeanour unless others tell me.'

Depression is characterized by the persistent loss of pleasure and energy or interest in things previously enjoyed and is a pervasive state of low mood which lasts for at least two weeks. In depression, the person's moods take on a 'life of their own', separate from the individual's life events and not under their conscious control. In contrast, significant mood changes (as described in RSD) in patients with ADHD are usually triggered by events, are quick in onset, and the mood is congruent to the trigger and relatively short-lasting (hours to a few days).

In our experience, patients find it helpful and reassuring to understand that the mood shifts of ADHD are *normal moods in every respect, other than in their intensity.* Whilst many individuals with ADHD frequently experience intense emotions, they fall within an accepted spectrum of 'normality' and function (to a greater or lesser extent) on a day-to-day basis alongside this. In contrast, individuals with bipolar disorder have prolonged periods of illness during which their behaviour does not fall within the 'normal' spectrum.

These episodes of sudden mood change either seem to run their course with spontaneous improvement, or quickly change when the individual becomes interested and engaged by something. This can be very confusing for the onlooker as the individual has gone from morose/hopeless or enraged, to being happy and engaged within just a few hours. Onlookers are still picking themselves off the floor whilst the patient now carries on with their new interest.

Significant mood instability and impulsive overspending may be mistaken for bipolar disorder if a careful history of the nature of the mood disturbance is not obtained. Helpful differentiating features between the over-stimulation of ADHD and bipolar disorder include the speed of onset of the mood change, and whether it is triggered and congruent, alongside its duration and offset. Bipolar disorder is episodic, with out-of-character prolonged episodes of high and low mood, whereas the mood instability and reactivity in ADHD is a trait and is how the person has always been. Of course, a patient may have both ADHD and bipolar disorder. Similarly, when emotional instability is often triggered by perceived rejection, it can be mistaken for borderline or emotionally unstable personality disorder.

> (Monday): 'Moods: been buzzing all day!!!!!!!!! Managed to clean bedroom but only because I wrote a list and had a break after each task was completed. Been practically bouncing off the walls!!!!!'

> (Tuesday): 'Been really lethargic and can't be bothered to do anything. Have been withdrawn and don't want to speak to or see anyone. Didn't eat anything until now (1am).'

Individuals with ADHD can also feel overwhelmed by sensory stimulation and/or when making decisions. It is sometimes useful to ask if the patient often feels overwhelmed or over-stimulated in busy places, such as large shops or at large social gatherings, or when faced with making decisions about non-urgent issues. Individuals with ADHD who feel overwhelmed under these circumstances often 'shut down', sometimes taking to bed, or 'zone out', unable to function for a while.

Tips for identifying the compensation strategies of women with ADHD

Many undiagnosed women with ADHD implement (almost unconsciously) strategies to help them function. A simple example of this is that a woman may respond that she does not lose objects or belongings. However, if asked, 'How do you respond if people move your stuff?', they may respond, 'I go ballistic!', as they have set places for storing objects to avoid them becoming lost.

They may be frequent list makers (although lists are often only partially helpful as they are not usually followed through to completion). High-functioning women may be excellent and appropriate delegators and have staff in the workplace that 'sweep up' after them for certain administrative and organizational tasks. However, when they change roles and that structure is no longer in place, they may be puzzled by how much they struggle. Occasionally, some women become excessively efficient with work-based paperwork, dealing with it immediately.

'My boss can't believe me; she's barely set the work and I've done it. I daren't leave it because otherwise I will forget to do it.'

Whilst these compensation strategies are helpful to an extent in the short term, they come at the cost of fatigue, burn-out and often constant worry and self-doubt.

'I have all these achievements, but I am not proud of them. I know how much extra work I have had to do to achieve these goals. Anyone would have achieved this if they had worked as hard as me.'

It can sometimes be helpful to ask questions such as:

- Do you spend a lot of time trying to catch up, or covering up mistakes or work not done on time?

- Do you feel that you are just about holding everything together?

- Do you have to spend a lot of time and energy doing extra work to stay organized and in control?

- Does this impact on your ability to relax and enjoy yourself?

Tips for identifying the impairments of ADHD in women

It is worth stressing that many women with ADHD appear to function relatively well. However, they have often underachieved *relative to their innate ability* in both education and in the workplace. They watch as others of equal or less education and experience pass them by on the career ladder, and become increasingly despondent. They know that they have ability and ideas, but they can't seem to 'get it together' to meet their goals.

'After a while I just thought that I was arrogant and deluded to think that I could do more.'

It therefore may be useful to ask, 'Do you feel that you underachieved academically?' or 'Do you feel that you are fulfilling your potential?' and if answered negatively, to then enquire what they think is getting in their way. Whilst anyone can feel that they could do more to achieve their goals, a characteristic feature of individuals with ADHD is that they are frequently distressed that no matter how hard they try, they are unable to come even close to realizing their potential. This discrepancy frequently leads to huge frustration, self-criticism, demoralization and a tremendous loss of self-esteem. Many individuals with ADHD describe that inefficiency in their academic work or occupation contributes to this relative underachievement. Eventually, just trying to work harder and harder becomes non-sustainable.

It is useful to sensitively enquire about romantic relationships and sexual function, as many women are embarrassed about raising this. Similarly, sensitive enquiry about their domestic situation and the extent of their social support outside of the home is often valuable. Many women stop inviting people over to their house. The reasons for this are multi-factorial; for example, it is 'yet another thing' to organize and becomes a stress and not a pleasure. Individuals with ADHD often live in the 'here and now' and find planning things in advance quite challenging as they don't know how they will feel about the event on the day itself (and therefore may regret issuing the invitation). Women often feel ashamed if their home is disorganized or messy, and feel embarrassed about inviting people over as a result. A controlling and abusive partner may not wish the woman to socialize with friends, either inside or outside of the home. It is therefore useful to ask, 'Do you often invite people over to your house to socialize?' and then to sensitively enquire further for the reason if not.

Finally, it is useful to gently enquire about the effect of the woman's ADHD on her self-esteem. Many women have a deep sense of shame that they are 'less than', 'imposters' or difficult, irrational people due to their relative underachievement and their emotional reactivity or lability. The accumulation of these experiences over decades can cause a significant loss of self-confidence and shame, which probably makes them less likely to seek help.

'By not being diagnosed till now, I have struggled massively. Suspected bipolar, depression. The downs are darker and more lonely than you can imagine. A number of times I have self-harmed during these. Very few people know – it's a way of punishing myself for being less than my potential, disappointing.'

🖐 KEY POINTS

» Attention in ADHD is *inconsistent* rather than *deficient*. Patients can concentrate on topics of interest to them, often with initial enthusiasm, until the interest associated with this new subject wears off.

» About 75% of adults with ADHD will have at least one other mental health disorder.

» Having three or more psychiatric disorders is associated with a ten-fold increase in the chance of having ADHD.

» Symptoms described as 'tension' or 'anxiety' may in fact be a presentation of the mental restlessness seen commonly in ADHD. The ceaseless mental activity common in ADHD can exacerbate rumination and insomnia.

» Mood instability and emotional over-reactivity are common in females with ADHD.

» Significant mood instability and impulsive overspending may be mistaken for bipolar disorder if a careful history of the nature of the mood disturbance is not obtained.

» Many patients use alcohol or cannabis to reduce the unpleasant internal hyperarousal and to facilitate sleep.

» ADHD is associated with learning difficulties, less years in education, frequent changes in job and underachievement at work.

» Individuals with ADHD have twice the risk of marital separation and divorce.

» Binge eating disorders and obesity are more common in patients with ADHD.

» Some women with untreated ADHD find it difficult to concentrate during sexual intercourse. One study (Bijlenga *et al.* 2018) found that 43% of female ADHD patients had symptoms of a sexual dysfunction.

» Treatment may be offered for other symptoms but with no thought given to the possibility that ADHD may be fuelling other mental health problems.

» Some patients may have read about the concept of 'rejection sensitive dysphoria (RSD)' and feel distressed by these features. RSD is described as the exquisite sensitivity to teasing, rejection, criticism, or their own perception that they have fallen short, real or imaginary.

THE ASSOCIATION BETWEEN ADHD AND SOMATIC MEDICAL CONDITIONS

It is important to recognize the presence of comorbid somatic conditions which may affect the patient with ADHD. These are outlined in Figure 7.5. A recent review described well-documented associations between ADHD and asthma, obesity and sleep disorders, and possible associations between ADHD and other conditions such as fibromyalgia and epilepsy (Instanes *et al.* 2018).

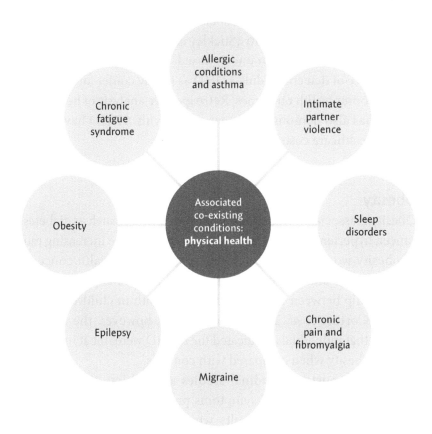

Figure 7.5 Physical health conditions that are
commonly comorbid with ADHD

Physical health conditions may be more likely to become chronic if patients are forgetful about aspects of their health (such as healthcare follow-up appointments) or have negative lifestyle factors, such as poor sleep or smoking (Kooij *et al.* 2019). A study of health outcomes in women demonstrated that women with ADHD had triple the prevalence of insomnia and chronic pain in comparison with women without ADHD, even after adjustments for age, race, education and income (Fuller-Thomson, Lewis and Agbeyaka 2016).

Another large study has shown that individuals with five or more diseases had over three times higher odds for possible ADHD and that this association was observed in all age groups. Stressful life events, disordered eating, depression and anxiety were shown to be significant mediators of this association between possible ADHD and physical multi-morbidity (Stickley *et al.* 2017). Given that many adults with ADHD remain undiagnosed, this study highlighted the importance of detecting adult ADHD as it may confer an increased risk of poorer health outcomes. Retrospective analysis of healthcare claims has also demonstrated that adults with ADHD have much higher healthcare costs.

Obesity

Obesity is associated with multiple chronic diseases such as diabetes, cancer, hypertension and cardiovascular disease. The increasing rate of obesity worldwide is therefore a major public health concern. A large meta-analysis of cross-sectional studies showed a clear relationship between ADHD and obesity, both in children and in adults (Cortese *et al.* 2016). Interestingly, however, the analysis showed that individuals medicated for ADHD were not at increased risk for obesity when compared with controls.

Whilst robust longitudinal studies are lacking, the available data suggests that ADHD symptoms predate the onset of obesity. Inattention may cause difficulty when planning meals, or binge eating may occur as a manifestation of impulsivity. Comorbid depression or anxiety may lead to unhealthy eating habits, whilst circadian rhythm disturbances or other sleep disorders leading to short sleep duration are also associated with obesity. The assessing physician needs to understand the extent of these contributing yet modifiable factors to optimally educate and manage the patient.

Sleep-related disorders

'I got a grand total of 1.5 hrs sleep last night, and I was still hyper for most of the day!! I only started to crash at about 8pm (it's now 11.34pm and although I'm starting to slow down a bit, I'm still awake, so perhaps tonight will be devoid of sleep as well…great, not!!).'

'People often marvel at my ability to stay awake for up to 48 hrs and not be a complete zombie, no caffeine required, but for me it's a curse… I can be awake all those hours, and still not complete a single task! Instead, I tend to start ten tasks and walk away halfway through. I've got piles of half-finished things, paperwork, books, dishes that were all supposed to be washed, clean clothes that are half put away and half strewn across the bed, jewellery-making equipment, etc., all over the flat. I can attempt to tidy a room, but ten minutes later I'm bored as hell, my mind is whirring and I end up leaving behind more mess than there was in the first place!'

Most adults with ADHD suffer with some form of sleep disturbance which is *central to the ADHD itself*. Associated medical conditions may also impact on sleep, alongside the behavioural consequences of ADHD and/or the presence of any comorbid mood disorder. The literature also documents an association between the use of stimulant medication and insomnia. Chronically impaired sleep restriction (or fragmentation due to multiple awakenings) causes excessive daytime fatigue and reduced cognitive-affective and physical functioning, thereby worsening ADHD symptoms and increasing the risk of road traffic accidents. The prevalence of sleep problems in patients with ADHD increases with age, with a notable increase in prevalence around the time of puberty.

'Exactly the same as yesterday, stayed up all night again and didn't fall asleep till 5pm today. I woke up around midnight, I am now writing this at 2am because I'm wide awake. I try so hard to sleep but my brain doesn't switch off!! I've cut out caffeine, but it doesn't help.'

Sleep and stimulant medication
The side effect of insomnia with stimulant medication is well described in the literature and most clinicians discuss insomnia as a potential side effect with patients prior to starting stimulant treatment for ADHD. However, it is crucial that a clear history of sleep function

is obtained *prior* to starting ADHD medication. Failure to do this may otherwise lead the clinician to assume that any subsequently reported disturbance of sleep whilst on ADHD medication is a side effect of treatment. Indeed, we have observed some patients admit to being too anxious to report sleep difficulties on treatment, for fear of the stimulant medication being discontinued. When further questioned, it is usually apparent that the sleep problems were present and entrenched well *before* starting any stimulant medication. It is therefore important to understand what has *changed* with regards to their sleep pattern since a new medication has been started. Many of these patients are very able to sleep in the afternoon whilst their stimulant medication is on board. This 'paradox' is worth highlighting with the patient, to reduce any anticipatory anxiety about night-time insomnia on medication. Indeed, some patients report that they sleep better at night-time when they have had a dose of stimulant medication in the second half of the day as this quietens the 'busy brain' at night-time and helps them 'switch off'.

The stimulant medication is extremely good at keeping patients 'on task'. Therefore, insomnia on stimulants can arise because the patient is simply 'on task' and engrossed in the interesting project that they are doing late at night, finding themselves still working on a project in the early hours. This is a different subjective experience to the inability to 'switch off' due to a busy, flitting and restless brain that arises as a core feature of untreated ADHD. If the patient is able to gain insight into this difference, then being 'on task' at night can sometimes be put to good use with the redirection of focus to the pursuit of excellent sleep hygiene and the use of meditation etc. However, sometimes even with these caveats and the implementation of the best sleep hygiene measures, some patients are simply unable to take a stimulant medication which is still 'in the system' at night-time, reporting significant initial insomnia. Alternative medical treatments for this problem are described in the following chapter.

Causes of sleep disturbance in patients with ADHD

Patients with ADHD can have difficulty with multiple components of sleep, including getting off to sleep, staying asleep and not feeling refreshed on waking in the morning. Sleep restriction or fragmentation may be secondary to a circadian rhythm disturbance disorder. Other associated medical causes of sleep disturbance include restless leg syndrome and periodic limb movements of sleep. Obesity associated with ADHD can lead to sleep apnoea secondary to intermittent partial or complete obstruction of the upper airways.

CIRCADIAN RHYTHM SLEEP DISTURBANCE

A circadian rhythm sleep disturbance (CRSD) is a problem relating to the timing of when a person sleeps and is awake. It is caused by changes within the endogenous circadian rhythm or how this intrinsic rhythm is aligned with the external environment. Over 70% of patients with ADHD have evidence of a CRSD. Many patients have delayed sleep phase syndrome (DSPS), which is characterized by the patient regularly going to sleep and waking over two hours later than normal. This association between CRSD and ADHD may be both biological and behavioural (Bijlenga et al. 2019).

Indeed, many patients with ADHD like being up late at night. They are 'night owls' and feel at their most productive in the evening when the rest of the household is quiet. Parents are exasperated that their teenage daughter who has done seemingly little productive work all day is now, at midnight, choosing to tidy her room with a missionary zeal not seen in daylight hours. Keeping these sorts of hours may be possible for several years but this pattern quickly becomes challenging with the added responsibilities of increasing work and family demands. Whilst a university student may be able to be productive until 3am, knowing that they can sleep in until midday the following day, this luxury is not afforded to most women who have families to look after alongside their own work. Having a chaotic sleep–wake cycle and not waking up until late morning also makes it more difficult for a patient to keep a consistent routine with medication. The patient perceives that they should not take their stimulant medication that day as it is now the mid-afternoon and they fear that it will keep them up all night again.

In the clinic, many patients describe not being able to 'switch off' at night-time to go to sleep, either at the start of sleep or if they wake in the night and then try to return to sleep. Patients commonly report it taking one to two hours to fall asleep. They report an over-active mind, which is often interpreted wrongly as anxiety. Many keep a pad of paper and a pen by the bed to note down thoughts that come to them for fear of forgetting them the next day. They report to the doctor, 'I'm not worried… I'm just awake… I can't switch off.' Often, they lie awake, becoming more and more frustrated by their inability to go to sleep, watching the clock until the early hours. Alternatively, they may wander downstairs and sit for an hour or two listening to the radio or play on their electronic device until they are so fatigued that they fall asleep. In the morning, patients often cannot wake despite the use of multiple alarms and multiple 'prods' by family members. They can be extremely irritable and cross with any calls from family who try to wake them (despite having asked the previous day to ensure that they are woken up in good time). Often the patient does not feel fully awake until noon.

Patients may benefit from good sleep hygiene, the use of sunrise lights (or more exposure to daylight) to reset their internal circadian rhythm, and/or the use of melatonin.

RESTLESS LEG SYNDROME AND PERIODIC LIMB MOVEMENTS OF SLEEP

Restless leg syndrome (RLS) is an urge to keep moving the legs (and, rarely, the arms) and is usually experienced when sitting resting in the evening and particularly when in bed at night-time. Patients describe having to get up and walk around the bedroom to relieve the unpleasant feelings. This is a very 'physical' and uncomfortable sensory experience affecting the legs and can, with careful enquiry, be separated from the internal sense of restlessness arising as a core feature of ADHD. Studies have shown that up to 44% of patients with ADHD have symptoms of RLS (Cortese *et al.* 2015) and this may further impede their ability to get off to sleep.

Patients with ADHD may also be more likely to suffer with periodic limb movements of sleep (PLMS), which is the frequent movement of the legs during sleep. The patient is not bothered by this unless they happen to wake up in the night feeling cold and realize that the duvet is on the floor. However, any bedfellow is usually very bothered by being repetitively kicked and usually decamps to an adjacent bedroom.

If RLS or PLMS are problematic, then referral to a neurologist for expert advice is recommended.

OBSTRUCTIVE SLEEP APNOEA

In obstructive sleep apnoea (OSA), intermittent partial or complete obstruction of the upper airways leads to a history from a bedfellow of loud snoring, gasping or pauses in breathing (apnoeas) during sleep. The patient reports excessive daytime sleepiness and feeling unrefreshed after sleep. Intermittent hypoxia is associated with arousals and sleep fragmentation. Obesity is associated both with OSA and with ADHD. Cognitive impairment may be driven by the fatigue from chronically poor sleep associated with OSA and so it is an important differential diagnosis to consider.

The diagnosis of OSA is established by clinical evaluation and specialist sleep tests. Treatment with continuous positive airway pressure may improve cognitive symptoms, if they are due to OSA and not ADHD. Medical complications of untreated OSA include hypertension and other cardiac problems alongside metabolic syndromes.

Asthma and allergenic conditions

Asthma is a chronic inflammatory disorder of the airways with episodic worsening. Reversible airflow obstruction and bronchospasm cause wheeze and cough. Asthma commonly starts in childhood and is associated with anxiety and depression. Morbidity and mortality from asthma is associated with poor attendance for routine medical asthma follow-up and poor self-management. A meta-analysis of clinical and registry data studies demonstrated that adults with ADHD were more likely to have a comorbid diagnosis of asthma when compared with controls. A further large population-based study also showed that there was a significant association between asthma and ADHD, even when controlling for multiple cofounding variables (Cortese *et al.* 2018).

A possible link between ADHD and other allergic conditions has been suggested by a large study which showed that patients with ADHD were more likely to have allergenic disorders (asthma, allergic rhinitis, atopic dermatitis and allergic conjunctivitis) when compared with healthy controls (Instanes *et al.* 2018).

Epilepsy

Epilepsy occurs in up to 1% of the general population and is defined as an enduring predisposition to generate epileptic seizures. Several studies have demonstrated an increased prevalence of ADHD in adult patients with epilepsy when compared with control subjects, with ADHD occurring in 10–30% of patients with epilepsy.

Manufacturers have cautioned against the use of stimulant medication and atomoxetine in patients with a history of epilepsy. A large study of adult patients with ADHD showed that both male and female patients with ADHD had a higher risk for any seizure compared with non-ADHD controls (odds ratio >2.3). However, a within individual comparison showed that the prescription of ADHD medication was concurrently associated with a *lower* risk of seizures (odds ratio 0.71), with or without a prior history of seizures. Furthermore, a long-term within individual comparison analysis showed no evidence of an association between medication use for ADHD and seizures (Wiggs *et al.* 2018). A second large study also showed no evidence that the prescription of ADHD medication was associated with an increased rate of acute seizures (Brikell *et al.* 2019). These two studies suggest that a diagnosis of epilepsy should not automatically prevent patients with epilepsy from receiving treatment for their comorbid ADHD.

Fibromyalgia and chronic pain

Fibromyalgia syndrome (FMS) is a common and chronic pain disorder which is much more common in women. Common clinical manifestations include chronic widespread pain, muscle tenderness and joint stiffness, poor sleep and fatigue, mood disturbance and cognitive symptoms. The cognitive impairment is often described by patients as 'brain fog' or 'fibro-fog' and this can sometimes be the most disabling aspect of the condition.

Since FMS is frequently comorbid with anxiety or depressive disorders, it is conceivable that associated cognitive symptoms may be both under-appreciated and attributed to a co-existing mood disorder. However, it is possible that the cognitive (and mood) symptoms are sometimes due to the presence of ADHD. Studies which have examined the comorbidity between FMS and ADHD, whilst being relatively small and exploratory in nature, have demonstrated a high prevalence of ADHD symptoms in patients with FMS. One of the largest studies (n = 123) which used a screening tool for ADHD indicated that the co-occurrence of adult ADHD in FMS may be highly prevalent (44%) and may also significantly impact the morbidity of FMS (Van Rensburg *et al*. 2018). To date, there have not been any randomized controlled trials which have looked at the effect of ADHD treatment on FMS core symptoms in patients with comorbid ADHD and FMS.

It is unclear whether adults with ADHD symptoms have an increased likelihood for experiencing significant pain from conditions other than fibromyalgia. However, one large study of the general adult population (n = 7403) looked at the relationship between a self-reported screen for ADHD and the presence of pain (assessed by the degree to which it had interfered with work activity in the previous month). After adjusting for socio-demographic and physical health conditions, the authors reported a significant association between a high ADHD symptom score and extreme pain, which remained significant even after adjusting for common comorbid mental disorders (Stickley *et al*. 2016).

Chronic pain can have a significant impact on quality of life. A recent small prospective longitudinal follow-up study of females diagnosed with ASD and/or ADHD prior to adulthood demonstrated that 77% of women reported chronic pain and that this was associated with a particularly poor health-related quality of life. The authors also interestingly observed that women with ADHD who had ongoing treatment with stimulants had a lower prevalence of chronic widespread pain than those not treated. Further work is required to evaluate these preliminary findings.

Patients with Ehlers-Danlos syndrome (EDS) and hypermobility syndrome (HS) frequently report musculoskeletal pain. A large population-based cohort study of individuals with EDS or HS and their unaffected siblings showed that these individuals with HS or EDS are at a significantly increased risk of being diagnosed with psychiatric disorders including ADHD. The interesting observation that unaffected siblings of patients with EDS or HS also had an increased risk of ADHD suggests that this may be due to early environmental and/or genetic factors (Cederlöf *et al.* 2016).

Chronic fatigue syndrome (CFS)

Chronic fatigue syndrome is a disorder characterized by significant fatigue which worsens with physical or mental activity, which does not improve with rest, and which is not explained by any underlying medical condition. The cause of CFS is unknown, although it may possibly be triggered by events such as psychosocial stress or a viral infection. The diagnosis is made clinically. Manifestations may include fatigue, impaired memory and concentration, unexplained musculoskeletal pain, sore throat, flu-like symptoms, unrefreshing sleep, and extreme and prolonged exhaustion after physical or mental exertion. Possible treatments include supportive management, cognitive behavioural therapy and graded exercise programmes.

A study of 158 patients with CFS, assessed for the presence of childhood and adult ADHD by clinical interview and ADHD-specific scales, showed that 30% of CFS patients had childhood ADHD, with ADHD persisting into adulthood in 21% of patients. This study suggested that CFS patients with comorbid ADHD may have a more severe psychopathological clinical profile, with more severe anxiety and depressive symptoms and a higher risk of suicide than CFS patients without ADHD (Sáez-Francàs *et al.* 2012).

✋ KEY POINTS

» Obesity and binge eating disorders are more common in patients with ADHD.

» ADHD and asthma are also associated.

» Patients with ADHD can have difficulty with getting off to sleep, staying asleep and waking in the morning.

» Some patients report that they sleep better at night-time when they have had a dose of stimulant medication in the second half of the day as this quietens the 'busy brain' and helps them 'switch off'.

» Other possible associations are between ADHD and epilepsy, allergic conditions, fibromyalgia and chronic pain as well as chronic fatigue syndrome.

» Manufacturers have cautioned against the use of ADHD medication in patients with a history of epilepsy. Yet ADHD medication has been associated with a *lower* risk of seizures.

CONCLUSION

The discrepancy in prevalence between childhood and adult ADHD indicates that girls are not being referred for an assessment in childhood but are more likely to be diagnosed in adulthood, perhaps due to an increase in difficulties coping and more public knowledge leading to self-presentation as an adult.

There are specific barriers to the recognition of ADHD in girls and women. These include different patterns of behaviours compared with men, gender biases due to stereotypical expectations, other disorders being more likely to be diagnosed, and the ways that women can compensate, which mask or overshadow the effects of ADHD. There is a misunderstanding that ADHD is a behavioural disorder that primarily affects males.

Females with ADHD remain more likely to be unrecognized

or misidentified, leading to lower rates of referral, assessment and treatment for ADHD and with implications for long-term social, educational and mental health outcomes. The focus on broader symptoms, especially those of emotional regulation, as part of an assessment, as well as considering DSM-5 criteria, allows for a more complete understanding of your patient. Symptoms that are part of ADHD-related emotional dysregulation may be responsive to ADHD medication (Asherson 2005). This approach will very probably promote better clinical care and prevent the need for additional psychotherapeutic or pharmacological approaches due to the misidentification of a comorbid disorder.

A better understanding of ADHD in girls and women is needed among clinicians that refer, as well as better assessment skills among specialists, if we are to improve the longer-term well-being and functional clinical outcomes of these women.

'The dots are starting to come together and for the first time at 28, I'm starting to feel hopeful. Because of this diagnosis, I am starting to believe that I am worth more. I'm not thick, or an idiot, or mad!...I am sort of mourning the last ten years. Want to give the small me a big hug. Better late than never though isn't it?...Actually, just try and avoid the "late", so that this expression doesn't have to be said. That expression is usually said when you're really saying something else in your head. It seems to me that "late" shouldn't be a possibility.'

REFERENCES

American Psychiatric Association (2013) *Diagnostic and Statistical Manual of Mental Disorders: DSM-5*, 5th edn. Arlington, VA: American Psychiatric Association.

Andreassen, C.S., Billieux, J., Griffiths M.D., Kuss, D.J. *et al.* (2016) 'The relationship between addictive use of social media and video games and symptoms of psychiatric disorders: A large-scale cross-sectional study.' *Psychology of Addictive Behaviours 30*, 2, 252–262.

Antshel, K.M., Biederman, J., Spencer, T.J. and Faraone, S.V. (2016) 'The neuropsychological profile of comorbid post-traumatic stress disorder in adult ADHD.' *Journal of Attention Disorders 20*, 12, 1047–1055.

Asherson, P. (2005) 'Clinical assessment and treatment of attention deficit hyperactivity disorder in adults.' *Expert Review of Neurotherapeutics* 5, 4, 525–539.

Bijlenga, D., Vollebregt, M., Kooik, S. and Arns, M. (2019) 'The role of the circadian system in the etiology and pathophysiology of ADHD: Time to redefine ADHD.' *Attention Deficit Hyperactivity Disorder* 11, 1, 5–19.

Bijlenga, D., Vroege, J., Stammen, A., Breuk, M. *et al.* (2018) 'Prevalence of sexual dysfunctions and other sexual disorders in adults with attention-deficit/hyperactivity disorder compared to the general population.' *Attention Deficit Hyperactivity Disorders* 10, 1, 87–96.

Brikell, I., Chen, Q., Kuja-Halkola, R., D'Onofrio, B.M. *et al.* (2019) 'Medication treatment for attention-deficit/hyperactivity disorder and the risk of acute seizures in individuals with epilepsy.' *Epilepsia* 60, 2, 284–293.

Cederlöf, M., Larsson, H., Lichtenstein, P., Almqvist, C., Serlachius, E. and Ludvigsson, J.F. (2016) 'Nationwide population-based cohort study of psychiatric disorders in individuals with Ehlers-Danlos syndrome or hypermobility syndrome and their siblings.' *BMC Psychiatry* 4, 16, 207.

Cortese, S., Konofal, E., Lecendreux, M., Arnulf, I. *et al.* (2015) 'Restless legs syndrome and attention-deficit/hyperactivity disorder: A review of the literature.' *Sleep* 28, 8, 1007–1013.

Cortese, S., Moreira-Maia, C.R., St Fleur, D., Morcillo-Peñalver, C. *et al.* (2016) 'Between ADHD and obesity: A systematic review and meta-analysis.' *American Journal of Psychiatry* 173, 1, 34–43.

Cortese, S., Sun, S., Zhang, J., Sharma, E. *et al.* (2018) 'Association between attention deficit hyperactivity disorder and asthma: A systematic review and meta-analysis and a Swedish population-based study.' *Lancet Psychiatry* 5, 9, 717–726.

Diva Foundation (n.d.) *DIVA-5 (Diagnostic Interview of Adult ADHD).* Accessed on 27 July 2020 at https://www.divacenter.eu/DIVA.aspx.

Dodson, W. (2020) 'How ADHD ignites rejection sensitive dysphoria.' Accessed on 27 July 2020 at https://www.additudemag.com/rejection-sensitive-dysphoria-and-adhd.

Driver and Vehicle Licensing Agency (n.d.) *Attention Deficit Hyperactivity Disorder (ADHD) and Driving.* Accessed on 07 September 2020 at www.gov.uk/adhd-and-driving.

El Ayoubi, H., Brunault, P., Barrault, S. and Maugé, D. (2020) 'Posttraumatic stress disorder is highly comorbid with adult ADHD in alcohol use disorder inpatients.' *Journal of Attention Disorders* 43, 300–304.

Fuller-Thomson, E., Lewis, D.A. and Agbeyaka, S.K. (2016) 'Attention-deficit/hyperactivity disorder casts a long shadow: Findings from a population-based study of adult women with self-reported ADHD.' *Child Care Health & Development* 42, 6, 918–927.

Guendelman, M.D., Ahmad, S., Meza, J.I., Owens, E.B. and Hinshaw, S.P. (2016) 'Childhood attention-deficit/hyperactivity disorder predicts intimate partner victimization in young women.' *Journal of Abnormal Child Psychology 44*, 1 155–156.

Instanes, J., Klungsøyr, K., Halmøy, A., Fasmer, O. and Haavik, J. (2018) 'Adult ADHD and comorbid somatic disease: A systematic literature review.' *Journal of Attention Disorders 22*, 3, 203–228.

Kessler, R.C., Adler, L., Ames, M., Demler, O. *et al.* (2005) 'The World Health Organization Adult ADHD Self-Report Scale (ASRS): A short screening scale for use in the general population.' *Psychological Medicine 35*, 245–256.

Kooij, J.J.S., Bijlenga, D., Salerno, L., Jaeschke, R. *et al.* (2019) 'Updated European Consensus Statement on diagnosis and treatment of adult ADHD.' *European Psychiatry 56*, 1, 14–34.

Kooij, S., Michielsen, M., Kruithof, H. and Bijlenga, D. (2016) 'ADHD in old age: A review of the literature and proposal for assessment and treatment.' *Expert Review of Neurotherapeutics 16*, 12, 1371–1381.

Polanczyk, G., Silva de Lima, M., Horta, B.L., Biederman, J. *et al.* (2007) 'The worldwide prevalence of ADHD: A systematic review and metaregression analysis.' *American Journal of Psychiatry 164*, 6, 942–948.

Reimherr, F.W., Roesler, M., Marchant, B.K., Gift, T.E. *et al.* (2020) 'Types of adult attention-deficit/hyperactivity disorder: A replication analysis.' *Journal of Clinical Psychiatry 81*, 2. DOI: 10.4088/JCP.19m13077.

Rucklidge, J.J, Brown, D.L., Crawford, S. and Kaplan, B.J. (2006) 'Retrospective reports of childhood trauma in adults with ADHD.' *Journal of Attention Disorders 9*, 4, 631–641.

Sáez-Francàs, N., Alegre, J., Calvo, N., Ramos-Quiroga, J.A. *et al.* (2012) 'Attention-deficit hyperactivity disorder in chronic fatigue syndrome patients.' *Psychiatry Research 200*, 2–3, 748–753.

Stickley, A., Koyanagi, A., Takahashi, H. and Kamio, Y. (2016) 'ADHD symptoms and pain among adults in England.' *Psychiatry Research 246*, 326–331.

Stickley, A., Koyanagi, A., Takahashi, H., Ruchkin, V., Inoue, Y. and Kamio, Y. (2017) 'Attention-deficit/hyperactivity disorder and physical multimorbidity: A population-based study.' *European Psychiatry 45*, 227–234.

Swanson, E., Owens, E. and Hinshaw, S. (2014) 'Pathways to self-harmful behaviors in young women with and without ADHD: A longitudinal examination of mediating factors.' *Journal of Child Psychology & Psychiatry 55*, 5, 505–515.

Van Rensburg, R., Meyer, J., Hitchcock, S. and Schuler, C. (2018) 'Screening for adult ADHD in patients with fibromyalgia syndrome.' *Pain Medicine 19*, 9, 1825–1831.

Ward, M.F., Wender, P.H. and Reimherr, F.W. (1993) 'The Wender Utah Rating Scale: An aid in the retrospective diagnosis of childhood attention deficit hyperactivity disorder.' *American Journal of Psychiatry 150*, 6, 885–890.

Weiss, M.D. (n.d.) *Weiss Functional Impairment Rating Scale – Parent Report (WFIRS-P)*. Accessed on 27 July 2020 at https://www.caddra.ca/wp-content/uploads/WFIRS-P.pdf.

Wender, P.H. (1995) *Attention-Deficit Hyperactivity Disorder in Adults*. New York, NY: Oxford University Press.

Wiggs, K.K., Chang, Z., Quinn, P.D., Hur, K. *et al.* (2018) 'Attention-deficit/ hyperactivity disorder medication and seizures.' *Neurology 90*, 13, e1104– e1110.

Young, S. (n.d.) *ACE+: A Diagnostic Interview of ADHD in Adults*. Psychology Services. Accessed on 07 September 2020 at https://www.psychology-services.uk.com/adhd.

Chapter 8

Treatment of ADHD in Women

—— DR SALLY CUBBIN ——

Attention deficit hyperactivity disorder (ADHD) is one of the most misunderstood, underdiagnosed and yet treatable disorders in psychiatry. Once settled on a dose that suits the individual, the majority obtain a rapid reduction in symptoms as a result of taking medication which, together with the new understanding of their life to date, can be described as 'life-changing'. The pharmacological treatment of ADHD has also been shown to *significantly reduce* many *serious* adverse outcomes such as road traffic accidents and criminality.

How then is it possible, that only 1 in 20 adults with ADHD ever receive a diagnosis and treatment?

For women, it is likely that the statistics are even more staggering. A girl with ADHD is far less likely to receive the correct diagnosis and treatment than a boy, despite the known adverse trajectory associated with ADHD in female girls and adolescents. Whilst the gender ratio for diagnosis in adulthood is more equal, the prescribing patterns in the UK suggest that *the prescription rate in males is probably almost five times that of females* (Renoux *et al.* 2016).

There is no difference between the specific treatments that can be offered to males or females for their ADHD. However, there are several factors which are either unique or more common in women, which do impact on the treatment approach. Women with

ADHD are more likely to have received an incorrect diagnosis (and therefore incorrect treatment) of another mental health condition (e.g. depression) prior to being diagnosed with ADHD. Therefore, women are often already on some form of psychiatric medication at presentation which may require review.

Many women report that their ADHD medication does not seem to work as effectively in the week prior to their menstrual period, or at the time of the menopause. If so, this can result in sub-optimal symptom control for a significant part of their life. Medication usually confers a significant benefit on the core symptoms of ADHD. However, allied approaches, including psychological support, coaching and the acquisition of organization skills, are also integral to the successful management of women with ADHD. The clinician should be aware of the issues which are specific to females and be prepared to adapt to their specific needs whenever possible.

A BRIEF OVERVIEW OF ADHD TREATMENTS

'The chatter in my head is gone. I might hear the comment, but I don't say it. My thoughts and actions are linear instead of bouncing.'

'My thoughts line up, one by one.'

'I thought stimulants would make me twitchy but instead I feel a sense of deep calm and order.'

There are several published guidelines on the treatment of ADHD, including in the UK, the National Institute for Health and Clinical Excellence (2018), which was last updated in 2019. Advice seen across guidelines is similar. Other guidelines include the British Association for Psychopharmacology (BAP) (Bolea-Alamañac et al. 2014), the (recently updated) consensus statement from the European Network Adult ADHD (Kooij et al. 2019) as well as the new version of the Canadian ADHD Practice Guidelines (CADDRA 2020).

NICE recommends pharmacological (drug) treatment following 'psycho education and environmental modification' – although there is no evidence that either psychoeducation or environmental modification will have a lasting effect on core ADHD symptoms. When a person seeks help for ADHD, almost invariably they will have 'tried everything' to adapt their environment. Medication should then be the treatment of choice. It is well tolerated, generally safe, and most medicines have an extremely low potential for abuse. Medication is effective at reducing the symptoms of ADHD and improving the ability to function in life, and can lead to wider benefits (Chang *et al.* 2019) (Figure 8.1).

Meta-analysis of functional benefits of ADHD medication (Chang *et al.* 2019)

Reduction in road traffic accidents

Increased educational achievement (test scores, grades)

Reduction in criminality (32% for men and 41% for women)

Reduction in substance misuse (27–35%)

Reduced rate of unplanned hospital visits due to depression (20%)

Reduced risk of injury (9–32%)

Further benefits shown in other research

Reduction in sexually transmitted infections in men (41%)

Reduction in violent reoffending (42%)

Improved self-report scores for daily functioning, general well-being and productivity

Figure 8.1 Functional benefits of ADHD medication

Medication often has a positive effect on mood and even suicidality. Adler *et al.* (2013) showed that medication improved self-report scores for daily functioning, general well-being and productivity. Lichtenstein *et al.* (2012) studied 25,656 patients with ADHD from 2006 to 2009 and showed that being *on* ADHD medication (compared with periods being *off* medication) led to a reduction in criminality of 32% for men and 41% for women. Chang *et al.* in 2017 studied 2.3 million patients in the United States with ADHD. Patients with ADHD had a higher risk of a motor vehicle crash (MVC) than a control group of people who did not have ADHD. The use of medication in patients with ADHD was associated with a reduced risk for MVC in both female and male patients. Female patients with ADHD had a 42% lower risk of MVCs and male patients had a 38% lower risk of MVCs in months when receiving ADHD medication.

In the ideal world, a combination of environmental changes and psychological interventions including education, coaching and therapy should be offered alongside medication. Some patients do not wish to use medication, whilst a small number may not receive any significant benefit from pharmacological treatment. Success with medication, however, does appear to make it easier to implement changes suggested from therapy or from self-help resources.

PHARMACOLOGICAL TREATMENTS

'After the medication kicked in, I felt a quiet in my mind I had never felt before. My partner laughed at me when I asked him if his mind was that quiet. I understood why he couldn't comprehend how hard it was for me to transition from task to task, or sit quietly – his mind was this quiet all the time, and he didn't feel anxiety or excess energy that he needed to channel into something. I realized that I had a constant stream of noise in my head all the time, which the medication quieted down. I felt a sense of calm wash over me. That week I could sit down at my desk and start writing (something that had taken agony to do each time before). It also has become a lot easier to keep my mood stable, although not perfect. And I have to be careful not to fall into hyperfocus – I would say the medication has made it a thousand times easier to start work, but a little harder to break out of hyperfocus if I accidentally fall into it. I don't want to sound clichéd, but it has been life-changing.'

There is no difference in the drugs available to be prescribed for women compared with men. Women respond to the same medications and at the same doses as men (i.e. dose does not vary according to gender, weight, age, height, ADHD scale scores or severity of impairments). The two groups of ADHD medicines are outlined in Figure 8.2.

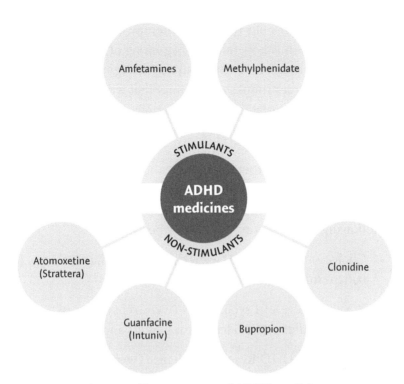

Figure 8.2 The two groups of ADHD medicines

Stimulants are the most effective ADHD drugs. About seven out of ten people will have a good response to either stimulant medication (methylphenidate or lisdexamfetamine); more when both medicines have been tried. Anecdotally this leaves around 15% (one in every seven people) who do not tolerate and/or respond to stimulants. Non-stimulants drugs are options for those who do not respond to stimulants or where a combined approach (using more than one ADHD drug) would be appropriate to trial. A combined approach is usually considered when stimulants have had a helpful but incomplete effect (e.g. they help focus but not emotional symptoms), or work for only part of the day. Non-stimulants could also be used for those who do not want to trial stimulants or if a clinician does not want to consider them, for example if there is evidence that ADHD stimulants are being diverted and sold illegally.

Despite the high success rate of ADHD drugs, it is useful to always emphasize that 'pills don't build skills' and building on strategies using self-help resources, therapy or coaching is also needed. Medication is hopefully the beginning of a long process of continuous improvement. A clinician should signpost a woman to a variety of resources (books and online) that will help. Education about ADHD is essential to improve compliance and optimal use. ADHD symptoms will not go away; drugs are not a cure, and lifelong management of ADHD is essential.

Prescribers should provide patients (and family members) with oral and written information about the medicines being proposed as well as information about ADHD and any local self-help groups. The following webpages on ADHD may be useful:

- Choice and Medication (www.choiceandmedication.org – for patient information leaflets)

- Royal College of Psychiatrists (www.rcpsych.ac.uk – adult ADHD leaflet, ADHD leaflet for parents and carers)

- Canadian ADHD Resource Alliance (www.caddra.ca – free questionnaires and information leaflets)

- National Attention Deficit Disorder Information Support Service (ADDISS) (www.addiss.org.uk – for information and resources)

- AADD-UK (www.aadduk.org – a UK site run by and for those with ADHD)

- ADDitude (https://www.additudemag.com – an American site with some useful podcasts and further information on what is described as 'rejection sensitive dysphoria (RSD)')

- 'King's College London: Neurobiology Animation' (www. youtube.com/watch?v=4r3XWj269_g – a useful and easily understood animation on the neurobiology of ADHD from King's College London)

In terms of physical health monitoring, NICE guidelines (National Institute for Health and Clinical Excellence 2018) suggest a cardiovascular examination and a baseline blood pressure, pulse and weight. A cardiovascular examination can be difficult to organize for patients under mental health services. Neither blood tests nor an ECG is needed routinely unless there are relevant clinical concerns.

NICE recommends a referral for a cardiology opinion before starting medication for ADHD if any of the following apply (although in most clinics, a discussion with the GP is likely to be the first port of call):

- history of congenital heart disease or previous cardiac surgery

- history of sudden death in a first-degree relative under 40 years suggesting a cardiac disease

- shortness of breath on exertion compared with peers

- fainting on exertion or in response to fright or noise

- palpitations that are rapid, regular, and start and stop suddenly (fleeting occasional bumps are usually ectopic and do not need investigation)

- chest pain suggesting cardiac origin

- signs of heart failure

- a murmur heard on cardiac examination

- blood pressure that is classified as hypertensive for adults.

🖐 KEY POINTS

» ADHD may be more common in boys than girls and yet, in adulthood, the male:female ratio is closer to 1:1.

» ADHD is under-recognized in women, who are more likely to have previously received an incorrect diagnosis of another mental health or neurodevelopmental condition.

» When a person seeks help for ADHD, almost invariably they will have 'tried everything' to adapt their environment. Medication should then be the treatment of choice.

» Medication is effective at reducing the symptoms of ADHD and improving the ability to function in life, and can lead to wider benefits. It often has a positive effect on mood and even suicidality.

» Despite the high success rate of ADHD drugs, it is useful to always emphasize that 'pills don't build skills' and building on strategies using self-help resources, therapy or coaching is also needed. Medication is hopefully the beginning of a long process of continuous improvement.

Stimulant drugs

'The whole experience has been like the lifting of a "cloud". Instead of approaching anything I do with the expectation I will fail, I am more confident that it is within my abilities to succeed. Medication has provided an opportunity to re-enter a career with confidence.'

'Previously, making a decision was like trying to cross a dual carriageway: you know you could do it but the distance is far and fraught with risk. Whereas now the road seems like a small and quieter country lane. It feels closer, less busy and less overwhelming and I can cross easily rather than putting it off or giving up as it is just too difficult.'

Deciding to start ADHD stimulants does not mean a permanent or long-term commitment to continue the drug. Stimulant medications are usually effective within an hour, that is, as soon as they get to the brain. Therefore, a trial of stimulants is often relatively quick and easy, with the woman being able to begin to assess her response to a particular preparation and dose on the day that she takes the medication. A drug does not need to be continued for two or three weeks to see if a benefit may occur. Some trial and error is needed with dosing; low doses should be initiated, with careful subsequent dose titration to determine the most effective dose. Clinicians vary as to how quickly they titrate doses, but most studies use a relatively fast titration with one to three dose changes per week. Slower titration is recommended with some comorbidities, especially anxiety, bipolar disorder, a history of psychosis, substance misuse and autistic spectrum disorders, or with patients with physical health concerns that may heighten side effects.

ADHD medications do not lead to a 'personality change' as some people fear. Instead, they should allow a woman with ADHD to focus more and to stay on task, feel less restless or overwhelmed, and improve her general ability to function in life, ideally with minimal or no side effects. Whilst she should feel better able to sustain attention when engaged in tedious, repetitive or boring tasks, not all women report improvement in overcoming the procrastination to start such tasks. The main benefits are outlined in Figure 8.3.

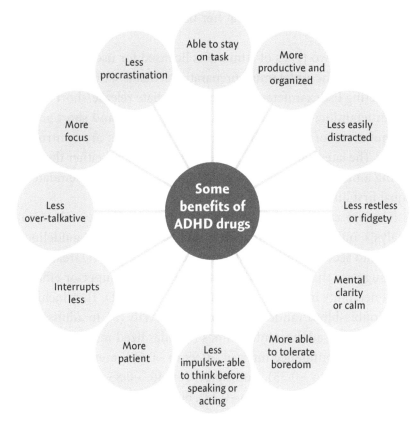

Figure 8.3 The main benefits of ADHD drugs

Although stimulants are licensed for regular daily use, some women choose to omit them occasionally. This is because some women prefer to take the drugs as needed to reduce ADHD symptoms and enhance performance when they have specific tasks to do that are more challenging. Flexible dosing like this is not an evidence-based approach but it is quite common; and, although it is not proven, some clinicians theorize that that having breaks from the drug helps reduce the risk of tolerance. There are no randomized controlled studies that support the flexible use of stimulants in adults. If as needed dosing were found to be as effective as regular medication, advantages might include enhanced doctor–patient communication, reduced side effects and cost savings (Caisley and Müller 2012). If she does have a break from ADHD medicines, the drugs should work as well when restarted at her usual dose. Re-titration is not required.

There are two types of stimulants licensed for use in ADHD in the UK: first, the amfetamine preparations, that is, extended release/long acting lisdexamfetamine, plus immediate release/short acting dexamfetamine; and second, various long acting and short acting formulations of methylphenidate. All stimulants are controlled drugs. The latest 2018 NICE guidelines recommend either the long acting amfetamine drug lisdexamfetamine or methylphenidate as equal first line treatments.

Cortese *et al.*'s (2018) systematic review and network meta-analysis, published after the latest update of the NICE guidelines, takes into account both the efficacy and safety of ADHD treatments and suggests that amfetamine-based drugs have superior efficacy and tolerability in adults for the treatment of ADHD. They included 133 double-blind randomized controlled trials (51 in adults) and found that for adults, amfetamines (standardized mean difference −0·79, 95% confidence interval −0·99 to −0·58), methylphenidate (−0·49, −0·64 to −0·35), bupropion (−0·46, −0·85 to −0·07), and atomoxetine (−0·45, −0·58 to −0·32), but not modafinil (0·16, −0·28 to 0·59), were better than placebo.

All stimulants need to be titrated starting at low doses. Regular monitoring for side effects is needed in order to obtain the optimal dose that gives maximum effect with minimum side effects. The dose should always be gradually increased according to response and tolerability. Medication should be reduced or stopped if unwanted side effects, which outweigh benefits, occur. It is a matter of trial and error and if one stimulant does not work, usually it is worth trialling the other type of stimulant.

Once daily dosing with extended release/long acting formulations provides more consistent and stable symptom control due to more consistent levels of medication in the blood. In comparison, immediate release/short acting preparations are in and out of the body rapidly so the effect is not sustained for long. Women with ADHD find it hard to remember to take multiple doses so once daily use is easier and is usually taken more reliably. This is not just because they are forgetful, but also because women with ADHD have a poor sense of the passage of time. Fewer side effects may also be experienced with long acting formulations as the levels of medication are not rising and falling as quickly as with repeated dosing of short acting formulations. This is especially the case at the end of the day when the benefits are wearing off. Some women describe a 'crash' or 'rebound'. Long acting formulations will help smooth out the ups and downs and help prevent or reduce this 'crash'. It is also more discreet and less embarrassing for women to take medication before going to work or college than having to take repeated doses during the day.

✋ KEY POINTS

» Stimulants are the most effective ADHD drugs. About seven out of ten people will get a good response to either stimulant medication (methylphenidate or lisdexamfetamine); more when both medicines are tried.

» Stimulant medications are usually effective within an hour, that is, as soon as they get into the brain. Therefore, to trial a stimulant is relatively quick and easy, with the woman being able to begin to assess her response to a particular preparation and dose on the day that she takes the medication. A drug does not need to be continued for two or three weeks to see if a benefit may occur. Some trial and error is needed with dosing; low doses should be initiated, with careful subsequent dose titration to determine the most effective dose.

» Medication should allow a woman with ADHD to focus more and to stay on task, feel less restless or overwhelmed, and improve her general ability to function in life, ideally with minimal or no side effects.

» Amfetamine-based drugs appear to have superior efficacy and tolerability in adults for the treatment of ADHD.

» Some women prefer to take stimulant drugs 'as needed' to reduce ADHD symptoms and enhance performance when they have specific tasks to do that are more challenging.

Amfetamine preparations

In Europe, the extended release/long acting drug lisdexamfetamine is somewhat confusingly available as two branded formulations – Elvanse for children and Elvanse Adult for adults. For adults, it may be easier to prescribe the brand Elvanse (despite its technically being licensed only for children), as this is more likely to be stocked by pharmacists and the medicine in the packet is the same as Elvanse Adult. Elsewhere in the world, Elvanse is branded Vyvanse or Tyvense. Vyvanse is available as both capsules and chewable tablets.

Amfetamines act predominantly as 'releasing agents', stimulating the release of dopamine and noradrenaline into the synapse from the pre-synaptic nerve terminal. Amfetamines also block the reuptake of dopamine (DA) and noradrenaline (NA) by the dopamine and noradrenaline transporters. Rapid increases in DA and NA underpin the early onset and the large effect size of both methylphenidate and dexamfetamine, and this accounts for the potential for recreational abuse. This is not thought to be a risk for lisdexamfetamine as it is an extended release pro-drug. After absorption, the L-lysine portion of the molecule is cleaved off, leaving the active substance dexamfetamine. As this takes around an hour, there is no rapid onset and it is thought that this prevents its use as a recreational drug. Formulations of amfetamines available in the USA and not in Europe include chewable lisdexamfetamine tablets, various brands of mixed amfetamine salts (i.e. various brands including Adderall – long and short acting), as well as short acting dextroamfetamine and medium acting dexedrine. Lisdexamfetamine is approved for the treatment of binge eating disorder in the US so is a good choice in those with ADHD and comorbid binge eating disorder or bulimia.

Lisdexamfetamine dosing starts at 30mg once in the morning for adults. However, some patients achieve their optimal response at a lower dose. If there are concerns about sensitivity to side effects, a 20mg capsule is available (as well as a 10mg capsule outside of Europe); or the contents of a capsule can be dissolved in water or orange juice so that the patient can start with a half capsule or less by drinking a fraction of the liquid solution. The dose can then be titrated in 10–20mg increments to a maximum of 70mg once each morning if tolerated and if needed. Although it is licensed for once daily use, occasionally twice daily dosing is needed if it appears the drug is metabolized quickly and only has an effect for half a day. The side effect of insomnia may mean this is not possible for some women; but for others, using a stimulant later in the day may improve sleep.

The drug dexamfetamine is a short acting/immediate release amfetamine formulation and can usually be used if lisdexamfetamine causes insomnia, or if a 'top up' of a short acting amfetamine is needed, for example if lisdexamfetamine wears off too early in the day – as long as there is no concern about misuse or diversion. Dosing starts at 5mg tablets. If this is used as the only stimulant (rather than as a top up after lisdexamfetamine wears off), it may be needed twice to three times a day. Each dose can be increased in 5mg increments to a maximum of 20mg per dose and a total daily dose of 60mg in divided doses for adults, 40mg (as per the licence) for adolescents. Dexamfetamine tablets are not a first line treatment as this is the medicine most vulnerable to misuse as a recreational drug.

✋ KEY POINTS

» Lisdexamfetamine is a good choice in those with ADHD and comorbid binge eating disorder.

» Occasionally, twice daily dosing of a long acting stimulant drug is needed if it appears the drug is metabolized quickly and has an effect for only half a day.

» The side effect of insomnia may mean twice daily dosing is not possible for some women – but for others, using a stimulant later in the day may improve sleep by calming a busy mind that otherwise prevents sleep onset.

» The contents of a capsule of lisdexamfetamine can be dissolved in water or orange juice and this feature can help speed dose titration.

» In the UK dexamfetamine tablets are the only stimulant that is not a first line treatment choice as this is the medicine most vulnerable to misuse as a recreational drug.

Methylphenidate

Formulations of methylphenidate available in the UK include immediate release/short acting brands such as Ritalin, Tranquilyn and Medikinet tablets as well as various extended release/long acting formulations of methylphenidate. These include Equasym XL and Medikinet XL capsules (medium acting – about 8 hours' effect) as well as long acting osmotic release Concerta XL (about 12 hours' effect). Since Concerta XL is no longer patented in the UK, other similar formulations have become available, for example Xaggitin XL, Xenidate XL, Matoride XL and Delmosart tablets at the time of writing. Formulations available in the USA, and not in Europe, include methylphenidate transdermal patches and dexmethylphenidate (i.e. Focalin immediate and extended release). A clinical effect is usually evident by one hour; sooner for immediate release formulations. In terms of its mode of action, methylphenidate blocks the reuptake of DA and NA by the dopamine and the noradrenaline transporters (DAT and NAT).

Long acting, extended release formulations (e.g. Concerta XL, Xaggitin XL, Xenidate XL, Matoride XL and Delmosart tablets) claim to last up to 12 hours. Generally, dose titration starts at 18mg once daily in the morning (which is equivalent to 5mg three times a day of immediate release methylphenidate) and increases in 18mg increments at approximately weekly intervals (more quickly early on if there is no therapeutic effect and no adverse effects), according to response. The maximum total daily dose recommended in adults is 108mg, if this is needed and tolerated. Dispensing of the drug may be faster if the prescription is written generically as 'methylphenidate modified release' because brands stocked will vary between pharmacists.

Medium release formulations (e.g. Medikinet XL and Equasym XL capsules) claim to last around eight hours. Equasym XL has a smoother continuous profile of drug release, whereas Medikinet XL releases half of its contents immediately so has a bias towards delivery of more medication early on. These two drugs are usually prescribed as a specific brand rather than generically, depending on which release profile is suitable. Medikinet XL is more suited to someone who finds mornings particularly difficult and wants the drug to have a more sudden initial effect. Usually, it would be reasonable to prescribe 10mg doses once or twice a day, increasing in 10mg increments to a maximum of 100mg total daily dose – usually as a maximum of 50mg twice a day or 60mg in the morning followed by a 40mg second dose in adults who can tolerate a second dose without insomnia.

An alternative to twice daily dosing for extended release formulations, especially if a second dose of stimulant causes insomnia, is to top up with a shorter acting immediate release formulation to provide a few hours of afternoon or evening cover.

Immediate release methylphenidate (e.g. Ritalin, Medikinet and Tranquilyn tablets) is usually prescribed generically as 'methylphenidate' (rather than as a specific brand). The formulation dispensed, therefore, will depend on which brand that particular pharmacist stocks. Their effect usually lasts three to four hours. Start with 5mg twice a day after breakfast and lunch, moving to three times a day dosing by adding in a mid to late afternoon dose if needed, but initially avoiding taking a dose too late in the day in case of insomnia. Increase to 10mg doses, if needed and if tolerated, after a few days; and then, if needed and if tolerated, increase each dose again by further 5mg increments at around weekly intervals – sometimes sooner, if there has been no therapeutic effect and no adverse effects. The maximum total daily dose is 100mg. More frequent small doses may be needed, for example every three hours, if the drug wears off quickly. Such regular dosing is inconvenient for most patients and greater compliance will be achieved with extended release formulations. Because it is easier to remember, effectiveness is usually better with once daily long acting medication. However, students with less routine to their schedule sometimes prefer the flexibility of repeated dosing of immediate release formulations.

🤚 KEY POINTS

» Regular dosing of short acting medication is inconvenient for most patients and greater compliance will be achieved with extended release formulations.

» Because it is easier to remember, effectiveness is usually better with once daily long acting medication.

» Students with less routine to their schedule sometimes prefer the flexibility of repeated dosing of immediate release formulations.

» An alternative to twice daily dosing for extended release formulations, especially if a second dose of stimulant causes insomnia, is to top up with a shorter acting immediate release formulation to provide a few hours of afternoon or evening cover.

» Sometimes extended release stimulant drugs designed to be taken once daily do not last long enough and are needed twice daily.

Side effects, tolerance, stopping and swopping

If needed, dosages of stimulants can be titrated up (within the licensed range) until either there is no further clinical improvement or side effects become significant; and then the dose is reduced to the lowest effective dose. Potential side effects of stimulants include reduced appetite, weight loss, insomnia, headache, anxiety, low mood, an increase in pulse and blood pressure, palpitations, dry mouth, diarrhoea, abdominal pain, nausea, irritability, feeling jittery and fatigue. The complaint of fatigue is sometimes reported when the drug wears off but occasionally, soon after taking it. Stimulants have been reported to exacerbate motor and vocal tics and Tourette's syndrome; but for some women, tics can improve with stimulants. Their presence should not be a reason to decline an informed trial of these drugs.

Some patients experience an initial enhanced effect in the first few days which is not sustained. Significant benefits may continue, but not at the initial level. Some women or their clinician may be cautious at the start of treatment and may be using a sub-optimal dose, being delighted at any mild improvement in symptoms. Therefore, some subsequent requests to increase the dose may not reflect tolerance, but that the optimal dose was not reached at the start. The woman and her clinician may, with more confidence, realize that she obtains an even better response on a higher dose if this is tolerated. Tolerance occurs in some individuals and future cautious dose increases (within the licence) may be needed. A break from the medication may help. Tolerance, however, is not a universal problem. After some initial changes, once a regime is finely tuned to suit an individual, then most women stick with that dose or regime; but sometimes women do return asking for a higher dose than they originally settled on, and may benefit from increases.

In cases of significant adverse effects, stimulants can be stopped abruptly if needed. Manufacturer advice is usually cautious and advises that when stopping after long-term use, drugs are tapered off or are stopped 'under careful supervision'. But the author's experience is that many people with ADHD take stimulants flexibly and may start and stop them regularly, with no adverse effects. Some patients do report that, on days when they do not take their stimulant, they experience more fatigue. This sometimes reflects the difference in their level of functioning on the drug and so may represent a return to previous lower levels of functioning and elevated levels of fatigue.

If a woman needs to swop from one stimulant to another, this can be done with no cross tapering, that is, she can stop one stimulant on one day and move straight to the alternative on the following day.

KEY POINTS

» Stimulant doses can be gradually titrated up (within the licence) until either there is no further therapeutic gain or adverse effects become significant; and then the dose is reduced to the lowest effective dose.

» Some patients experience an initial enhanced effect in the first few days which is not sustained. Significant benefits may continue, but not at the initial level.

» Some women or their clinician may be cautious at the start of treatment and may be using a sub-optimal dose. Therefore, some requests to increase the dose may not reflect tolerance but that the optimal dose was not reached at the start.

» If a woman needs to swop from one stimulant to another, this can be done with no cross tapering, that is, she can stop one stimulant on one day and move straight to the alternative on the following day.

» Stimulants may exacerbate or improve motor and vocal tics. The presence of tics should not be a reason to decline an informed trial of these drugs.

Non-stimulant drugs

NICE guidelines suggest that the non-stimulant drug atomoxetine can be effective and form second line management, and should be offered if trials of the stimulants lisdexamfetamine and methylphenidate do not provide benefit or are not well tolerated. NICE suggests that other medications (e.g. clonidine, bupropion, guanfacine) should be used in adults only by ADHD specialists. These non-stimulant drugs are outlined below. Non-stimulant drugs do not work as quickly as stimulants, need to be taken regularly and not stopped suddenly, and are therefore less flexible.

Atomoxetine

The non-stimulant atomoxetine is recommended in the NICE guidance as a second line drug treatment for ADHD in both children and adults. It is therefore used mostly if stimulants have not been tolerated or are not effective. It is not a controlled drug. An advantage is that, when it is effective, it has a 24-hour effect. The drug is a specific noradrenergic reuptake inhibitor (NARI) and may take 2–4 weeks to have any positive effect and may not reach its optimal effect for 6–12 weeks, sometimes longer. Its lower rate of success compared with stimulants (Cortese *et al.* 2018), and its higher drop-out rate due to side effects, makes it less popular. If there is a comorbid anxiety disorder, it is sometimes a good choice as stimulants are not always tolerated in this group of people. One study provided evidence that atomoxetine can reduce symptoms of social anxiety (Adler *et al.* 2009). However, an effective stimulant may also reduce anxiety. Being less impaired by ADHD symptoms may enable a woman to function better socially, so this positive effect on social anxiety may not be exclusive to atomoxetine.

Historically, atomoxetine was thought to be a better drug choice when there are concerns about substance misuse or diversion. However, with the development of the prodrug lisdexamfetamine, this can be a safe and more effective first line choice, even for this group of patients.

About 7% of the Caucasian population and 1% of the Asian population are considered 'poor metabolizers' of atomoxetine, experiencing higher than usual concentrations of the drug in their blood (Sauer *et al.* 2003). This leads to more side effects and a greater risk of harm in the case of overdose.

Although manufacturer guidance on its use states that atomoxetine should be initiated at 40mg once a day, doubling to 80mg after a week, atomoxetine is more likely to be tolerated if a smaller dose is used initially, alongside more gradual titration. One option is to initially provide a one-month supply of 28 x 18mg capsules and suggest that the patient take 1 x 18mg for the first three days, increasing if tolerated to 2 x 18mg (i.e. a 36mg dose) for five days. If this is tolerated, then increase to 3 x 18mg (i.e. a 54mg dose) for five days. As long as a telephone review can be conducted at the two-week point, before the initial supply runs out, then a judgement can be made as to whether further titration to 40mg, 60mg or 80mg is appropriate. If there is evidence that the patient is a slow metabolizer, then lower maintenance doses of 25mg or 40mg may be considered. Once the patient has reached the highest tolerated dose, a trial of at least six weeks should be allowed to fully evaluate effectiveness. Most patients who do respond notice an initial small improvement after about two weeks on a maintenance dose. An optimal response may not be achieved until at least three months. The usual maintenance dose is 80mg but doses of 100mg and 120mg/day can be considered subsequently, given in one or two divided doses (e.g. morning and late afternoon or early evening). Once daily dosing is more likely to be taken reliably. Slower titration than recommended by the manufacturer often improves tolerability and also helps identify this small percentage who are 'poor metabolizers' and are more sensitive to side effects and are likely to need a lower dose.

Patients who are prescribed atomoxetine should be informed about the risk of suicidal ideation and liver dysfunction, which are both uncommon. Common side effects include reduced appetite, nausea, vomiting, abdominal pain, tiredness and headaches in the first few weeks, which are minimized if the drug is started at low doses, and usually settle if it is titrated gradually. Regarding stopping the drug, no distinct withdrawal symptoms have been described. In cases of significant adverse effects, atomoxetine may be stopped abruptly; otherwise, it is usually tapered off over a week or so, but with much less difficulty than stopping most antidepressants.

Treatment with atomoxetine need not be indefinite. At an annual review, re-evaluation of the need for continued therapy and a 'drug holiday' (i.e. a few weeks without the drug) could be performed, especially if the benefits are mild. Conversely, if a woman is happy with its effect and wants to continue it, then continuous use would also be reasonable.

✋ KEY POINTS

» Non-stimulant drugs do not work as quickly as stimulants, need to be taken regularly and not stopped suddenly, and are therefore less flexible.

» Patients who are prescribed atomoxetine should be informed about the risk of suicidal ideation and liver dysfunction, which are both uncommon.

» Atomoxetine is used mostly if stimulants have not been tolerated or are not effective.

» Its higher drop-out rate, and lower effect size due to side effects, makes it less popular.

» One study provided evidence that atomoxetine can reduce symptoms of social anxiety but an effective stimulant may also reduce anxiety. Being less impaired by ADHD symptoms may enable a woman to function better socially, so this positive effect on social anxiety may not be exclusive to atomoxetine.

» Historically, atomoxetine was thought to be a better drug choice when there are concerns about substance misuse or diversion. However, with the development of the prodrug lisdexamfetamine, this can be a safe and more effective first line choice, even for this group of patients.

Guanfacine

Extended release guanfacine is licensed in the UK for use in children with ADHD (branded Intuniv). It is a selective alpha$_{2A}$ adrenergic receptor agonist. It is sometimes used off licence in adults by specialists. A recent double-blind, placebo-controlled study (Iwanami *et al.* 2020) assessed guanfacine in adults with ADHD and concluded that it improved ADHD symptoms without any major safety concerns. Studies in children have found that it is useful for comorbid ADHD and tics (Chappell *et al.* 1995). There is some evidence that augmenting a stimulant with guanfacine may be the best approach for patients suffering from ADHD and oppositional symptoms (Stahl and Mignon 2011). These patients can be argumentative, aggressive and exhibit temper tantrums. There is anecdotal evidence that guanfacine can help about a third of those who complain of 'rejection sensitive dysphoria (RSD)'. Guanfacine may be useful for patients with ADHD and treatment resistant hypertension, but further research is needed.

Although the manufacturer recommends a baseline ECG to screen for QT prolongation and arrhythmia, an amendment to the NICE guidance in 2019 indicated that an ECG is *not* needed 'if cardiovascular history and examination are normal and the person is not on medicine that poses an increased cardiovascular risk'. Monitoring is necessary at the start of treatment for a history of syncope, low blood pressure and bradycardia. Patients should be advised that sedation can occur, particularly early in treatment or with dose increases, but usually settles. The dose may be increased by 1mg per week from a starting dose of 1mg once a day usually to 2–3mg once a day, in the author's experience, when benefits have been seen within the first few weeks. The maximum licensed dose is 7mg. During dose titration, monitor weekly and before dose increases for signs and symptoms of sedation, hypotension and bradycardia.

Taking guanfacine with high-fat meals or grapefruit juice increases levels and exposure to the drug so should be avoided. When discontinuing treatment, the manufacturer advises avoiding abrupt withdrawal (taper by 1mg per week) due to the risk of rebound hypertension. It suggests monitoring blood pressure and pulse during downward titration. Anecdotally, the author has not seen any problems when stopping guanfacine, even in patients who have stopped the drug suddenly.

👋 KEY POINTS

> » Extended release guanfacine is licensed for use in children with ADHD. It is sometimes used off licence in adults by specialists, especially for comorbid oppositional and emotional symptoms.

> » Studies in children have found that it is useful for comorbid ADHD and tics.

> » Guanfacine in adults with ADHD has been shown to improve ADHD symptoms without any major safety concerns.

> » A 2019 amendment to the NICE guidance indicated that a routine baseline ECG is not needed in patients with no cardiac clinical concerns.

Bupropion

Bupropion is approved in the UK only for use as a smoking cessation agent (branded Zyban). In the USA, it is also licensed for the treatment of depression (branded Wellbutrin) and there is some evidence for its use in patients with ADHD (Maneeton *et al.* 2011). Bupropion is a noradrenaline and dopamine reuptake inhibitor. It falls into the category of medications that NICE states should be started only by a specialist service or following a second opinion. Its use in ADHD is supported by the Cortese *et al.* (2018) systematic review and the BAP 2014 guidelines (Bolea-Alamañac *et al.* 2014). Positive results typically favour higher doses (300–450mg per day). It may be useful with comorbid depression, anxiety, substance misuse disorder, or if the patient is also keen to give up smoking.

Clonidine

In the UK, clonidine is not approved for the treatment of ADHD so is occasionally used off licence. Like guanfacine, clonidine is an alpha$_2$ adrenergic agonist, increasing noradrenaline release; but it is not selective to alpha$_{2A}$ receptors. It may reduce hyperactivity and impulsivity but has limited impact on inattention. It may be a useful option in ADHD patients who also suffer from tics or Tourette's syndrome. However, it has a much higher incidence of side effects compared with guanfacine. Sedation can exacerbate concentration and a reduction in blood pressure can also limit its use. A rebound hypertension can occur if a dose is forgotten, which can be dangerous for chaotic and forgetful patients. It is not included in any treatment guidelines.

Modafinil

Modafinil is licensed for narcolepsy and is known to be one of the 'smart drugs' misused by students in attempts to achieve cognitive enhancement, being more available than controlled drugs used for ADHD. It increases alertness. There is no good evidence it is effective in adults with ADHD.

Antidepressants

It has been suggested that tricyclic antidepressants and monoamine oxidase inhibitors may improve ADHD symptoms, but evidence is weak (Spencer *et al.* 2002). Specific serotonin reuptake inhibitor (SSRI) antidepressants have not been found to be beneficial in the management of ADHD. Trazodone or amitriptyline may be useful to help insomnia, and mirtazapine in theory may reduce appetite loss caused by stimulants and also help with sleep and anxiety.

Combination treatment

There is a lack of evidence for the efficacy of combining stimulant and non-stimulant drugs in the treatment of ADHD in adults, but this can sometimes have a useful role. Where stimulants produce a good effect, but for only part of the day, and sometimes where the addition of a 'top-up' dose of a short acting stimulant or a second dose of a long acting stimulant is not successful or is not tolerated (often due to insomnia), then non-stimulant drugs may help. They may enhance symptom reduction, especially in the evening when stimulants have worn off.

Sometimes a second drug may be used to target a different symptom type. For example, if a patient reports an improvement in focus and cognitive symptoms with stimulants, but if other ADHD symptoms or emotional dysregulation remain problematic, then it may be useful to trial the addition of a non-stimulant. Atomoxetine has a severe theoretical interaction with lisdexamfetamine. Guanfacine is an alternative that is increasingly used in combination by ADHD specialists. An eight-week study in children combined immediate release guanfacine with stimulants and showed small but consistent benefits (McCracken *et al.* 2016). There is recent evidence that guanfacine is helpful and safe for adults mentioned above.

Anecdotally, the combination of a stimulant and guanfacine can be helpful for tic disorders, oppositional symptoms and in those who describe symptoms of emotional over-reactivity or specifically of 'rejection sensitive dysphoria (RSD)'. In terms of the management of comorbid tics, Ogundele and Ayyash's (2018) meta-analysis did not support an association between new onset or worsening of tics and normal doses of psychostimulant use, although supratherapeutic doses of dextroamfetamine have been shown to exacerbate tic disorders. They suggested that there is some evidence supporting the use of clonidine and guanfacine as well as atomoxetine and stimulants for the treatment of tics and comorbid ADHD. Severe tic disorders may require antipsychotic treatment (e.g. aripiprazole). Aripiprazole may help severe tics but antipsychotics do not help ADHD and so are likely to be needed in combination with ADHD drugs.

Monitoring

Monitoring of the dose titration is commonly completed by telephone or online video in ADHD clinics. Initially, frequent, brief consultations every few weeks may be required. Attending outpatient clinics may not be practical and appointments may not be available, given common resource limitations. Telephone or video follow-up for appropriate patients can provide good support and monitoring.

Issues to explore at follow-up include:

- the current dose, frequency and timing of medication use, positive effects and response of patient's key symptoms

- the development of adverse effects such as appetite loss, insomnia, dry mouth, anxiety or cardiac symptoms

- the effect of missed doses/periods of no treatment

- the emergence of psychiatric symptoms, such as changes in mood or anxiety or any worsening of existing psychiatric disorder(s)

- any substance use concerns including prescribed medication misuse or diversion

- the opinions of carers/partners on treatment response

- the use of questionnaires may be helpful (e.g. the ASRS, Weiss or WRAADDS; see Chapter 7); these are usually used at assessment.

NICE guidelines suggest blood pressure (BP), pulse and weight at baseline, after dose changes and then six-monthly. The results of physical health monitoring should be discussed. If it is felt to be clinically appropriate, BP, pulse and weight in low-risk individuals can be monitored between clinic visits remotely, if the patient is able to measure BP and pulse at their local GP surgery or by using a home monitor. If using a home monitor, they should take the BP at least two hours after taking a dose and after sitting down for 10–15 minutes. They should be told to record the lowest of three readings and capture their pulse reading.

Annual reviews

An evaluation of the need for continued therapy should be made annually as should efforts to ensure a woman is still taking the optimal and most effective drug and dose.

NICE suggests that the annual review include a discussion about:

- the patient's individual treatment preference

- benefits, including how well the current treatment is working throughout the day

- adverse effects

- whether medication has been optimized

- impact on education and employment

- effects of missing a dose, the outcome of any dose reductions or periods of no treatment

- effect of medication on existing or mental health, physical health or neurodevelopmental conditions

- the need for support and type of support.

Long-term use of medication

'I'm actually enjoying my work now. So much of the daily angst has gone, as have the feelings of worthlessness when another day passes with no progress/nothing done! I feel on top of my life for the first time in my recorded history!'

Following titration and dose stabilization, prescribing often continues under locally agreed shared care agreements with primary care, but this currently varies between areas and GPs. The European Medicines Agency (EMA) review of the safety of medicines containing methylphenidate has concluded that their benefits outweigh the risks associated with cardiovascular, cerebrovascular and psychiatric safety and long-term effects (European Medicines Agency 2009). The BAP guidelines (Bolea-Alamañac *et al.* 2014) suggest drug treatment should be continued for as long as is clinically useful. Cortese *et al.* in their 2018 systematic review highlight that new research should be funded to assess long-term effects of ADHD drugs. Pharmacoepidemiological studies have investigated real-life longer-term effects of ADHD medication (Chang *et al.* 2019). Prescribed ADHD medication reduced the higher risk, usually seen in ADHD, of criminal offending (Lichtenstein *et al.* 2012), road traffic accidents and physical injuries. Similar studies found that ADHD medication was associated with a reduced long-term risk for depression with the occurrence of depression being 20% less during periods when patients received ADHD medication compared with periods when they did not.

UK drug licences

In the UK, at the time of writing, lisdexamfetamine, Medikinet XL and atomoxetine are approved for treatment initiation of ADHD in both children and adults. Other brands either have an adult continuation licence for individuals first treated for ADHD as a child or adolescent or are licensed for the treatment of ADHD in childhood and adolescence only. Therefore, many prescriptions of ADHD medication in adults are used off licence but supported by NICE and BAP guidance and the British National Formulary.

✋ KEY POINTS

» ADHD is a highly treatable condition yet is commonly confused with other mental health disorders.

» It is estimated that less than 1 in 20 women who suffer from ADHD are being prescribed treatment for this...and yet medicines for ADHD are among the most effective psychiatric drug treatments available.

» Drug treatment should be continued for as long as is clinically useful.

NON-PHARMACOLOGICAL TREATMENTS
Psychological therapies, coaching and signposting

The goal of psychological interventions is to arrive at an appreciation of the many ways in which ADHD has adversely affected the individual's life, how it affects the lives of others, and to support individuals to develop and improve skills and coping strategies. Psychological treatments are often conducted in groups, both because it is financially more affordable and because it creates a buddy system to help a participant reach their goals and make changes. Including spouses and significant others in the group may be helpful. Current evidence, however, shows that pharmacological (drug) treatment is more effective at changing core ADHD symptoms. Studies have shown that psychological therapies alone are inferior in effect to medication. Evidence suggests that the best outcomes will be achieved using a combination of both pharmacological and psychological approaches (Philipsen *et al.* 2015).

Treatments may involve psychological, educational, behavioural, social and lifestyle interventions. A detailed guide as to how to deliver this is beyond the scope of this chapter, but for best results this type of treatment should be offered in combination with medication. Medication may help a woman concentrate on therapy sessions, help her put ideas into practice and maintain new, consistent skills. NICE guidance emphasizes the need to provide a comprehensive, holistic, shared treatment plan that addresses psychological, behavioural, occupational and educational needs. Specifically, NICE suggests that 'if, following medication, there is either residual impairment or no response, or if medication is not an option, or if the person chooses to avoid medication, then cognitive behavioural therapy (CBT) should be considered' (National Institute for Health and Care Excellence 2018). CBT can be provided on an individual or group basis.

Interventions also need to address the potential for women with ADHD to be vulnerable in terms of their sexual behaviour and relationships. In combination with low self-esteem, ADHD may render a woman vulnerable to sexual harassment, exploitation, and abusive or inappropriate relationships. The Adult Psychiatric Morbidity Household Survey (McManus *et al.* 2009) conducted in England found that 27% of females who experienced extensive physical and sexual violence had ADHD traits. Support should therefore be offered to address the more complex situations adult females may face, such as multitasking, occupational demands, home management and family/parenting responsibilities, as well as to address their sexual health and safety.

Whatever type of therapy is delivered, it should address core ADHD symptoms, executive dysfunction, comorbid conditions and dysfunctional strategies (e.g. substance abuse or deliberate self-harm). It should help the patient to develop a more reflective and goal-oriented approach to everyday activities and help with problem solving. It is important to identify and focus on a woman's strengths and positive attributes rather than solely on her perceived weaknesses and failures, as self-esteem is commonly low and other mental health problems may be present. Comorbid symptoms such as low mood and anxiety may also respond to psychological therapy and should be addressed.

Coaching, although an unregulated industry, may be helpful, as may mindfulness therapy and other specialist sources of support (e.g. relationship/marital counselling, family therapy, educational study skills support or vocational counselling), although further research is needed.

At the very least, information should be offered to all women and should include:

- information on adult ADHD and the medication that has been suggested

- signposting to self-help resources and local groups when available

- advice on planning and structuring activities using diaries, reminders and lists

- advice on educational or employment adjustments as relevant.

Educational adjustments
Students should be offered a letter confirming the diagnosis and supporting their entitlement to the disabled students' allowance. If

appropriate, suggestions can be made such as extra time (usually 25% extra) or use of a separate room and extra breaks for exams, use of a mentor and study skills support.

Occupational adjustments
Women who disclose ADHD as a disability to their employer are entitled to reasonable adjustments to the workplace in relation to their needs. Additional support may be available to help a woman manage through her employer or the government access to work scheme (www.gov.uk/access-to-work).

Using technology
Technology can help provide reminders to start or complete tasks, or check that one is still on track and has not become distracted. It can also be used to improve compliance with medication. Reminders and alarms on smart phones or using discrete vibrating wrist watches can help, as can calendar and reminder apps on computers or using pill boxes with timers.

Stigma, shame and self-help groups
Sadly, psychological treatments are not widely available in the UK. Some areas have developed self-help groups. These can do a lot to help women with ADHD. Despite evidence to the contrary, many people still do not believe that ADHD is a proper medical condition. Some family, friends or work colleagues may see ADHD as an excuse for sloppiness or laziness. The fact that ADHD symptoms fluctuate, depending on the situation or the time of the month, feeds the scepticism of others. Sharing experiences with other sufferers can help provide validation and support and reduce shame, frustration and embarrassment. Sometimes there are criticism and negative feelings from others about the use of psychiatric drugs, especially as there has been a well overdue growth in the number of people taking ADHD medication in recent years. This leads to stigma and shame. Self-help groups or group psychotherapy and psychoeducation can help overcome this.

THE INFLUENCE OF FEMALE HORMONES ON THE SEVERITY OF ADHD SYMPTOMS

Emerging evidence suggests that hormonal factors may play an important role in understanding ADHD in females. Women with ADHD very often report that their ADHD symptoms are affected by hormonal changes, both within their menstrual cycle and in the perimenopausal period. These changes can have a significant impact on the severity of a woman's ADHD symptoms throughout her life and have treatment implications. Figure 8.4 outlines the ways in which hormones can affect ADHD.

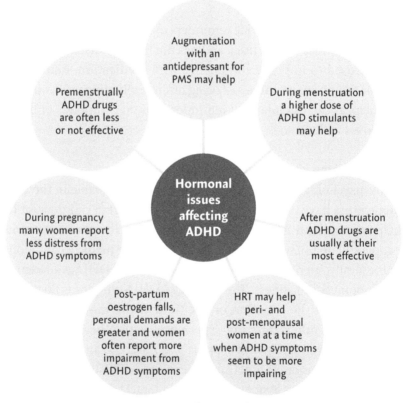

Figure 8.4 Hormonal issues affecting ADHD

Clinical practice suggests that women with ADHD are particularly vulnerable to experiencing premenstrual syndrome, with more irritability, emotional lability and feelings of low self-worth alongside physical complaints such as breast tenderness. In addition, some women report that their stimulant medication becomes noticeably less effective in the week before their period (when progesterone levels are higher and oestrogen levels are falling), and also in the perimenopausal period.

Levels of oestrogen and progesterone have been shown to affect the response to psychoactive stimulant medication. One small study examined whether oestrogen affects the response to an amfetamine in healthy young women (Justice and Wit 1999). In this study, during the follicular phase (during and immediately after a menstrual period), the effects of amfetamine were greater and subjects reported feeling more 'energetic and intellectually efficient' after amfetamine than during the luteal phase (premenstrually). Further analyses showed that during the follicular phase, but not the luteal phase, responses to amfetamine were related to levels of oestrogen. Therefore, once menstruation starts, it seems that rising oestrogen levels are associated with greater clinical effects from amfetamines. However, premenstrually, during the luteal phase, in the presence also of high progesterone, the oestrogen levels were not associated with greater therapeutic effects from amfetamines.

This may help explain the anecdotal evidence that raising the dose of an ADHD stimulant to try and gain a greater benefit premenstrually for many women is unsuccessful. It seems that oestrogen can enhance the response to a stimulant drug, but that this effect may be masked in the presence of progesterone. Many women report more benefit from an increased dose of an ADHD drug once they start menstruation. At this time, when oestrogen and progesterone levels are both low, a higher dose of an ADHD drug may have a greater effect. In comparison, premenstrually, when oestrogen is low but progesterone is higher, then ADHD drugs may be less effective and their effect may not be boosted by an increase in dose. After menstruation has ended, when oestrogen levels are rising but progesterone remains low, women may notice that their ADHD drugs are at their most effective – and they may even need to reduce their dose of ADHD medication. Clinicians may need to provide options for tailoring ADHD drugs to accommodate these changes (Quinn 2005).

For a comprehensive treatment approach, an enquiry should be made into additional symptoms, for example of premenstrual syndrome or features of the menopause, as well as into the variability in impairment due to ADHD that may be related to hormonal factors. Treatment adjustment around the menstrual cycle, including successful augmentation with an antidepressant during the premenstrual period, has been shown to reduce problems with moodiness, irritability and inattention, normally well controlled through stimulant medication alone (Quinn 2005). Fluoxetine is a usual favourite for this but it interacts with lisdexamfetamine (as does paroxetine, although this is not recommended for intermittent use) so another antidepressant, such as low dose citalopram or sertraline, may be used.

Many peri- and post-menopausal women find that their ADHD symptoms become more intrusive, with worsening cognitive, affective and sleep-related symptoms. Shanmugan and Epperson (2014) suggest that this lower executive functioning may be due to the effect of lower levels of oestrogen, which importantly interacts with different neurotransmitter systems. Unfortunately, increasing the dose of the stimulant medication at these times may not always confer any additional benefit. The use of HRT in peri- and post-menopausal women may be helpful.

🖐 KEY POINTS

» Greater awareness on the part of healthcare professionals regarding the impact of female hormones on the response to ADHD treatment as well as comorbidities such as premenstrual syndrome is needed to optimize successful outcomes.

» It is almost impossible to accurately fine tune ADHD medications in the week prior to menstruation.

» For many women with ADHD, their stimulant medication does not work, or works less well, at this time.

» Using contraception to avoid premenstrual syndrome may help.

» The arrival of the menopause may be associated with more symptomatic ADHD as well as ADHD medications working less well. Raising the dose may not always help.

» Many post-menopausal women benefit from HRT, which may improve sleep and cognitive symptoms.

TREATING COMORBIDITIES

Women with ADHD are highly likely to be misdiagnosed with, or suffer from, another mental illness. This can include substance use disorders. Sometimes mood symptoms, emotional instability or volatility may be misattributed to depressive disorders, bipolar disorder or personality disorders, or may have been given the label 'cyclothymia'. Sometimes a comorbid disorder exists and may be seen as complicating ADHD treatment choices. Common examples are discussed below. Treatment of ADHD may improve the comorbidity and help to improve longer-term functional, health and mental health outcomes.

Substance use

Clinicians need to be mindful of, and discuss with their patients, the risks around alcohol and drug use whilst on ADHD medication, but the presence of a substance use problem should not prevent a person from successfully seeking treatment for ADHD. There is increasing evidence that treatment with ADHD medication does not increase the risk of substance misuse. In fact, there appears to be a benefit from ADHD treatment with regards to reducing substance use and its complications. One study (in commercial healthcare) showed reduced claims for emergency department visits related to substance use disorders when patients were being prescribed treatment for ADHD (Quinn *et al.* 2017). A Swedish study of male prisoners with ADHD and amfetamine dependence were treated with high doses (up to 180mg) of methylphenidate and CBT, and had significantly higher proportions of negative drug urine screens in comparison with the placebo group (Konstenius *et al.* 2014). Another RCT demonstrated that treatment with mixed amfetamine salts increased urine-confirmed abstinence among patients with ADHD and cocaine dependence (Levin *et al.* 2015).

Although there are risks of misuse or diversion to consider and manage, the potential benefits of treatment must be viewed in the context of lifetime adverse outcomes associated with poorly managed ADHD and ongoing substance use (poor mental health, educational and occupational impairment, financial problems, arrests, early pregnancy and relationship failure) and, if at all possible, treatment should be offered. NICE (National Institute for Health and Care Excellence 2018) recommends cautious prescribing of stimulants for ADHD if there is a risk of diversion for cognitive enhancement or appetite suppression, and makes one of the few 'do not' recommendations: 'Do not offer immediate-release stimulants that can be easily injected or insufflated [snorted] if there is a risk of stimulant misuse or diversion.'

A recent European consensus statement on the treatment of ADHD and substance misuse (Crunelle *et al.* 2018) suggested a range of strategies for the treatment of both ADHD and SUD which included combining psychotherapy and pharmacotherapy. The authors suggest that the abuse potential is limited with slow-onset agents so recommend long-acting methylphenidate, extended-release amphetamines (e.g. lisdexamfetamine in Europe), and atomoxetine for the treatment of comorbid ADHD and SUD, and that up-titration to higher dosages may be considered in some patients.

Depression
For women with ADHD in whom depressive mood symptoms are present but not severe, it is usually advisable to treat the ADHD

symptoms first, as this may lead to a secondary improvement in mood. Low mood may be due to demoralization driven by ADHD and its impairments. Indeed, ADHD is associated with treatment-resistant depression (Sternat *et al.* 2018), and regular treatment for ADHD may reduce treatment resistance (Chen *et al.* 2016). Clinicians, however, still need to be mindful of potential interactions with other drugs, as patients are often already prescribed psychiatric drugs when first seen for an ADHD assessment. Usually, the practice of making one change at a time means that ADHD drugs may be started alongside existing treatments. If ADHD treatment improves mood, it may be that medication regimes could be simplified in due course and an antidepressant weaned off when no other changes to medicines are being made simultaneously. A particular interaction to be aware of and to avoid is between the antidepressants fluoxetine and paroxetine with lisdexamfetamine.

Anxiety

Women who suffer from anxiety do not always tolerate stimulant drugs. Some may also need a separate treatment for anxiety. Sometimes psychological treatments such as cognitive behavioural therapy help, but for someone prone to anxiety, a stimulant may exacerbate this. Some women need a second drug (e.g. an antidepressant or, if this is unsuccessful, pregabalin) in order to be able to tolerate stimulants. Beta blockers (eg propranolol or bisoprolol) reduce heart rate and are sometimes useful, as the side effect of a raised pulse caused by stimulants can exacerbate physical symptoms of anxiety.

Bipolar disorder

ADHD drugs should never be initiated during a manic or hypomanic episode of bipolar disorder. Unstable bipolar disorder must be controlled with mood-stabilizing drugs before treating ADHD. In patients with (stable) bipolar disorder, Viktorin *et al.* (2017) found an increased rate of manic episodes within three months of starting methylphenidate (hazard ratio = 6.7). By contrast, for patients taking mood stabilizers, the risk of mania was lower after starting methylphenidate (hazard ratio = 0.6). It is therefore appropriate to treat ADHD in a patient with stable comorbid bipolar disorder, but the patient should be made aware of the risk of stimulant treatment triggering mania. Continuation of a mood stabilizer is essential for these patients alongside ADHD drugs.

Personality disorder

Symptoms or problems experienced by women with ADHD may also overlap with those indicating a personality disorder, such as borderline or emotionally unstable personality disorder. Sometimes ADHD as a cause of emotional symptoms, such as mood instability, has been disregarded. This will have implications for treatment, as ADHD treatment differs significantly from treatments offered for personality disorder. Clinicians again need to be mindful of potential interactions with the drugs, as patients are often already prescribed psychiatric drugs when first seen for an ADHD assessment. If ADHD treatment improves other symptoms, it may be that medication regimes could be simplified in due course.

Eating disorders

Binge eating disorder and bulimia are more common in patients with ADHD. Lisdexamfetamine is approved for the treatment of binge eating disorder in the USA so is a good choice of ADHD treatment in those with ADHD and comorbid binge eating disorder or bulimia (McElroy 2017). Caution is needed in those with anorexia nervosa as many ADHD drugs cause appetite and weight loss.

Sleep problems

As described in Chapter 2, adults with ADHD commonly struggle to sleep well, and report initial insomnia, intermittent waking and a tendency to a delayed sleep phase pattern. Some of this is due to the ceaseless mental activity as patients cannot switch their minds off at night.

How to get to sleep with ADHD

'Sleep hygiene' considers all the things that assist the initiation and maintenance of sleep. This set of conditions is very personal. For example, some people need absolute silence. Others need white noise, such as a TV, radio, some background music or other white noise to mask disturbances. Figure 8.5 outlines a range of approaches for poor sleepers.

Figure 8.5 Tips for poor sleepers

Basic sleep hygiene involves avoiding stimulants, including nicotine and caffeine (including foods containing caffeine), for several hours before bedtime; avoiding alcohol around bedtime; taking regular exercise, especially in the late afternoon or early evening; allowing adequate time to unwind and relax before going to bed; ensuring that the environment is conducive to sleep – making certain that the mattress and bedding are comfortable, the room is dark and quiet, and the temperature is controlled and not too warm; and avoiding clock-watching during the sleep period. Use the bed only for sleep or sex, not as a place to confront problems or argue. Most importantly, patients should attempt to maintain a regular sleep schedule, with consistent bedtime and rise times, and avoidance of daytime naps. If a woman does nap, she should try to avoid this or, at worse, finish it by no later than 4pm. She may need to set an alarm to go to bed and try to get to sleep.

Many people with ADHD are at their most productive at night. Unfortunately, they may have commitments to which they must attend in the morning.

Treatments to help insomnia

Sometimes a low dose of a stimulant 30–45 minutes before bedtime helps calm a wandering, overactive mind that otherwise struggles to switch off. This course of action, however, can exacerbate insomnia for others. To determine whether this may be useful, the woman could try to nap in the day. If she can, she may find that taking a small dose of a stimulant at night may help her to fall asleep. For those for whom the reverse is true, stimulant medication at bedtime is not helpful. For a woman with insomnia who is taking a once daily long acting stimulant, unless she already senses that taking her drug later in the day exacerbates insomnia, then a trial of a small dose of a short acting stimulant at night may be useful.

There are, however, some other medicines that may help induce sleep. These medications are not tolerated by some people as, unfortunately, they can produce undue sedation the next day and may make getting up in the morning harder than ever:

- Diphenhydramine is sold without prescription, is present in some over the counter sleep formulas and is not habit-forming.

- Sedative antihistamines such as promethazine are also available over the counter and may help sleep.

- Melatonin is a naturally occurring peptide released by the brain as light fades and has some function in setting the circadian rhythm. It is available on prescription in the UK but without prescription in the USA. Licences in the UK include a prolonged release formulation for use in adults over the age of 55 years (branded Circadin), a prolonged release formulation for children with autism spectrum disorder and/or Smith-Magenis syndrome (branded Slenyto), or as melatonin tablets or oral solution (licensed for the short-term treatment of jet lag). It is often used for children and adults.

- Most clinicians avoid sleeping pills because they are potentially habit-forming. People quickly develop tolerance to them and require ever-increasing doses.

- Antidepressant medications with significant sedation as a side effect are non-habit-forming and may be useful. For example, trazodone 50–100mg, amitriptyline 25–50mg or mirtazapine 15mg at night are used by some clinicians for their sedative side effects. Due to a complex mechanism of action, lower doses of mirtazapine are more sedative than higher ones.

Solutions to help those who struggle to wake

One solution is to set an alarm to go off an hour before the woman actually plans to rise so that she takes her ADHD medication and then snoozes for the next hour until it starts working. When a second alarm goes off, an hour later, she should be more able to get up and start her day. A second approach involves the use of light. Sitting beside a light box each morning may help some people but is time consuming. Light therapy glasses are available which can continue this exposure to light whilst on the go. These lights, however, are experimental and expensive. Cheaper and probably more effective is to expose yourself to natural light as much as possible. Open the curtains wide and then get outside for ten minutes or more as soon as possible. Natural light and outside air are alerting and refreshing and may help.

✋ KEY POINTS

> » Missed diagnosis of ADHD in women and girls may occur when anxiety or depression presents in association with ADHD. These co-existing conditions may improve with ADHD treatment.

> » For effective treatment of ADHD, a holistic approach should be taken including addressing common sleep disorders and offering both pharmacological and behavioural treatment options.

> » In some women, stimulants help reduce the ceaseless mental activity and promote sleep but in others stimulants promote wakefulness and hinder sleep so need to be avoided later in the day.

TREATING ADHD DURING PREGNANCY AND BREASTFEEDING
Using ADHD drugs during pregnancy

Historically, prescribing ADHD medication during pregnancy or breastfeeding has not been advised due to a lack of evidence for safety and risks concerning unknown adverse effects to the baby. However, a recently published systematic review and meta-analysis reported that exposure to ADHD medication during pregnancy does not appear to be associated with serious adverse maternal or neonatal outcomes (Jiang *et al.* 2019). Nevertheless, most clinicians are cautious, especially regarding prescribing during pregnancy, and feel that it should be avoided, given the potential risks to the developing baby.

Oestrogen levels rise during pregnancy and then fall post-partum. Some women report spontaneous improvement in ADHD symptoms during pregnancy, and especially in these patients, stopping drugs is an easier decision. There may be situations, however, where the risks of not treating ADHD may outweigh the potential risks to the foetus and continued prescribing may be necessary, subject to more careful obstetric monitoring. In these cases, women with ADHD need to be informed of these risks.

Using ADHD drugs during breastfeeding

Perhaps due to hormonal changes, fortunately many women with ADHD report less distress from their symptoms during pregnancy. This is not the case after birth, however. The post-partum fall in oestrogen, as well as the added complexity of coping with a newborn, means that more thought needs to be given as to whether to prescribe during breastfeeding.

The request to restart ADHD medication once the child has been born is a common one as a woman struggles with the extra responsibility and energy needed to look after a newborn. The postnatal period is a stressful and challenging time for women with ADHD. A great deal of organization and planning is required to meet the demands of a new child. Women may find their ADHD symptoms worsen or become particularly difficult to manage while breastfeeding, given additional life pressures that occur in the presence of a new baby. Prescribers should be aware that mothers with ADHD may experience difficulties in managing their own symptoms alongside the increased demands from family life, and these difficulties may be augmented by the presence of ADHD in their own children. As a result, many women with ADHD will request to be restarted on medication after delivery.

If ADHD drugs are requested by the mother, Orney (2018) suggests that the benefits to the mother may outweigh the risk to the child, especially as the child may benefit indirectly from the positive effect on the mother's behaviour. If medication is used during breastfeeding, potential effects of the drug on the child should be monitored, in particular for any evidence of irritability and agitation, hyperactivity, sleeping difficulties, poor weight gain, weight loss and tremor. However, in all of the documented cases to date, no adverse effects have been observed (Marchese, Koren and Bozzo 2015). The child's GP or paediatrician should be informed of any concerns. The mother should be informed of the risks; in particular, she should be made aware that the long-term neurodevelopmental effects have not been adequately studied.

A comprehensive source of information on lactational pharmacology is *Hale's Medications and Mothers' Milk: A Manual of Lactational Pharmacology* (Hale 2019). A further invaluable and freely available resource is LactMed, a free online database. It facilitates a search of any medication and summarizes the data available on the safety of that drug in breastfeeding.

If a drug is requested for ADHD during breastfeeding, current evidence suggests that the least damaging option is methylphenidate, which seems relatively safe. *Hale's Medications and Mothers' Milk* (2019) summarizes the relevant literature on breastfeeding and suggests that the average relative infant dose (RID) derived from a variety of case studies of women taking methylphenidate whilst breastfeeding is low at 0.2–0.4%. It suggests these levels are probably too low to be clinically relevant. In one study, no drug was detected in breast milk 20–21 hours after the maternal dose. No adverse effects were noted in any of the infants. An RID of under 10% is felt to be low and could be considered for use in breastfeeding. The RID for methylphenidate is significantly less than for dexamfetamine (RID 2.46–7.25%) and so methylphenidate is thought to be the safest option in a mother who is breastfeeding. Hale's textbook (2019) suggests that infant monitoring is needed to observe for agitation, irritability, poor sleeping patterns, changes in feeding and poor weight gain.

CONCLUSION

ADHD often places a significant psychological, emotional and economic burden on families as well as the individual. Children with ADHD have poorer long-term outcomes as adults than controls with respect to academic achievement and attainment, occupational rank and job performance, risky sexual practices and early unwanted pregnancies, substance use, relationship difficulties, marital problems, traffic violations and car accidents (Usami 2016).

Due to the differences in how ADHD presents, and the lack

of understanding that surrounds the condition in females, many women remain undiagnosed or misdiagnosed. It is thought that in the UK less than 1 in 20 women who suffer from ADHD are currently offered a treatment that could be life changing (Renoux *et al.* 2016). This should not be the case.

ADHD treatment does not just help with the core ADHD symptoms, but can often help with emotional instability and wider mental and physical health problems. Oestrogen levels can greatly affect women, making them more susceptible to severe premenstrual mood swings and menopausal changes, and can cause ADHD medication to be ineffective or less effective at certain times of the month.

For optimal treatment, a clinician needs to understand the range of ADHD symptoms in women and how treatment should be tailored individually. Ideally, a range of strategies to help women with ADHD should be available – pharmacological and non-pharmacological. Technology can help improve compliance by providing reminders using alarms on smart phones or via discreet vibrating wrist watches, using calendar and reminder apps on computers or using pill boxes with timers.

Lastly, don't forget the wider family. ADHD is highly genetic and often runs in families. A child may be more able to cope if their parent is also treated and vice versa. Look out for ADHD in relatives and consider screening others in the family and signposting them to appropriate help.

REFERENCES

Adler, L.A., Dirks, B., Deas, P., Raychaudhuri, A. *et al.* (2013) 'Self-reported quality of life in adults with attention-deficit/hyperactivity disorder and executive function impairment treated with lisdexamfetamine dimesylate: A randomized, double-blind, multicenter, placebo-controlled, parallel-group study.' *BMC Psychiatry 13*, 253.

Adler, L.A., Liebowitz, M., Kronenberger, W., Qiao, M. *et al.* (2009) 'Atomoxetine treatment in adults with attention-deficit/hyperactivity disorder and comorbid social anxiety disorder.' *Depression & Anxiety 26*, 3, 212–221.

Bolea-Alamañac, B., Nutt, D.J., Adamou, M., Asherson, P. *et al.* (2014) 'Evidence-based guidelines for the pharmacological management of attention deficit hyperactivity disorder: Update on recommendations from the British Association for Psychopharmacology.' *Journal of Psychopharmacology 28*, 3, 179–203.

CADDRA (2020) *Canadian ADHD Practice Guidelines*, 4.1 edn. Accessed on 27 July 2020 at https://www.caddra.ca/canadian-adhd-practice-guidelines.

Caisley, H. and Müller, U. (2012) 'Adherence to medication in adults with attention deficit hyperactivity disorder and pro re nata dosing of psychostimulants: A systematic review.' *European Psychiatry 27*, 5, 343–349.

Chang, Z., Ghirardi, L., Quinn, P.D., Asherson, P., D'Onofrio, B.M. and Larsson, H. (2019) 'Risks and benefits of attention-deficit/hyperactivity disorder medication on behavioral and neuropsychiatric outcomes: A qualitative review of pharmacoepidemiology studies using linked prescription databases.' *Biological Psychiatry 86*, 5, 335–343.

Chang, Z., Quinn, P.D., Hur, K., Gibbons, R.D., Sjölander, A. *et al.* (2017) 'Association between medication use for attention-deficit/hyperactivity disorder and risk of motor vehicle crashes.' *JAMA Psychiatry 74*, 6, 597–603.

Chappell, P.B., Riddle, M.A., Scahill, L., Lynch, K.A. *et al.* (1995) 'Guanfacine treatment of comorbid attention-deficit hyperactivity disorder and Tourette's syndrome: Preliminary clinical experience.' *Journal of the American Academy of Child & Adolescent Psychiatry 34*, 9, 1140–1146.

Chen, M.H., Pan, T.L., Hsu, J.W., Huang, K.L. *et al.* (2016) 'Attention-deficit hyperactivity disorder comorbidity and antidepressant resistance among patients with major depression: A nationwide longitudinal study.' *European Neuropsychopharmacology 26*, 11, 1760–1767.

Cortese, S., Adamo, N., Del Giovane, C., Mohr-Jensen, C. *et al.* (2018) 'Comparative efficacy and tolerability of medications for attention-deficit hyperactivity disorder in children, adolescents, and adults: A systematic review and network meta-analysis.' *Lancet Psychiatry 5*, 9, 727–738.

Crunelle, C.L., van den Brink, W., Moggi, F., Konstenius, M. *et al.* (2018) 'International consensus statement on screening, diagnosis and treatment of substance use disorder patients with comorbid attention deficit/ hyperactivity disorder.' *European Addiction Research 24*, 1, 43–51.

European Medicines Agency (2009) 'Methylphenidate.' Accessed on 8 September 2020 at https://www.ema.europa.eu/en/medicines/human/referrals/methylphenidate.

Hale, T.W. (2019) *Hale's Medications and Mothers' Milk: A Manual of Lactational Pharmacology*, 18th edn. New York, NY: Springer.

Iwanami, A., Saito, K., Fujiwara, M., Okutsu, D. and Ichikawa, H. (2020) 'Efficacy and safety of guanfacine extended-release in the treatment of attention-deficit/hyperactivity disorder in adults: Results of a randomized, double-blind, placebo-controlled study.' *Journal of Clinical Psychiatry 81*, 3. DOI: 10.4088/JCP.19m12979.

Jiang, H.-Y., Zhang, X., Jiang, C.-M. and Fu, H.-B. (2019) 'Maternal and neonatal outcomes after exposure to ADHD medication during pregnancy: A systematic review and meta-analysis.' *Pharmacoepidemiology and Drug Safety* 28, 3, 288–295.

Justice, A.J. and Wit, H. (1999) 'Acute effects of D-amphetamine during the follicular and luteal phases of the menstrual cycle in women.' *Psychopharmacology* 145, 1, 67–75.

Konstenius, M., Jayaram-Lindström, N., Guterstam, J., Beck, O., Philips, B. and Franck, J. (2014) 'Methylphenidate for attention deficit hyperactivity disorder and drug relapse in criminal offenders with substance dependence: A 24-week randomized placebo-controlled trial.' *Addiction* 109, 3, 440–449.

Kooij, J.J.S., Bijlenga, D., Salerno, L., Jaeschke, R. *et al.* (2019) 'Updated European Consensus Statement on diagnosis and treatment of adult ADHD.' *European Psychiatry* 56, 1, 14–34.

LactMed (Drugs and Lactation Database) Accessed on 27 July 2020 at https://www.ncbi.nlm.nih.gov/books/NBK501922/.

Levin, F.R., Mariani, J.J., Specker, S., Mooney, M. *et al.* (2015) 'Extended-release mixed amphetamine salts vs placebo for comorbid adult attention-deficit/hyperactivity disorder and cocaine use disorder: A randomized clinical trial.' *JAMA Psychiatry* 72, 6, 593–602.

Lichtenstein, P., Halldner, L., Zetterqvist, J., Sjölander, A. *et al.* (2012) 'Medication for attention deficit-hyperactivity disorder and criminality.' *The New England Journal of Medicine* 367, 21, 2006–2014.

Maneeton, N., Maneeton, B., Srisurapanont, M. and Martin, S.D. (2011) 'Bupropion for adults with attention-deficit hyperactivity disorder: Meta-analysis of randomized, placebo-controlled trials.' *Psychiatry & Clinical Neurosciences* 65, 7, 611–617.

Marchese, M., Koren, G. and Bozzo P. (2015) 'Is it safe to breastfeed whilst taking methylphenidate?' *Canadian Family Physician* 61, 9, 765–766.

McCracken, J.T., McGough, J.J., Loo, S.K., Levitt, J. *et al.* (2016) 'Combined stimulant and guanfacine administration in attention-deficit/hyperactivity disorder: A controlled, comparative study.' *Journal of the American Academy of Child and Adolescent Psychiatry* 55, 8, 657–666.

McElroy, S. (2017) 'Pharmacologic treatments for binge-eating disorder.' *Journal of Clinical Psychiatry* 78 (suppl. 1), 14–19.

McManus, S., Meltzer, H., Brugha, T., Bebbington, P. and Jenkins, R. (2009) *Adult Psychiatric Morbidity in England 2007: Results of a Household Survey.* Leeds: The NHS Information Centre.

National Institute for Health and Care Excellence (2018) *Attention Deficit Hyperactivity Disorder: Diagnosis and Management (NICE Guideline NG87).* Accessed on 27 July 2020 at https://www.nice.org.uk/guidance/ng87.

Ogundele, M.O. and Ayyash, H.F. (2018) 'Review of the evidence for the management of co-morbid tic disorders in children and adolescents with attention deficit hyperactivity disorder.' *World Journal of Clinical Pediatrics 7*, 1, 36–42.

Orney, A. (2018) 'Pharmacological treatment of attention deficit hyperactivity disorder during pregnancy and lactation.' *Pharmaceutical Research 35*, 3, 46.

Philipsen, A., Jans, T., Graf, E., Matthies, S. *et al.* (2015) 'Effects of group psychotherapy, individual counselling, methylphenidate, and placebo in the treatment of adult ADHD: A randomized controlled trial.' *JAMA Psychiatry 72*, 12, 1199–1210.

Quinn, P.D., Chang, Z., Hur, K., Gibbons, R.D. et al. (2017) 'ADHD medication and substance-related problems.' *American Journal of Psychiatry 174*, 9, 877–885.

Quinn, P.O. (2005) 'Treating adolescent girls and women with ADHD: Gender-specific issues.' *Journal of Clinical Psychology 61*, 5, 579–587.

Renoux, C., Shin, J.-Y., Dell'Aniello, S., Fergusson, E. and Suissa, S. (2016) 'Prescribing trends of attention-deficit hyperactivity disorder (ADHD) medications in UK primary care, 1995–2015.' *British Journal of Clinical Pharmacology 82*, 3, 858–868.

Sauer, J.-M., Ponsler, G.D., Mattiuz, E.L., Long, A.J. *et al.* (2003) 'Disposition and metabolic fate of atomoxetine hydrochloride: The role of CYP2D6 in human disposition and metabolism.' *Drug Metabolism and Disposition 31*, 1, 98–107.

Shanmugan, S. and Epperson, C.N. (2014) 'Estrogen and the prefrontal cortex: Towards a new understanding of estrogen's effects on executive functions in the menopause transition.' *Human Brain Mapping 35*, 3, 847–865.

Spencer, T.J., Biederman, J., Wilens, T.E. and Faraone, S.V. (2002) 'Novel treatments for attention-deficit/hyperactivity disorder in children.' *Journal of Clinical Psychiatry 63* (suppl. 12), 16–22.

Stahl, S.M. and Mignon, L. (2011) *Stahl's Illustrated Attention Deficit Hyperactivity Disorder.* Cambridge: Cambridge University Press.

Sternat, T., Fotinos, K., Fine, A., Epstein, I. and Katzman, M.A. (2018) 'Low hedonic tone and attention-deficit hyperactivity disorder: Risk factors for treatment resistance in depressed adults.' *Neuropsychiatric Disease & Treatment 14*, 2379–2387.

Usami, M. (2016) 'Functional consequences of attention-deficit hyperactivity disorder on children and their families.' *Psychiatry & Clinical Neurosciences 70*, 8, 303–317.

Viktorin, A., Rydén, E., Thase, M.E., Chang, Z. *et al.* (2017) 'The risk of treatment-emergent mania with methylphenidate in bipolar disorder.' *American Journal of Psychiatry 174*, 4, 341–348.

Chapter 9

A Collection of Voices

This chapter brings together stories of life directly from girls and women with attention deficit hyperactivity disorder (ADHD). The task was to tell a piece of their life story in order to help clinicians, parents, relatives, friends and other girls and women understand. Each report portrays a person's personal journey and may not reflect the experiences of other girls and women with ADHD.

As a collection of experiences, they provide important and powerful messages. There are themes in these accounts which resonate with every chapter in this book: a late diagnosis, developing mental health problems, choosing medication, the strengths of ADHD, as well as the ability to develop strategies and skills to overcome obstacles. Whilst many of the themes are common, the variety, colour and depth of these personal accounts describe the vast array of presentations of ADHD.

So here is a great example of my ADHD, with a smile as I try to keep my humour. Woke this morning to recall the article I had hoped to contribute and panicked!! I had missed the deadline...because although I had launched myself into writing with the enthusiasm of a whippet dog chasing the wind, it was followed by totally forgetting to finish what I had started. In my defence, I have recently begun three 'online' short courses, so my mind is deeply submerged not only in various topics but in various eras. Not being able to find the piece of paper I had so carefully noted the date on, I had to think, 'Which website did I see the original post on? Ah, here it is, the 10th of May – phew.' I wonder what others will write and look forward to reading a copy of the book. If I remember to buy a copy!

Virginia

I don't actually know what not having ADD is like. Absolutely no idea. For all my imagination, I can't imagine not having ADD.

I know that my attention span is interest based, and that's why the quality of my work used to vary based on my interest in the topic – something that baffled my teachers in primary school who I think were convinced I was being inconsistent to spite them. I know that I have rejection sensitivity – light-hearted teasing feels like an attack on my very soul, no matter how illogical I know that is. Right now, I'm writing this without a plan like I really should have done and am writing this like a stream of consciousness instead – I'm pretty sure that's my ADD too.

Before I was diagnosed, I remember going to school, being told off by every teacher, being excluded by the other kids (not out of malice but just because I wasn't exactly easy to talk to. Looking back, I think some people actually wanted to be my friend but I wasn't paying attention!), losing my coat, hat, gloves or all three, and then coming home, to be told off again for having forgotten however many things I had forgotten on the given day.

I remember being told off in reception, being told, 'You know what you're doing!' and having not the faintest clue. I told the teacher as much – how am I supposed to stop doing it if I don't know what it is? – and was firmly dragged out of the classroom. It felt very unfair, and I was certain that if the teachers just heard me out, we could come to an understanding. This sort of thing happened a lot.

I'm actually surprised no one noticed my ADD sooner – I wasn't a quiet kid at the back of the class – I was consistently talking back to teachers, getting into trouble and not understanding why and with an attention span that was about as stable as a nuclear reactor.

Once I was diagnosed, three things happened. First, arguments at home dropped dramatically. Second, after a bit of explaining, teachers started treating me and my antics with more understanding – and I felt much safer from those dreaded telling-offs that hurt each time like it was the first (I now know that was rejection sensitivity!). Finally, I started taking medication, and with that I could suddenly do the things I had to do without making such a massive effort.

Not everyone understands ADD – I think some of the girls thought the pill I took in the afternoon was to prevent me from going crazy, and I've had a teacher tell me, 'But it doesn't say in your notes you need to listen to music to stay focused!' and that she 'knew what ADHD was'. But I know what it is for me and that's helped me understand how to work with it.

(Curse this word count I have so much to say...)

Anna, aged 18 years

Living with undiagnosed ADHD for most of my school days was somewhat of a minefield. One of the first things I learned in my reception class aged five was that if I asked to go to the toilet, I was able to give myself a five-minute break from the perils of concentration with a brief relaxing stroll and a quick catch-up with my friends. I indulged happily in this rule-bending defiance for months until the concerned head teacher asked my mother if I had bladder condition.

From then on, I had a fairly tumultuous relationship with my teachers at school. On the one hand, my quick-witted one-liners (thanks, ADHD) would make them laugh and get me off the hook for quite a lot of bad behaviour, but I battled with my defiance on a daily basis. A Year 7 Latin lesson springs to mind: we were completing some grammar exercises before the end of class and I was bored out of my mind. Incidentally, this lesson took place in a physics laboratory and in the corner was an Airzooka toy that shot out air at high pressure. I quietly rose from my seat, grabbed the toy and shot my unwitting teacher point blank in the face with a blast of cold air. She asked to see me after class but miraculously I managed to talk my way out of any trouble!

Shortly after this, my family's lives were turned upside down: my mother was diagnosed with cancer on my 13th birthday. I wish I were proud of how I reacted to this, but I was not capable of behaving maturely at the time. I became incredibly angry at my parents and I projected my defiance onto them, engaging in series of precocious and unhealthy behaviours that I could not comprehend the consequences of at the time. I became very impulsive and no one could persuade me to behave otherwise. We would not know I suffered with ADHD for another two years.

Shopping over recent weeks has drawn to my attention that my supermarket habits were not perhaps as organised as the majority...

Alexa arrived at the end of the first week of lockdown; no surprise to hear it was an impulse buy when seeing it on offer! I had a love-hate relationship with the idea of Alexa, it's one that still stands! I love the fact that I can ask Alexa to add things to my 'To Do' list as they randomly pop into my head in no logical order and at no particular time of the day or night. I love the fact I can ask her to remind me to follow through the said reminder at a seemingly more appropriate time. I hate the fact that I don't join the dots so Alexa has reminded me to 'collect your HRT from the chemist' and 'don't forget to pay credit card bill', both in the middle of a Zoom meeting with a client. I have too many reservations to allow her access to my diary.

I like the fact I can keep a running shopping list that is stored on my phone so it actually accompanies me into the supermarket. The various sticky notes often failed to make it into the handbag. Those that did often absconded from the handbag and could be found rolling round the car (alongside various other things). Thanks to Alexa, this is a thing of the past.

Next is learning the new supermarket etiquette in place as a result of Covid-19. Some have adapted more easily than others. The challenge of waiting for people with ADHD has been well enough documented. The instinct is to jump into any free gap as quickly as possible in order to move on to the next thing. I've had a couple of reminders to 'wait' before starting to unpack the trolley onto the conveyor belt. One wasn't delivered very courteously. It's not that I don't get the need or am deliberately ignoring measures, I really do, but my spatial awareness is a little challenged and it feels frustratingly like shopping is in 'slow mo'.

Social distancing means when I realise I have forgotten something, and swing the trolley round 180° to double back on myself, there is a reduced chance of a near collision. Many supermarkets have introduced a one-way system, a safe and logical measure. However, it's made me more aware of the extent to which I darted between aisles. When something I needed (which may not have made it to Alexa's list) popped into my head, I would go straight to wherever it's located before returning to the aisle I was last in. This was repeated frequently. I probably did four times the necessary step count as I boomeranged between the aisles. This aisle hopping isn't as easy with the one-way system as it's even more obvious you are going against the tide of the other shoppers, and people are less tolerant of it. Sadly, to my knowledge, Alexa does not organise shopping lists into the same order as the supermarket aisles.

Take out the undertone of anxiety that can on occasions be sensed, the experience once inside feels calmer and more organised – until I arrive that is!

Brooke, mum with ADHD

I'm Leila, I'm in my late 30s and I'm a mum to an 8-year-old boy who has recently been diagnosed with ADHD. I too have recently been diagnosed with ADHD following the diagnosis of my son. Researching the subject and how it affects people both young and old really resonated with me. As I researched coping strategies for my son, I realised that I also ticked all of the boxes and I decided to get myself assessed. If I was diagnosed, I felt that not only would it help my son to come to terms with having ADHD, it would also help me to understand some of the most confusing and difficult times in my life. Unsurprisingly, I was diagnosed with all aspects of ADHD.

As a child, I played a lot of sports and this really helped me with my energy levels. I was a very energetic, talkative girl, with a head full of ideas and things I wanted to do. I struggled to focus at school and although I didn't do badly, my report always read 'Leila is a very enthusiastic member of the class but could do better if she applied herself.' Story of my life!

As I grew older and discovered my loves in life, I flourished. For me, I loved to be around other people and to help others. My career has been mainly focused on customer service and sales. These days, I'm a software tester as I'm a great team player, a lateral thinker and I have excellent attention to detail (when I want to). These qualities are quite typical of people with ADHD and, as a result, I've progressed very quickly in this new profession.

The biggest challenge I've found with my ADHD has been the impulsive side of things. I may speak out of turn unintentionally or make decisions without properly thinking about the possible outcomes. My emotions can be very up and down and always have been since I was a child. I care deeply about things and feel the need to fix things and struggle to rest until I've done everything I can. When I'm low, I struggle really badly with motivation and have found that I turn to online shopping or similar to give me that boost I need, but it's a short-term fix. I'm prone to panicking and worrying, and worst of all, I overthink everything! I've learned to deal with these issues a lot better in the past few years by using mindfulness techniques. Cognitive behavioural therapy has also really helped me understand how I think and what strategies work best for me.

There are far more positives than negatives for me with my ADHD. It makes me who I am, it makes me good at what I do, and now that I understand my 'quirks', I love and accept who I am. I embrace my ADHD and have learned to use it to my advantage!

Leila

In 2004, I was on the phone to the Samaritans. I thought, 'That's it, I've lost it, I'm going crazy.'

My brother would have been diagnosed with ADHD but sadly he self-medicated and was dead at age 35 years.

I was in an unhappy marriage, trying to support my son who had been diagnosed with ADHD that same year, hold down a job and run a family home. Life had been challenging; the worst part was school as we had corporal punishment in those days. Teachers could hit you, throw things at you, and use the two-pronged leather strap. Children did not have a voice in those days and if you were abused, there was no one to tell. My family were very supportive and encouraging except when it came to authority. I was sexually abused but never told my parents.

Now I felt like I was in a dark pit and knew I had to somehow pull myself out. I had been thinking about starting to sing again and plucked up the courage to join a small group, and that's when it started to change. I began to get my voice back. My singing teacher was approached as Celebrity Fame Academy needed stand-ins for their celebrities and so I applied, not thinking anything of it at the time. I received a phone call at work asking me to go for an audition so off I went after work with my shopping bags (LOL!). I was subsequently asked to be a stand-in for Jenny Eclair and was sent the songs to learn.

My husband said I couldn't go because I had a son to look after but by that time I had become more myself and told him I was going. So off I trotted to this studio, which they were still erecting. I lost the key to my little suitcase so they had to cut the padlock off it. That was the start of many differences I had with the other stand-ins. There was so much going on around me that I was getting distracted every second.

Then the lightbulb moment: OMG that's it, I have ADHD too. I broke down and told David Grant, the voice coach, and he was so supportive as his friend whom he had known from school days has ADHD. After that, the production team made sure they had eye contact with me when giving out instructions. I wish they had told me about the teleprompter and how it worked, but that's another story.

So when I returned home I went to see my GP to deliver the news. She said I couldn't have ADHD because I was a professional person. I stuck to my guns and so she asked me for more evidence. I told her my husband says it's like looking after two children. She got it and referred me to the Maudsley Hospital in London, and nine months later, in December 2005, I was diagnosed with combined ADHD. This totally changed my world for the better as I started taking Concerta XL. I am now taking Elvanse, which is even better, and I have been helping others to change their lives ever since.

I am so grateful for this diagnosis and treatment. I am not crazy, I am blessed.

Sheena

For me, ADHD resembles that feeling you get when you know, you know the answer to something – you've forgotten it – but it's on the tip of your tongue. It's like always being on the brink of something brilliant but, a lot of the time, not quite getting there. Any of my friends or family can tell you my most used phrase is 'Wait. What?' or 'I forgot, never mind' – it would be an understatement to say that clarity isn't an attribute of mine.

I've always had a huge imagination that I'm sure ADHD expands the boundaries of – I dream vividly, creating whole universes in my head. But I've only learnt over time that there's a time and a place for daydreaming and, apparently, it's not school. The thing is, whilst I do believe ADHD has enhanced my creativity and aided me in a lot of other ways, it's not exactly been my friend in a classroom setting. Zoning out often translated to 'not listening' to my less than knowledgeable teachers, who often thought I just didn't care. I was labelled as the 'misbehaved troublesome one' from the get-go, and my naturally excited and chaotic demeanour was always met with the same 'You'd do better if you talk less' or 'Stop disrupting the class!'

I remember when I was in Year 11, the school called my mum to tell her that (complete news to me) I'd apparently missed over *four* detentions, and was due an hour-long one for my 'disgraceful behaviour'! The whole thing was quite amusing, considering I had absolutely no idea what they were even for. Thankfully, my mum was well-versed on the topic of my inattentiveness and general foolishness, so she understood that I never, knowingly, 'took the piss'. She scolded my teachers for their ignorant attitudes towards my ADHD-fuelled actions and managed to get me out of it! Funnily enough, I actually never found out what I was in trouble for, which sums up my life pretty well.

All of that aside, though, I don't wish I was 'normal'. I don't want to mute my personality with medication for the convenience of others! I may have too much energy and an *abysmal* attention span but I am certainly *very* entertaining. The best thing about ADHD is meeting people who love my energy; who see my faults as what makes me who I am: lively and hilarious! If you can catch what I'm saying in my rapid flow of speech, I'll hopefully make you laugh. Or at least curious and somewhat confused.

Jessie

My experience with having ADD has been challenging throughout my life. From a very young age, I have always found it difficult to concentrate and stay on task, especially when I first started school in reception. I just couldn't understand how everyone else knew what to do, and how they were thriving and progressing in school while I was still struggling to bring the right equipment to school and remember my homework. I knew that I was bright, and I loved reading and learning about the world, but I found it so difficult to organise myself. As I progressed into secondary school, this became more and more challenging, as I had to adapt to new environments that I had no prior experience of. I moved schools in Year 8, shortly after being diagnosed with ADD. I found that being formally diagnosed was a relief in some ways, as it finally meant that I knew exactly why I was the way I am, and could work out ways to make life easier and more manageable for myself.

Molly

Growing up with ADHD has been an odd one. I remember when I was constantly daydreaming in class and not being able to understand what people were saying even though I knew exactly what they were saying and could hear them from a very young age. There were a lot of issues like this but as I got older there were more and more instances of major mistakes from what seemed like either a lack of care, extreme emotion or lack of memory.

Each time the fallout from it got bigger and bigger. When I was doing my AS-levels, I had a large meltdown after having not completed about three weeks' worth of artwork due to freezing up from stress. That's another thing as well, I used to freeze up when there was a task that required either large or sometimes small amounts of emotional or physical exertion. Anyway, after this particular meltdown I started looking things up online because I knew that something was 'off', as it were. I kept being told over and over again that I 'didn't care' and was 'lazy' and that I 'just had to get on with it', yet I was trying to do the tasks every time but my body wouldn't listen to what I wanted to make it do. So, I looked it up online and found a couple of things about ADHD. I did as many tests as I could find; all came back with percentages of over 80%. So I thought it would be a good idea to go have an assessment. It came back as just being on the verge but not quite ADHD. This diagnosis stuck until six months after the end of my A-levels when I had another meltdown that left me catatonic for about 30–60 minutes and then in an incredibly low mood for the next week. I remember saying something along the lines of, 'I can't keep going like this' and, 'I don't want to have to keep going'. It was a really awful time.

So I went somewhere else for a second opinion and told them about the previous assessment, and then they assessed me and it came back that I in fact had ADHD (combined type) and rejection sensitive dysphoria. I was really relieved when they told me as this, as it affirmed that I wasn't just 'lazy' or 'didn't care' (which, as I have grown up, I have always equated to being a bad person who doesn't care about others). They also explained to me that in the first assessment they had said I didn't have it because I wasn't bad academically and that I wasn't as bad as their other clients with ADHD, but that this was not really valid and that sometimes people (especially women) with ADHD can fly under the radar academically and that everyone's symptoms of ADHD are different.

Since this diagnosis, I have been on Elvanse and I have seen incredible improvement in many areas including my self-confidence, which had always been low as I felt out of place among my peers, especially with the girls. The difference between my first and second assessments was evident as well: in the first, the questions and forms given out were not (as many of my teachers commented) suitable for my age or maturity, and my personality traits were not taking into context; however, in the second, the questions were well-suited to me and everything was taken into consideration.

Evelyn

Growing up, I was the 'naughty' one. I used humour as a way to cope; I was the class clown, but really, I was shy, awkward and weird. I used it unwittingly to mask my unease and to deflect from feelings of inadequacy. One of my better coping skills!

Early on in secondary school, I began to drink alcohol to deal with socialising. I self-harmed and developed an eating disorder to deal with intense emotions, self-esteem issues, feeling stupid, not good enough, a failure. Where I struggled socially and academically, I excelled in arts and sports. I played in all the school teams (which often got me out of classes), competed in dance, swimming, trampolining, gymnastics and athletics, and loved musical theatre. I was creative, I drew fashion, and I wrote short stories and song lyrics.

When I was asked not to return to my school for sixth form, I took dance in college. I thrived and got a distinction in a Performing Arts BTEC, which was mainly practical. In university, there was lots of theory and essay writing, and as I had never had to write one before, I struggled; I dropped out twice. There was no support.

I got a job in a supermarket; I didn't enjoy handling money and when panic attacks stopped me going there, I worked for my brother for a while. I tried office temping, but the anxiety got the better of me; having to take calls and manage new systems was too much. So, I quit.

My mental health declined. I made several suicide attempts from age 18 onwards. My family didn't understand me. Learning difficulties and abuse are a potent mix for mental illness. I left home, and I sofa surfed and lived in a caravan for over a year before getting a council property.

I was diagnosed with generalised anxiety disorder, borderline personality disorder and post-traumatic stress disorder. The depression and medication stripped me of my creativity. I relied on alcohol and weed to get though the lonely days. My sensory issues got worse and were triggered often; I was unaware that a simple pair of earphones could help so much! I developed agoraphobia, became paranoid, had psychotic episodes, and my rock bottom was getting aggressively sectioned and physically assaulted. Navigating the benefits system and mental health teams was so stressful (and still is). I was ashamed. I didn't like myself. I didn't want to be here. It is a miracle I survived.

After lots of therapy, I was still struggling with life when I took an online mental health course that mentioned ADHD. I had always joked I had ADHD, but now I was convinced. I immediately looked for a local support group and have been fortunate to find Fastminds.

Now I have a diagnosis, I'm learning coping skills that could have been taught to me as a child. You can't help but wonder if things would have been different for me if it had been recognised earlier. Would I have graduated? Would I have a job rather than being unemployed for a decade?

Sara

The word count is limited so I will glaze over much and ensure I leave you intrigued with a cliff-hanger at the end!

My name is Rachel Banks, 29 years old, diagnosed with severe, combined type ADHD at 21 years old. This late diagnosis, of course, occurred after the short process of seven years! And inevitably at this stage, I was a bit all over the place in many areas of my life... However, I will shed some light on another aspect of ADHD.

Extremely exuberant and passionate about pretty much everything is probably what most people would say I was like. And I can't really say otherwise, and it has been both a blessing and burden... A 'unique' individual is probably the most-used term.

This energy has led to some productive and/or cool things such as: raising money for charities by means of walking on fire and free-fall abseiling, etc. Trying many sports, for example snowboarding, ice-skating, BMX or boxing. Writing to companies, TV producers, athletes, etc. to tell them how much I like their products/packaging or if I feel they have helped or inspired me in some way (many of which have responded!). I started my own tennis racket stringing business after impulsively buying a machine, having never strung a racket before...fortunately, I taught myself and ran a very successful business! A career in tennis coaching with a focus on coaching those with disabilities and people with no self-confidence; for example, I taught a boy how to play tennis through his love of *Star Wars*, so we no longer had tennis lessons, we had lightsabre lessons with force fields and shooting droids and all sorts!

In school, I would fidget and doodle the entire time and was apparently 'disengaged from the learning process'. I was kicked out of college for many reasons, including talking continuously, throwing chairs/tables, never being on time, not paying attention, not handing in my work on time...the list is endless. Yes, my time management is horrendous and my organisational skills are not exactly orthodox, and when not channelled well, my energy is nothing less than a ticking time bomb. However, my fidgeting and doodling helped me concentrate and know what was going on, plus, the doodles were pretty awesome and eventually my doodles have ended up being incorporated into much of my work.

Eventually, I got into university after returning to college on stimulant medication, which made me a much calmer, more organised person. However, medication is not a cure and my struggles led to a rather turbulent journey, to say the least, trying to juggle all areas of life and taking on more and more. However, after three leaves of absence, I went back to smash it and graduate with a first class honours degree and... an outstanding academic achievement award! I learnt to work with my ADHD instead of trying to change and learn like others, which I simply couldn't do. I doodled away, used an exercise bike with makeshift desk, worked when I could, accepted the nothing days and didn't overdo the good ones. I walked and talked with people instead of sitting and stewing, I learnt to trust that my brain knew what it was doing and that what appeared to be a chaotic mess and a lot of faffing was actually creative chaos and productive faffing which would eventually lead to finished, successful projects!

And now for that intriguing cliff-hanger I warned you about. I have been built with an abundance of energy but without any internal signal to tell me to stop or, as I was to find out in a scary way, that there is no actual available energy left to use! Prior to returning to finish university unmedicated, I had spent three months in hospital after not waking up one day. My heart and liver had gone all over the place and I was left with absolutely no muscle, fat or anything to become the lightest person the hospital had ever seen.

ADHD can be challenging in ways we don't realise and my passion, care and energy overrode the warning signals. Although ADHD can bring about a storm, in itself, ADHD does not determine any particular outcome; it is how the individual approaches the storm which determines how long it will last and how to deal with the aftermath.

Rachel Banks

The good parts of having ADHD is that it makes you more unique as a person. It's nice to have a challenge – it's not always easy because people often misunderstand what it's like. There are loads of opportunities for people with ADHD – I'm glad it doesn't have any effect on what job I could have. I like the ocean because it's calm and it's quiet so maybe I'll do something 'aquamariney'. I want to be a mum because I know I'm going to relate to how my child's feeling. I'm grateful there's no physical pain. It's good because you often have a sense of humour. Because you don't focus on the boring things as much, you tend to go off on tangents which people find funny. My friends support me just like they'd support anyone and they never ask me if I'm ok, they treat me like a normal person. People like asking questions and I like to share and answer their questions, and often it's nice because when you have therapy for it, you get to talk about other things which don't have anything to do with ADHD, so you can talk to people who will listen. *But,* sometimes people will blame things on my ADHD, when it's nothing to do with that.

The bad. People always minimise it, like it's nothing. People think it's like having hay fever, when it really isn't. It has a lot of impact on your mental state – it's not just physical. You feel vulnerable because people often misuse the term and aren't considerate of people with ADHD.

My parents say, 'Don't have that sugar, that will make you crazy.' That drives me mad. You make lots of noise and you're moving all of the time and people look at you as though you are crazy. Sometimes it's a bit overwhelming – the ADHD symptoms can become bigger than who you actually are as a person. People are constantly telling me to shush. It's not their fault, but it is quite hard to do. Or I don't stick to the subject and people find that annoying. Some people put themselves in a position where they think they can tell me what to do about it. That's frustrating because it feels as though they are being nosy and annoying.

I hated primary school because the teachers' perspective was I was just fidgety and attention seeking. They didn't recognise ADHD and were often making fake accusations that I was naughty and loud (although that's actually my personality – when I'm happy, I am loud). I get really buzzy. When people feel excited – for example, because they're getting a new cat – my excitement would be times ten. When I need to do something – I'm not that great at that – the ADHD makes it much worse. You often have to make friends with people who are just like you; I have friends who are pretty nuts because it's easier to have friends like that, and we share jokes. For example, I have a jellyfish called Bernard and he's friends with my flower seeds called Susan and Jessop and Arnold. I like making nicknames for things – making them my friends because they don't judge you.

Beth, aged 11 years

Chapter 10

Concluding Remarks

—— DR JOANNE STEER ——

It is not new news that girls and women can have attention deficit hyperactivity disorder (ADHD); after all, our colleagues in America have been talking about this for years, particularly Patricia Quinn and Kathleen Nadeau. However, in the UK we are still at the beginning of our journey. The accounts of the girls and women throughout this book highlight that the battles are still very real. These battles are to be referred, to be seen by the right team, to be supported at school, to be offered appropriate treatment, to be given quality information and advice, to be supported in the workplace, to receive physical health care and fundamentally to be taken seriously (girls, their parents and women).

It is important to remember that whilst symptoms of ADHD can present differently in girls and women compared with men and boys, this is not always the case. Whatever the clinical picture, those symptoms are no less impairing in females than in their male counterparts, and sometimes more so. It is absolutely critical that those girls and women are able to access high-quality and relevant information about ADHD alongside appropriate, evidence-based treatment.

We hope that this book will provide further focus on the issues for girls and women with ADHD. We hope that girls and women may read some, if not all, of the book and feel a connection with others who are walking similar paths. We hope that parents and carers will read this book and take new understanding, new ideas and energy to push on and carry on the often thankless task of parenting their daughter with ADHD. We hope that general practitioners, paediatricians, psychiatrists, child mental health teams, adult mental health teams and therapy teams read this book and take time to reflect on their own practice and their own potential biases, and develop their own understanding of girls and women with ADHD. We hope that doctors, nurses and staff who work in a physical health focused setting can take inspiration from Dr Allyson Parry and consider the part they could play in identifying and supporting girls and women with ADHD. We hope that school staff read this book and are able to reflect on those quiet daydreamers who don't cause too much fuss, to reconsider their assumptions about the teens who are always late, answer back and still manage to get the grades, and that they find new ways to work with girls with ADHD. We all need to work together to raise awareness and improve our understanding of ADHD in girls and women, so that future generations don't have to wait nearly half of their lifetime for the right diagnosis and support.

It is clear that we need to identify girls with ADHD earlier, in order to support them in the best way possible and reduce the impact of ADHD on their lives. Early identification can mean that parents, schools and other professionals are in a position to support these girls with their challenges and harness their strengths. This could mean channelling the energy of a hyperactive girl into sport, encouraging the creativity of a daydreamer into art or science, or supporting the impulsive risk-taking girl into entrepreneurial activities or even law like Eva Akins!

About the Contributors

Dr Joanne Steer

Dr Joanne Steer (BSc, PsychD) is a Clinical Psychologist and has specialised in working with children and adolescents with mental health difficulties. Joanne's interest in children with ADHD started with her doctoral research on ADHD and attachment at the University of Surrey. Joanne has worked in Child and Adolescent Mental Health Services (CAMHS) in London for the last 16 years. Joanne is the Associate Director for Emotional Health Services at Achieving for Children who provide services on behalf of Kingston and Richmond borough councils in South West London. Joanne has developed and leads a large service which provides psychological therapy to children and their families alongside training and consultation to the children's workforce. Joanne co-authored the practical workbook *Helping Kids & Teens with ADHD in School* in 2009. Ten years (and three children) later, Joanne returned to authorship and published the workbook *Supporting Kids & Teens with Exam Stress*. Joanne has held a range of committee positions in the Faculty for Children, Young People & their Families part of the British Psychological Society. Joanne contributed to the NICE Quality Standards for ADHD in 2012/13. Over recent years, Joanne has developed a special interest in working with girls with ADHD and providing training to schools and health professionals on the key issues. See www.drjosteer.com.

Claire Berry

Claire Berry qualified from King's College London as a Mental Health Nurse in 2009. Since qualifying, she has worked in several Child and Adolescent Mental Health Services (CAMHS) in London including community teams and inpatient settings. Claire has completed further studies including a Master's in Child and Adolescent Cognitive Behavioural Therapy (CBT) at University College London. She is a British Association for Behavioural and Cognitive Psychotherapies (BABCP) accredited CBT Therapist. Claire currently leads on the delivery and implementation of a new Neurodevelopmental service within the Emotional Health Service at Achieving for Children in South West London. This has involved providing assessments of ADHD and ASD to children and young people in the boroughs of Richmond and Kingston, the aim of which has been to reduce waiting times and provide a more local service to families. Claire's current role also includes providing training and consultation to professionals in the children's workforce on a range of mental health issues. Alongside this, Claire provides psychological therapy to young people under the age of 18 years.

Jess Brunet

Jess Brunet is trained as a Mental Health Nurse, having qualified in 2012, and currently works clinically as an Advanced Nurse Practitioner within the Community Paediatric Team and Neurodevelopmental Service at Norwich Community Hospital. Her background is working as a highly specialist Child and Adolescent Mental Health Nurse, having trained and worked in various boroughs around London as an ADHD specialist. Currently, Jess leads an ADHD nursing team and focuses on quality improvement; developing assessment and treatment pathways within ADHD services in which she is embedded. She trained as a non-medical prescriber in 2016 and has been running nurse-led ADHD medication clinics since then, but also enjoys developing and running groups for families. Alongside her clinical work, she is currently studying for an MSc in Neuroscience at the Institute of Psychiatry,

Psychology and Neuroscience, King's College London, building on her undergraduate degree in Psychology with Neuropsychology obtained from the University of Wales, Bangor, prior to training as a Mental Health Nurse.

Professor Peter Hill

Professor Peter Hill trained in psychology, then general medicine, subsequently working in paediatric neurology, general adult psychiatry and ultimately, as he had always intended, in child and adolescent psychiatry. He has been a medical doctor for more than 50 years and an opinion leader in ADHD for over 30 years. He has been asked to lecture and advise on child mental health topics in every continent apart from Antarctica. Previously at St George's University of London and Great Ormond Children's Hospital, he is now retired from the NHS and London University and runs a private child and adolescent practice in London. Within this, he sees a large number of girls (and boys), mainly those that other clinicians have struggled with, so that his clinical work is often complicated. That's a good thing, as far as he is concerned.

Dr Alex Doig

Dr Alex Doig is a Consultant Psychiatrist in Child and Adolescent Mental Health. He has been working with children and young people with neurodevelopmental disorders and mental health difficulties for the past 20 years. He ran the Community Adolescent Team in Hounslow, West London for 11 years, where he managed a multidisciplinary team and saw adolescents with a range of difficulties including ADHD, eating disorders, anxiety, depression and psychosis. He has also been the Training Programme Director for Speciality Trainees within Child and Adolescent Psychiatry. He currently works part-time in a Child and Adolescent Mental Health Service (CAMHS) in Richmond, London, where he sees young people of all ages with a wide variety of difficulties and is the Named Doctor for Safeguarding Children for the Trust. He has particular interests in ADHD, trauma and safeguarding children. He is on the board of both a local child counselling charity and a local homeless charity, where he is the lead trustee for safeguarding. When not at work, he will usually be found in the garden wrestling with his gooseberry bushes.

Eva Akins

Eva Akins is Head of Education Law at Russell-Cooke, a Top 100 London law firm. She is named as a star associate in *Chambers UK 2020* and *The Legal 500 2020* and appeared in Thomson Reuters' 'Super Lawyers' list. She is repeatedly called upon by the media, including BBC News and Radio, for expert opinion on topical education issues. Eva advises on special educational needs, Equality Act claims, admissions, exclusions, complaints and school governance. Eva's first contact with the education law system came at the age of 11 years when she was first permanently excluded from school. As a teenage mother and whilst working part-time, Eva went on to gain a first class degree in law, completed her legal studies at The College of Law and was admitted to the Law Society in 1999. Eva was a successful criminal trial and extradition advocate for over a decade before her exasperation at getting her youngest ADHD child's needs met prompted her transition into education law. Eva specialises in championing the rights of neurodiverse children, and has a special interest in 'dual exceptionality' and gender variance. Eva remains concerned by inequality of opportunity and access to justice in education, and delivers free 'Empowering Parents' seminars and workshops to support groups.

Valerie Ivens

Valerie Ivens is a qualified ADHD coach. She spent 20 years establishing and developing the ADHD Richmond and Kingston support group. During that time, she worked with families, children and young people with ADHD as an advocate, representative and lobbyist both locally and nationally. Valerie moved from a professional career in international diplomacy to work in special needs when her own daughter's medical condition meant extensive international travel became unworkable. Working at a local charity, she recognised ADHD as a misunderstood and poorly supported condition, thereafter becoming a champion for ADHD awareness, and actively promoting the interests of parents and children both locally and nationally. Valerie has been an active member of both All Party Parliamentary Groups for ADHD. She has been a board member of UKAP and is a member of ADDISS. She was Chair and Lead of ADHD Richmond and Kingston, which she ran as a volunteer, and continues to support families through post-diagnosis training and a free support clinic. She has a special interest in late-diagnosed teenage girls.

Dr Sally Cubbin

Dr Sally Cubbin (MBChB, MRCPsych, MSc, DipCBT) is a Consultant Psychiatrist who has specialist clinical expertise in adult attention deficit hyperactivity disorder (ADHD), in terms of both its diagnosis and medical management. She is a member of the UK Adult ADHD Network (UKAAN) executive board and sits on their training committee. Her clinical interests are in the assessment of ADHD in adults and using pharmacological as well as psychological approaches to reducing symptoms. She holds a Diploma in Cognitive Behavioural Therapy from the University of Oxford. She runs workshops on the pharmacological treatment of ADHD for healthcare professionals and has written various book chapters on ADHD. She graduated from the University of Bristol and underwent specialist training in Oxford. She subsequently worked at the National Adult ADHD Service at the Maudsley Hospital, London, from 2008 to 2012. For almost ten years, she provided the NHS ADHD service to Hampshire and latterly Southampton City. She has also worked as a Consultant Psychiatrist in an NHS community mental health team and has spent two years as a neuropsychiatry inpatient consultant at the National Brain Injury Service in Northampton. She currently runs The ADHD Clinic (adhdclinic.co.uk), conducting face-to-face and online private ADHD assessments, and continues to provide the NHS Adult ADHD service to Southampton City.

Dr Allyson Parry

Dr Allyson Parry (DPhil, MRCP) is a Consultant Neurologist at the John Radcliffe Hospital, Oxford. She has a special interest in attention deficit hyperactivity disorder (ADHD) alongside her long-established practice in general neurology. Allyson is an associate member of the UK Adult ADHD Network (UKAAN), and has written and spoken about the importance of diagnosing and managing ADHD given the impact this may have on physical health and non-ADHD mental health symptoms. She is a passionate advocate for ADHD to be more widely recognised as an important, disabling and treatable disorder by doctors and other professionals working in all areas of healthcare provision.

Subject Index

Author Index